Contemporary Issues in International Security and Strategic Studies

Volume 2

Edited by
James D. Bindenagel, Matthias Herdegen,
Karl Kaiser and Ulrich Schlie

James D. Bindenagel

Germany from Peace to Power?

Can Germany lead in Europe without dominating?

V&R unipress

Bonn University Press

Bibliographic information published by the Deutsche Nationalbibliothek
The Deutsche Nationalbibliothek lists this publication in the Deutsche Nationalbibliografie;
detailed bibliographic data are available online: https://dnb.de.

**Publications of Bonn University Press
are published by V&R unipress.**

© 2020, Vandenhoeck & Ruprecht GmbH & Co. KG, Theaterstraße 13, 37073 Göttingen, Germany
All rights reserved. No part of this work may be reproduced or utilized in any form or by any means, electronic or mechanical, including photocopying, recording, or any information storage and retrieval system, without prior written permission from the publisher.

Cover image: Felix Mittermeier (https://pixabay.com/de/photos/bundestag-deutsche-fahne-reichstag-2463236/)
Printed and bound by CPI books GmbH, Birkstraße 10, 25917 Leck, Germany
Printed in the EU.

Vandenhoeck & Ruprecht Verlage | www.vandenhoeck-ruprecht-verlage.com

ISSN 2513-1591
ISBN 978-3-8471-1051-4

Contents

Foreword 9

Part One: Rethinking Germany's Sovereignty

Chapter 1: National Sovereignty and Territorial Integrity Restored
at Unification 17

Chapter 2: A Peaceful Revolution for Democracy: An Eyewitness
Account 33
   Asylum seekers in the U.S. Embassy: Freedom 34
   East Germany's 40th Anniversary and Crackdown on
   Counterrevolutionaries 40
   A Miracle of Peace in Leipzig: Courage for Freedom 44
   The Berlin Wall Falls, November 9, 1989: Self-Determination 50

Part Two: The German Problem: National sovereignty or sovereign obligation to Europe

Chapter 3: The German Problem 83
   Rethinking German Unification 83
   Germany's International Responsibility Doctrine 86
   Unilateralism or Leadership in Partnership 89
   Unraveling World Order 92
   Changing Roles 94

Chapter 4: Geopolitical Power Shifts and Germany's Place in Europe:
From a Geo-economic to a Geopolitical Power 101
   America's Withdrawal from International Leadership 102
   Geopolitical Power Shifts 103

President Donald Trump's Worldview 107
Germany's Leadership Responsibility 109
After the German Question now the German Problem 110
Reinventing Germany 112

Chapter 5: The Eurozone 115
Franco-German Leadership in Partnership 115
Georges Pompidou and Willy Brandt 116
Pieces of the EMU Puzzle 123
Sovereign Debt Crisis in the Eurozone: German Dominance 124
Foreign Ministers Group: Political Will and Vision 130
Emmanuel Macron and Angela Merkel: Vision for the Eurozone 134
Where is the EMU Headed? 137

Chapter 6: Civilian Power or Security Guarantor, Peacekeeper or
Peacemaker 141
Sovereign Obligation and Security Operations 141
What should Europe do? 161

Part Three: The Case for German Engagement – To Support Europe and Transatlantic Relations

Chapter 7: Germany's Inflection Point: From Crises Management to
Strategic Planning? 167
Germany's Strategic Deficit: Lack of Foresight and Scenario Building . 170
The German Problem: Germany Shies Away From Strategic Foresight . 173
In Uncertain Times: Recalibrating Germany's Foreign Policy Role . . . 179
Reluctance, Strategy, and Foresight 181
Strategic Foresight is not a Predictions' Plan 183
German and European Security Strategy 184

Chapter 8: An Independent Council of Experts to Support Strategic
Thinking 187
Overcoming Obstacles to a strategic future 188
Germany needs a European Security Strategy that supports the
European Union 195

Chapter 9: Germany From Peace to Power? 197

Acknowledgments 205

Bibliography 207

Foreword

> More than ever, one should study history to understand
> why nations and men succeeded and why they failed.
> – Henry Kissinger[1]

"Germany From Peace to Power," asks whether a prosperous and secure Germany can lead and make sacrifices to complete the work of European unity without dominating. The book contributes to the understanding of historical underpinnings from the 1989 Peaceful Revolution to Germany unification that helps explain Germany's changing role and responsibilities. It draws on Dr. Henry Kissinger's dictum that the study of history is needed to understand why nations succeeded and why they failed.

The peace to power argument is threefold: First, unification answered the age-old German Question of the country's place in Europe. However, Germany did not just become a larger West Germany. Unification changed Germany through a Peaceful Revolution of freedom for the East Germans, with self-determination that brought down the Berlin Wall, for political legitimacy for parliamentary democracy in united Germany. Second, now that the banality of good times has ended, the "German Problem," remains how Germany, which is prosperous and secure as never before, can be persuaded to take the political initiative/lead, and make the necessary economic sacrifices to complete the work of European unity without dominating. Third, a council of experts for strategic foresight can forge German leadership with its European partners through debates on myriad issues in the Bundestag. Those debates can inform politics without infringing on German policymaking. Germany needs greater cross-departmental cooperation, a shared vision for greater German international engagement, and strategic foresight. In solidarity with its European friends, Germany can govern domestically and become a leader with its international partners.

Consequently, acting in leadership with other Europeans, Germans can strengthen the two pillars of its foreign policy, Europe and the Transatlantic Partnership. Americans will have a European partner that may be more difficult in formulating a shared foreign policy but one that is true to democratic values.

"Germany From Peace to Power?" questions the obstacles that block Germany from leadership that peace brought Germany over the last thirty years. Germany and Europe are at peace, and Germany has power. How can Germany lead? The answer comes by examining German unification that resolved the German

---

1 Henry Kissinger in Niall Ferguson, *Kissinger: 1923–1968: The Idealist*, (Penguin Press: London, 2015).

Question, reviews decisions about European Monetary Union, and security policy with a strategic glimpse into foresight.

The origins of this book arise from the debate at German unification whether the 1989 'reform' movement in the German Democratic Republic was a revolution that led to the fall of the Berlin Wall and whether the East German accession to the West German constitution led to a changed Germany of a 'Berlin Republic.' That debate over the description of a revolution remained unresolved during most of the past thirty years. However, widespread acceptance came after President Joachim Gauck celebrated a "Peaceful Revolution" on its 25th anniversary. United Germany continued its role as a civilian power in a Paris Charter world surrounded by friends and allies in the banality of good times until 2014 when Russia invaded Ukraine and annexed Crimea, the rise of China-dominated Asia, and wars in the Middle East confirmed the end of the era. The banality of good ended suddenly, and the United States began its withdrawal from international leadership. That led to the question for this book whether Germany's past would be an insurmountable obstacle to its future.

Throughout these good times, I served President George H.W. Bush as Ambassador Richard Barkley's deputy chief of mission in East Germany during the revolution and unification of Germany. I returned to the State Department as Director for Central European Affairs that included Germany. After serving as deputy chief of mission in the U.S. Embassy to united Germany for Ambassador Richard Holbrooke, I was American Chargé d'Affaires in united Germany. The U.S. withdrew its military forces from western Germany, opened NATO, and promoted American investment in eastern Germany. Subsequently, I was appointed Ambassador and Special Envoy for Holocaust Issues to negotiate a settlement of forced labor claims from the National Socialist regime with Deputy Treasury Secretary Stuart Eizenstat to deal with German history. Under President George W. Bush, I concluded that Holocaust-era agreement. A decade later, I returned to Germany as the Henry Kissinger Professor at Bonn University shortly after President Joachim Gauck and ministers Ursula von der Leyen and Frank-Walter Steinmeier called on Germany to accept more international responsibility. Soon afterward, in 2014, Russian President Putin invaded Ukraine, signaling the end of the peaceful order in Europe. The book is an eyewitness account with historical and political analysis.

History is an array of tipping points. We are in a constant process of change and evolution. Sometimes we take two steps forward, one step back, but all in all, history is always on the move. If we want to influence events, it is good to think of Ernest Hemingway, who wrote in his book "The Sun Also Rises" on the question of how events occur. His example was of bankruptcy that in Hemingway's answer is condensed to: 'Gradually, then suddenly.'[2] Nations and international orders end that way as well.

In the case of East Germany, in the beginning, stood a reform movement in 1977 with Vaclav Havel in Czechoslovakia – Charter 77 – then came *Solidarity* with Lech Walesa in Poland at the beginning of the 1980s. It is in this 'gradually' phase when strategic foresight offers the opportunity to shape events as the slow process of erosion in which structures and systems slowly dissolve. When the 'then suddenly' phase arises, events become crises to manage, and options often become too fragile, everything crashes.

No one could have predicted the Berlin Wall would fall in 1989, or that Germany's division would end with national sovereignty restored, and that subsequently, the Soviet Union would dissolve. Perhaps strategic foresight could have brought doubt to the consensus that the Berlin Wall would stand for a century, as Honecker predicted, and offered options for responses to the end of the Cold War.

Today, thirty years later, on the anniversary of German unification, we stand in the shattering transatlantic relationship and the broken pieces of the rule-based liberal world order. Events have driven politics: The election and the impending re-election of an impeached President Donald Trump, the killing of Iranian Commander Soleimani, Brexit, the Rohingya crisis, or the global rise of China with its growing influence of the Belt and Road-Initiative. The Coronavirus is a pandemic that threatens the world order. It seems, time and again, that we fail to study history to understand why nations succeeded and why they failed. Are we already at the tipping point of the rise of great power politics and the return of authoritarian rule where chaos seems inevitable?

It may be uncontroversial to say that predictions are hard, especially of the future. Still, we can deal with the uncomfortable business of foresight, if not a prediction of the future. It is frustrating to be more often wrong than right, and in the end, foresight is often thankless. Nevertheless, it is a crucial obligation to look ahead.

By evaluating the common ground of knowledge, establishing new routes of thinking and, perhaps even bending the rules of the possible, we create options. Strategic foresight is a call to understand the drivers of events at a time where things are slowly evolving, to evaluate options before events reach the tipping point and become crises. Foresight can assess factors leading to events using current facts, analyzing different outcomes, and considering possible outcomes. That effort means that we must question our values, norms, and own identity, our actions, and responsibilities to prepare to act to shape the future and not just

---

2 Ernest Hemingway, *The Sun Also Rises* (Scribner Classics: New York City, 1966), first published 1926.

react to crises. It means that we must breach our comfort thinking zones and abandon the walls we have built in our minds about visions of the future.

A wall is not only a symbol of trying to keep something out; it is one to keep in something. We need to reassess the walls in our minds, just as the physical Berlin Wall fell 30 years ago. By learning from history, identifying past tipping points, and understanding the actions that lead to unprecedented events, we can formulate scenarios to think with foresight without trying to predict the future.

James Bindenagel, April 2020

Part One: Rethinking Germany's Sovereignty

The East German democratic election on March 18, 1990, paved the way for Lothar de Maizière as Prime Minister to lead the parliament in its mandate to accede to the West German constitution (*Grundgesetz* or Basic Law) at German unification. Events on the ground in East Germany, as we in the U.S. Embassy to the German Democratic Republic in East Berlin saw them, set the pace of unification as more and more East Germans fled the country and political chaos disturbed the domestic stability in the East. The path to unification in Article 23, Basic Law from the 1949 Basic Law of the Federal Republic of Germany, led the way to unification:

> Article 23, Basic Law: For the time being, this Basic Law shall apply in the territory of the Laender Baden, Bavaria, Bremen, Greater Berlin, Hamburg, Hesse, Lower Saxony, North Rhine-Westphalia, Rhineland-Palatinate, Schleswig-Holstein, Wuerttemberg-Baden, and Wuerttemberg-Hohenzollern. It shall be put into force for other parts of Germany on their accession.[3]

The East German Volkskammer voted on August 23, 1990, to accede to the West German constitution on October 3, 1990, unifying Germany under Article 23 of the Federal Republic of Germany's constitution. With that vote, the Peaceful Revolution had achieved German unification and provided the Berlin Republic with democratic legitimacy. The World War II victorious Four Powers relinquished their 'rights and responsibilities for Berlin and Germany as a whole,'[4] in the *Treaty on the Final Settlement with Respect to Germany*, known as the *2+4 Agreement* in which Germany gained full sovereignty. This full sovereignty is the defining characteristic of united Germany, the Berlin Republic.

---

3 The Basic Law of the Federal Republic of Germany, Art. 23, p. 6. Online: https://www.cvce.eu/content/publication/1999/1/1/7fa618bb-604e-4980-b667-76bf0cd0dd9b/publishable_en.pdf. Since the reunification of Germany in 1989 the Basic Law has been updated and rewritten. The current Article 23 reads very different from the original version in 1949. For reference, one can download the neweset version on the website of the German Bundestag.

4 The Federal Republic of Germany, the German Democratic Republic, the French Republic, the Union of Soviet Socialist Republics, the United Kingdom of Great Britain and Northern Ireland and the United States of America, *Treaty on the Final Settlement with Respect to Germany*, September 12, 1990. Art. 7 Online: https://usa.usembassy.de/etexts/2plusfour8994e.htm.

West Germany's merger with East Germany confirmed Germany as a beacon for democracy. The country is grounded in the rule of law, and West Germany was a leading civilian power for 40 years. United Germany's political identity and its *Staatsräson* rest on the pillars of democracy, the rule of law, and human rights in a united Europe. According to the preamble and Article 1 of the Basic Law Germans are, one, "conscious of their responsibility before God and man; Inspired by the determination to promote world peace as an equal partner in a united Europe,"[5] and two, that they believe that "human dignity shall be inviolable. To respect and protect it shall be the duty of all state authority."[6] Germany has taken these principles and applied them to its foreign policy, which has emphasized peacebuilding, premised on encouraging other states to build institutions based on individual dignity and human rights. These constitutional principles, anchored in Germany's understanding of its past and in its commitment to seeking a better future, have been crucial to establishing Germany's international role as a leader in partnership with other countries.

Unification answered the German Question. German President Richard von Weizsäcker eloquently described the German Question:

> The German Question will remain open as long as Brandenburg Gate remains closed. This gets at the core of the unresolved German Question. It concerns the freedom of the people. Nowhere can this be felt more clearly than in the center of the divided Berlin. But it affects all Germans and all Europeans no less.[7]

Freedom and democracy are the twin issues of German unification. Henry Kissinger reminds us that success as a statesman rests on the study of history to understand why nations succeeded and why they failed. It is essential for today's statesmen and women to reassess the 1989 Peaceful Revolution that ended Germany's division, restored national sovereignty, and brought about unification and territorial integrity through democratic elections. When the Brandenburg Gate opened in December 1989, the German Question was closing. Within months, the East German parliament acceded to the West German constitution and created a different Germany. There are three critical components, which make the core of that revolution in East Germany – freedom, self-determination, and parliamentary democracy – and they play a crucial role in the development of Germany's political identity. Today, the country's reluctant

---

5 Preamble of the Basic Law of the Federal Ruplic of Germany, 1949. Translated by Prof. Christian Tomuschat, Professor David P. Currie, Professor Donald P. Kommers and Ramyond Kerr, in cooperation with the Language Service of the German Bundestag.
6 Ibid. Art. 1 (1).
7 Richard von Weizsäcker, Was ist das eigentlich: deutsch? ["What is that actually: German?"], in Reden und Interviews [Speeches and Interviews], vol. 2, pp. 395–412, (Bonn, 1986). Translation: GHDT, Federal President Richard von Weizsäcker on the Meaning of Being German (1986), Online: http://germanhistorydocs.ghi-dc.org/docpage.cfm?docpage_id=2111, (Bonn).

leadership is a call for Germany to reinvent itself as a leader in partnership with Europeans to strengthen the values-based liberal order that has provided peace and prosperity. It is a path from peace in 1990 to power today to mobilize Europe to sustain, reform, and reshape the transatlantic relationship.

First, the thirst for freedom took courage to demonstrate in the streets against the East German Government, and courage was shown despite the expected violence on October 9, 1989. That the revolution of 1989 ended peacefully stood on the *Miracle of Peace in Leipzig.* The peaceful protests for freedom, accompanied by a mass exodus from the GDR, miraculously did not escalate into a violent massacre, as many had feared. The Monday peace vigils in the St. Nicholas Church (*Nikolaikirche*) in Leipzig and the continuing street demonstrations throughout the country became beacons for the people's courage to fight for freedom. Although the East German Politburo ousted East German leader Erich Honecker, his successor, Egon Krenz, failed to halt the revolution.

Second, the demand for self-determination manifested itself through the people's demand for the right to travel, which was blocked by the Berlin Wall. Could travel be allowed without East Germany collapsing? Answering the growing public pressure through weekly street demonstrations and thousands of East Germans escaping through Hungary, Czechoslovakia, and Poland, the Politburo tried to open an escape valve by allowing some travel. On the evening of November 9, 1989, as I returned from an Aspen Institute reception, Erich Honecker's lawyer Wolfgang Vogel[8] shared with me the Politburo's new, relaxed travel law planned for release on November 10, 1989. Vogel's news, however, was soon eclipsed by Politburo spokesman Günter Schabowski's public announcement that the Berlin Wall was to open immediately on the night of November 9, 1989. East German citizens themselves breached the Berlin Wall at Bornholmerstrasse and rushed to West Berlin, which was flooded by East Germans and, in some ways, became an East German city overnight.

Third, governance in East Germany disintegrated in December 1989. East German Prime Minister Hans Modrow seized uncontrolled weapons in Kavelstorf near Rostock that threatened violence. Modrow restrained the threat of chaos and descent into violent unrest in the aftermath of the uprising that had brought down the Berlin Wall. In parallel, U.S. President George H.W. Bush and German Chancellor Helmut Kohl worked with Soviet President Mikhail Gorba-

---

8 Wolfgang Vogel was Erich Honecker's lawyer and negotiator for the German Democratic Republic (GDR). The United States negotiated spy exchanges with Vogel who oversaw in 1962, the exchange of KGB spy Rudolf Abel and American pilot Gary Powers, in 1985, 23 people held by East Germany on charges of espionage for the United States, and in 1986, the Jewish dissident Anatoly Scharansky. Ambassador Barkley, in 1985, was his U.S. Embassy Bonn negotiating partner. Vogel was critical in resolving the emigration of the asylum seekers in the U.S. Embassy to the GDR in October 1989.

chev to keep calm amid the disorder in East Germany. U.S. Secretary of State James A. Baker III visited West Berlin to speak about German unification and then met Hans Modrow in Potsdam in December 1989. The United States supported German unification in self-determination, urged Germany's continued membership in NATO, and in Potsdam endorsed an East German free and fair election for a democratically elected parliament. Baker also met with Protestant Church leaders, Manfred Stolpe, and East German pastors to reaffirm America's commitment to German unification and to call for peaceful demonstrations.

Finally, the East Germans democratically elected, on March 18, 1990, Lothar de Maizière to become East Germany's first democratically elected prime minister and to lead the parliament in its mandate to accede to the West German constitution (*Grundgesetz* or Basic Law) that unified Germany. On October 3, 1990, the Peaceful Revolution achieved German unification and provided the 'Berlin Republic' with democratic legitimacy. When the World War II victorious Four Powers relinquished their rights and responsibilities for Berlin and Germany as a whole at unification, Germany gained full sovereignty. This full sovereignty brought with it responsibility and leadership. Constitutionally mandated responsibility for Europe needs German leadership. That is still the defining characteristic of the Berlin Republic thirty years after unification.

West Germany's merger with East Germany confirmed Germany as a beacon for democracy. The country is grounded in the rule of law, and West Germany has been a leading civilian power for 40 years. United Germany's more profound beliefs in democracy and human dignity as well as its status as a leading, if reluctant, foreign policy actor stem from the lessons of tyranny, nationalism, and the rift with human and civil rights of the National Socialists.

United Germany's political identity and its *Staatsräson* rest on the pillars of democracy, the rule of law, and human rights in a united Europe. According to the preamble and Article 1 of the Basic Law, Germans are called on to respect and protect human dignity, which is the duty of all state authority. Germany has taken these principles and applied them to its foreign policy, which has emphasized peacebuilding, premised on encouraging other states to build institutions based on individual dignity and human rights.

Chapter 1: National Sovereignty and Territorial Integrity Restored at Unification

> If the European project fails, then there is the question of how long it will take to reach the status quo again. Remember the German Revolution of 1848: When it failed, it took us 100 years to regain the same level of democracy as before.
> – Jürgen Habermas[9]

Habermas wrote those lines to warn Europe of the more than 100 years of struggle before Germany achieved parliamentary democracy through a peaceful and successful revolution. The unification of Germany is – at its core – also part of the European project. West and East Europe could unify after united Germany found its place among friends, to say it with the words of Chancellor Helmut Kohl. But unification could have only happened through an act of self-determination. In 1989 Germans in East Germany rediscovered Thucydides' secret of freedom: courage.[10] With courage, they brought down the Berlin Wall, elected a democratic parliament and voted to accede to the West German constitution, which had created a democracy based on respect for human dignity and commitment to Europe in West Germany. This step in East Germany, the Peaceful Revolution that fought for freedom and democracy and a mandate to unite Germany in 1990, was an act of national self-determination. It was, first and foremost, an act of East German self-determination.

Germany's evolving power and leadership have grown from the seeds of responsibility sown at unification in 1990. The end of communist dictatorship in the German Democratic Republic and the restoration of German sovereignty is a story worth retelling. It is a story of the Peaceful Revolution in East Germany. Germany's path from peace to power began in the year 1989 when dramatic events stirred a new sense of freedom in the world that would end the Cold War. In East Berlin, on the lines of the Cold War's Central Front, change came gradually out of the critical confrontation in that long, Cold War struggle for freedom and liberal democracy against East German communist dictatorship.

---

9 Jürgen Habermas in Georg Diez, Habermas, the Last European: A Philosopher's Mission to Save the EU, in: Spiegel Online: https://www.spiegel.de/international/europe/habermas-the-last-european-a-philosopher-s-mission-to-save-the-eu-a-799237.html Remember the German Revolution of 1848: When it failed, it took us 100 years to regain the same level of democracy as before. "A vague future and a warning from the past – that's what Habermas", (Hamburg, 2011).

10 Thucydides, Quoted literally: "having judged happiness freedom, freedom courage". Author filled the gap as eyewitness October 9, 1989 in East Germany, Online: http://www.bristol.ac.uk/classics/research/thucydides/ttt/text/.

East German First Secretary Walter Ulbricht erected the Berlin Wall in 1961 as much to keep people in as it was to keep people out; it divided Berlin for 28 years. The Berlin Wall symbolized East Germans' loss of freedom and its lack in the German Democratic Republic (GDR). Ulbricht's successor, Erich Honecker, stated in early 1989, that the Wall could stand for another 100 years.[11] Also, in the West, expectations that the Wall would fall were low; not in my lifetime was the echo heard that autumn in the entirety Berlin.

The 1975 *Helsinki Final Act* of *the Conference on Security and Cooperation* (CSCE) marked the beginning of the end of the Cold War. Signatories agreed borders in Europe could change only through peaceful means, and both sides promised non-interference in the internal affairs of the other. Recognition of human rights, including the right to travel, was embedded in the agreement.[12] Of course, in the 1980s, the cost of an arms race with new nuclear missiles, the Strategic Defense Initiative, and economic crises from rising oil costs and a declining economy in the Soviet Union played roles as well. The *Helsinki Final Act*, with its commitment to human rights, was a much sought-after document in the library of the U.S. Embassy to the German Democratic Republic. East Germans during 1989 carefully compared the German and English texts in the American Embassy as they demanded the right to travel by holding the East German government to the agreement it had signed.

The *Helsinki Final Act* was a first step bringing change to divided Europe, but the real story of the Peaceful Revolution began in the 1980s. Soviet General Secretary Gorbachev's "New Thinking" launched in Davos 1985 a debate about *glasnost* (political openness) and *perestroika* (economic restructuring) in the Soviet Union. Political openness and economic restructuring were designed to rescue Soviet communism from its political stress and economic exhaustion. One could perhaps see an example of such reform from President Franklin Delano Roosevelt's policies that were employed to save capitalism decades earlier. Gorbachev and President Ronald Reagan addressed Soviet reforms when they met in Geneva, Switzerland, in November 1985. They set an ambitious agenda to

---

11 Erich Honecker in Los Angeles Times, *Berlin Wall Will Stand 100 Years, Honecker Vows*, East Germany's official news agency, Online: https://www.latimes.com/archives/la-xpm-1989-01-20-me-1130-story.html, January 20, 1989.
12 High Representatives of Austria, Belgium, Bulgaria, Canada, Cyprus, Czechoslovakia, Denmark, Finland, France, the German Democratic Republic, the Federal Republic of Germany, Greece, the Holy See, Hungary, Iceland, Ireland, Italy, Liechtenstein, Luxembourg, Malta, Monaco, the Netherlands, Norway, Poland, Portugal, Romania, San Marino, Spain, Sweden, Switzerland, Turkey, the Union of Soviet Socialist Republics, the United Kingdom, the United States of America and Yugoslavia, *Conference on Security and Co-operation in Europe Final Act*. Online: https://www.osce.org/helsinki-final-act?download=true, (Helsinki, 1975), p. 3f., 6, 37f.

discuss increases in trade, cultural exchanges, human rights, the Iran-Iraq War, the Soviet conflict in Afghanistan, and other regional conflicts.[13]

Gorbachev's 1988 speech at the UN focused on security issues, and he stated: "Political problems must be solved only by political means; human problems, only in a humane way."[14] General Secretary Mikhail Gorbachev, with the rise of the Solidarity Movement (*Solidarność*) in Poland, promised to allow Warsaw Pact countries to decide their futures for themselves, including which security alliances to join. He renounced the Brezhnev Doctrine, in which Moscow decided policies of Warsaw Pact countries, enforced by threatened Soviet military intervention and martial law as done in the Soviet invasion of Czechoslovakia in 1968. Keeping to his word for the first Polish election, June 1989, Gorbachev did not use military force against Poland. Gorbachev's new principles would be put to the test repeatedly in 1989.

Change was in the air, but no one knew where it would end. Seeking self-determination for Eastern Europe was a long-held U.S. policy, but a Europe whole and free was just a vision, one that had long evaded reality. It was Gorbachev's policy changes that allowed the parliamentary election of the Polish parliament (*Sejm*) with non-communist participation on June 4, 1989. That summer, the Hungarians opened a path for East Germans to flee. After Hungary signed the UN Convention Relating to the Status of Refugees, East Germans began to escape communist East Germany to Hungary. Civil society in East Germany also discovered the civil courage that Solidarity in Poland had found, and began to face down their communist government through peaceful demonstrations and demands for the freedom of travel.

George H.W. Bush took office as President in the ninth year of the Polish Solidarity Movement and the fourth year of Gorbachev's leadership. Change had come to Soviet-dominated Eastern Europe, and in the United States, President Bush reasserted President Ronald Reagan's 1987 call for President Gorbachev to tear down the Berlin Wall. Bush made clear:

> [n]owhere is the division between East and West seen more clearly than in Berlin. And there this brutal wall cuts neighbor from neighbor, brother from brother. And that wall stands as a monument to the failure of communism. It must come down! We seek self-determination for all of Germany and all of Eastern Europe.[15]

---

13 U.S. Department of State, *Gorbachev and New Thinking in Soviet Foreign Policy, 1987–88*, Online: https://2001-2009.state.gov/r/pa/ho/time/rd/108225.htm, (U.S. Department of State Archive, 2001).
14 The New York Times The Gorbachev Visit; Excerpts From Speech to U.N. on Major Soviet Military Cuts, in: New York Times, December 8, (New York, 1988), p. 16.
15 Georg H. W. Bush,Remarks to the Citizens of Mainz, Federal Republic of Germany , Mainz, 31. May 1989. in: Public Papers of the President of the United States, (Washington D.C., 1989), p. 652.

In his speech in Mainz in May 1989, President George H.W. Bush presaging German sovereignty and leadership said to Chancellor Helmut Kohl:

> ... We are at the end of one era and the beginning of another. And I noted that regarding the Soviet Union, our policy is to move beyond containment. And for 40 years, the world has waited for the Cold War to end. And decade after decade, time after time, the flowering human spirit withered from the chill of conflict and oppression. And again, the world waited. But the passion for freedom cannot be denied forever. The world has waited long enough. The time is right. Let Europe be whole and free. To the founders of the alliance, this aspiration was a distant dream, and now it's the new mission of NATO...The Cold War began with the division of Europe. It can only end when Europe is whole. And as President, I will continue to do all I can to help open the closed societies of the East. We seek self-determination for all of Germany and all of Eastern Europe.[16]

German revolutions for two centuries failed to overthrow established governments. The 1848 European democratic revolution failed, and the 1918 German Revolution of the Socialist Republic was crushed.[17] This time it was different. Citizens' in a national self-determination movement launched a budding revolution that began in May 1989 with poll watchers who monitored municipal elections. At the same time, other East Germans voted with their feet, and an unstoppable wave of Germans from East Germany fled through Hungary to freedom. In Leipzig on October 9, a peaceful demonstration faced off against a massive armed force from the regime. Surprisingly, a revolution could be non-violent, and the 1989 revolution has become known as the Peaceful Revolution.[18]

The *Peaceful Revolution* that would later unite Germany confirmed the wisdom of Chancellor Konrad Adenauer's policy of *Westbindung* that committed West Germany to Western values of democracy, the rule of law, and the inviolability of human dignity. The policy of Westbindung was followed by Chancellor Willy Brandt's *Ostpolitik* outreach to the Soviet Union to ease tensions through *détente*. Europeans, Americans, and Soviets came together in the Conference on Security and Cooperation in Europe (CSCE), championed by Vice-Chancellor Hans Dietrich Genscher. The Helsinki Final Act created hope for peaceful change in Europe and agreed borders could only change peacefully. Then in the Cold War confrontation, NATO's 'Double Decision' (*Doppelbeschluss*), led by Chancellor Helmut Schmidt, included both easing of tensions (*détente*) and deterrence towards the Warsaw Pact and maintained stability allowing for diplomacy in those tense years. Finally, Chancellor Helmut Kohl followed Schmidt's foreign policy

---

16 Ibid., p. 651.
17 Ernst Piper, Deutsche Revolution, Online: https://www.bpb.de/izpb/274840/deutsche-revolution, (Bundeszentrale für politische Bildung: Bonn, 2018).
18 Andreas Malycha, Auf dem Weg in den Zusammenbruch (1982 bis 1990) [To the German Collapse (1982 to 1990)], Online: https://www.bpb.de/izpb/48560/auf-dem-weg-in-den-zusammenbruch-1982-bis-1990?p=all, (Bundeszentrale für politische Bildung: Bonn, 2011).

and agreed to the deployment of American nuclear Intermediate-Range Forces (INF) to ensure the United States security guarantee remained coupled to Western Europe. German leaders strongly supported strategic ideas in NATO and CSCE.

In the Soviet Union, Soviet President Mikhail Gorbachev announced his economic restructuring (*perestroika*) and political openness (*glasnost*) that changed the Cold War and opened some hope in Eastern Europe for reform. It was, however, the Berlin Wall that symbolized Europe's division. It was the hated symbol of communism. The Peaceful Revolution that brought it down was breathtaking. In 1989 thousands upon thousands fled from East Germany to the West. Nearly a million more were seeking to emigrate. Peaceful demonstrators in the streets of Leipzig, Dresden, Berlin, and numerous cities demanded the freedom to travel and that the government live up to commitments made in the 1975 CSCE or the Helsinki Agreement. Thucydides, writing of the Peloponnesian War, was correct to declare that the secret of happiness is freedom; the secret of freedom is courage. In Leipzig and other cities, people found the civil courage to fight for freedom. That courage proved to be stronger than the fear of the regime's oppression or bullets. Dissidents needed courage the Central Front in the Cold War, where two million soldiers still stood face-to-face across the inner German border, armed with nuclear weapons. In Berlin, the Cold War confrontation at the Berlin Wall always threatened war, as seen in the dramatic 1961 face-off of American and Russian tanks at Checkpoint Charlie. Peace and stability were not assured as the United States and NATO Allies stationed a million soldiers in West Germany to deter an expected communist attack from the Soviet and Warsaw Pact armies across the German-German border.

Divided Germany was on the Central Front with confronting armies representing the ideological conflict of the Cold War. Hope still kept the dream of German unification alive. Although France and Britain were skeptical of German unification, the West hoped that Soviet reforms would open the way for parliamentary nation-states, legitimized by the will of the people through free, fair, regular, and open elections to resolve the division of Germany. East Germany and the Soviet Union had rejected West Germany's parliamentary governance in the post-war period. However, after more than 40 years, the East German (and Soviet) communist order was changing. Soviet President Mikhail Gorbachev began his experiment *glasnost* and *perestroika* in hopes of reforming the communist regime to better compete with the West. Gorbachev's attempt to introduce Western parliamentary governance and market reforms instead of undermined rather than strengthened the legitimacy of the communist system. *Solidarność* in Poland forced a free and fair election for representation by the people in the Polish *Sejm*. East Germans watched throughout the 1980s and then began to test the political will of the East German government to uphold its communist ideology.

Seen from the Chinese perspective, the endeavor for freedom was proving to be risky. China had rejected Gorbachev's reforms. Students in Beijing also had seen East Europeans' demands for parliamentary representation, and they demonstrated for democracy on Beijing's Tiananmen Square in June 1989. On June 4, the Chinese government brutally crushed the democracy demonstrators in Tiananmen Square in Beijing. Honecker's government used the massacre on Tiananmen Square to foster fear of the consequences of demanding freedom, which fed a flood of East Germans fleeing from the GDR. The pace quickened during the summer of 1989.

Repression by the Chinese government was an ominous signal for dissidents in East Germany. Crushing dissent in a violent manner became known as the "China Solution" for the East German government to attack counter-revolutionary demonstrators. Honecker stressed the option of crushing counter-revolutionaries after China attacks on Tiananmen Square. In June 1989, the Honecker government invited to East Berlin Chinese Foreign Minister Qian Qichen to visit East Berlin. The visit reinforced the role Premier Li Peng, named *Butcher of Beijing*, played for his role in the events on Tiananmen Square, to show solidarity with the Chinese crackdown.[19]

In September 1989, the Chairman of the ruling Socialist Unity Party (SED) Honecker was ill. His second-in-command, Egon Krenz, traveled to China to reinforce solidarity between China and East Germany. Krenz's subsequent comment on the Chinese Tiananmen Square action was that something had to be done to uphold order ("Etwas getan worden, um die Ordnung wiederherzustellen"[20]). East Germans understood violence would confront any demonstration to enforce order and keep the communist party in power. The expectation in Leipzig and throughout the country was that the government would violently crackdown on protests, implementing the Chinese solution, following the October 7, 1989, 40th anniversary of East Germany.[21]

Civic unrest spread in the summer and autumn of 1989 from Poland across East Germany, Czechoslovakia, and Hungary. Despite President Gorbachev's July 1989 Strasbourg address with his appeal for Soviet entry into a common

---

19 Neues Deutschland, Freundschaftliche Begegnung mit dem Außenminister der VR China, in: Neues Deutschland, Organ des Zentralkommitees der Sozialistischen Einheitspartei Deutschlands, Online: https://www.nd-archiv.de/ausgabe/1989-06-13, (Ostberlin, 1989a), p. 1.
20 Andreas Malycha, Auf dem Weg in den Zusammenbruch (1982 bis 1990) [To the German Collapse (1982 to 1990)], Online: https://www.bpb.de/izpb/48560/auf-dem-weg-in-den-zusammenbruch-1982-bis-1990?p=all, (Bundeszentrale für politische Bildung: Bonn, 2011).
21 Henrik Pomeranz, Interview with Egon Krenz, "Also, dann hoch mit den Schlagbäumen!" in: Frankfurter Allgemeine Sonntagszeitung, (Frankfurt, 2019), Nr. 21, p. 6.

home and his acknowledgment of "European unification," conventional wisdom in the West expected the Soviet Union to crush uprisings like those occurring in East Germany.[22] The Soviets had crushed rebellion in East Germany in 1953, Hungary in 1956, and Czechoslovakia in 1968. The change came in Poland when Gorbachev hesitated to intervene militarily and allowed the imposition of martial law instead. The Gorbachev experiment went further by disclaiming the Brezhnev Doctrine that had denied sovereignty to Soviet satellite countries, instead offering to grant them their right to exercise national sovereignty, even permitting them to take charge of their security arrangements.

As pressure grew on the Honecker regime, uncertainty rose. At dinner on the evening of the anniversary of the Nazi invasion of Poland hosted by Ambassador Barkley on August 31, 1989, Franz Bertele, the head of the West German Permanent Representation to East Germany, East German Ministry for Foreign Affairs State Secretary Ernst Krabbatsch and I chatted in the living room drinking coffee. After a pause in the conversation, Krabbatsch turned to Bertele and simply asked: What will you do to us, hang us? Bertele looked at the SED lapel pin on Krabbatsch's suit coat, looked him in the eye, and turned away. That act foreshadowed for me the potential for conflict as the revolution continued.

Did Gorbachev have another plan that could avoid conflict? Michael Beschloss and Strobe Talbott wrote later that the critical decisions by Gorbachev to allow East Bloc countries to decide their fate might have given Hungarians "tacit consent" to open the Iron Curtain already in May. Would that opening for East Germans to flee put pressure to encourage the ouster of Honecker in October?[23] A more likely driver of the peaceful challenge to Honecker would be a statement by Gorbachev in Berlin on October 7 during the October 1989 40th Anniversary of the German Democratic Republic, when Gorbachev warned publicly that "life punishes those who come too late."[24] (Wer zu spät kommt, den bestraft das Leben.) That statement was a hint for Honecker to step down. Gorbachev's words seemed implicit to support demands for changes similar to those he implemented in the USSR.

Gorbachev gave what was necessary for the peaceful weekend when he expressly ordered the Soviet troops in East Germany to stay in their barracks during the anniversary. That decision also meant Honecker was not going to be able to

---

22 Council of Europe – Parliamentary Assembly. Official Report. Forty-first ordinary session. 8–12 May and 3–7 July. Volume I. Sittings 1 to 9. 1990. Strasbourg: Council of Europe. "Speech by Mikhail Gorbachev", (Straßbourg, 1990), p. 197–205.
23 Michael R. Beschloss and Strobe Talbott, *At the Highest Levels: The Inside Story of the End of the Cold War*, (Little, Brown and Company: Boston, 1993).
24 Gorbachev never actually said those words, but they are a fragment of a translation from Russian to German, as described in: Claus Menzel, "Wer zu spat kommt, den bestraft das Leben" Vor 20 Jahren sagte Gorbatschow das Ende der DDR voraus, Online: https://www.deutschlandfunk.de/wer-zu-spaet-kommt-den-bestraft-das-leben.871.de.html?dram:article_id=126749, (Deutschland Funk, 2009).

rely on the almost half a million Soviet troops stationed in the country to support him in quelling the unrest.[25] Subsequently, Kurt Hager, East Germany's chief ideologist, ominously went to Moscow on Oct. 12, 1989, and discussed the mode of removing Honecker with Gorbachev.

In East Germany, reformers in Leipzig organized resistance with peaceful Monday evening vigils, including those held by Pastor Christian Führer at the *Nikolaikirche*. The rebellion reached a peak on the fateful night of October 9, 1989, when demonstrations grew, and the Berlin government demanded the Leipzig Communist Party block the counter-revolutionaries with violence, if necessary. The police moved into position; doctors were ordered to remain on duty and to stockpile blood supplies. However, after political leaders and Gewandhaus Orchestra Conductor, Kurt Masur intervened to call for non-violence; no violence was unleashed by police or demonstrators, eroding the legitimacy of the Honecker regime. The call for no violence (*Keine Gewalt*) won the day. After a second Leipzig demonstration on October 16, the Politburo deposed Honecker two days later and named Egon Krenz to succeed him. Nevertheless, pressure from demonstrators in the streets throughout East Germany exploded as demonstrators demanded the freedom to travel.

East German dissidents throughout the country were willing to risk their jobs, families, and even their lives to set the flames of reforms that would lead to the revolution. Sparks of change in May 1989 had ignited a revolution, and the fire for change grew higher when tens of thousands and then hundreds of thousands of Germans in the GDR took to the streets of many cities, including Leipzig, Dresden, and Berlin in a Peaceful Revolution to challenge the regime. Surprisingly after the next Leipzig demonstration on October 16, 1989, with more than 100,000 citizens, Egon Krenz, Honecker's likely successor, intervened to signal tolerance of dissent in the country.[26] The revolution could be peaceful despite the fear of reprisals.

After that second major demonstration in Leipzig, the Politburo met and deposed Erich Honecker. Egon Krenz took charge and offered a political turnaround (*Wende*) in an attempt to legitimize the SED. The citizens' movement vehemently protested this effort to deny them their freedom. It rejected Krenz's changes to the East German travel law that eased but did not guarantee the freedom to travel. Krenz was only in office for a few days when East German government spokesman and Politburo Member, Guenther Schabowski's statement at a press conference covered by television on the night of November 9,

---

25 Spiegel Online, Oct. 7, 1989. How 'Gorbi' Spoiled East Germany's 40th Birthday Party, in: Spiegel Online, Online: https://www.spiegel.de/international/germany/oct-7-1989-how-gorbi-spoiled-east-germany-s-40th-birthday-party-a-653724.html, (Hamburg, 2009a).
26 Konrad H. Jarausch, The Rush to German Unity, (Oxford University Press: Oxford, 1994), p. 45.

1989, set the revolution ablaze. Schabowski told the world that the Politburo agreed to more liberal changes in the restrictive East German travel law that would allow East Germans to obtain visitor visas quickly (*in kurzem*) for travel to the West from their local People's Police (*Volkspolizei*).

Schabowski also announced that the GDR would open a new processing center to handle emigration cases immediately. In other words, he announced the East Germans were free to travel. A journalist asked when this new policy would go into effect, and Schabowski mumbled "immediately" ("Das tritt nach meiner Kenntnis ... ist das sofort, *unverzüglich*").[27] That inaccurate statement opened the flood gates, and East Germans took to the streets and stormed checkpoints crossing the Berlin Wall to West Berlin. That night the division of Berlin and Germany was breached. This grass-roots democracy movement would prove unstoppable as it confronted the guards at the Berlin Wall and breached it in the drama of November 9, 1989. Communist rule in East Germany would end, along with the structures of government, the economy, and social life built under the Socialist Unity Party (SED).

After frantically confirming the news of the opening of the Berlin Wall to Washington, we in the U.S. Embassy in East Berlin returned to our East Berlin homes and, on the way, witnessed the confrontation between demonstrators and the border guards at Bornholmerstrasse. Demonstrators had besieged the Berlin Wall at the Bornholmerstrasse checkpoint between East and West Berlin, while others challenged the border guards at the Brandenburg Gate. Within minutes the Berlin Wall was breached. First, a wave of East Berliners came through the Bornholmerstrasse checkpoint signaling freedom of travel for all East Germans. As they streamed across the bridge over the Berlin Wall, television pictures flashed the chaotic scene around the world. The guards had standing orders to defend the Wall, and many East Germans over the years had died when the border guards shot those trying to flee. But the guards on Bornholmerstrasse that night refused to carry out the shoot-to-kill order. It would take time before we learned why the guards did not fire on their fellow citizens.

Although the events in Berlin on November 9, 1989, overshadowed the Leipzig October 9, 1989 confrontation, the freedom movement spread so quickly that observers recalled a quip attributed to Bismarck that "when the world comes to

---

[27] Schwaboski, Günter, Internationale Pressekonferenz von Günter Schabowski (in Begleitung der SED-ZKMitglieder Helga Labs, Gerhard Beil und Manfred Banaschak), 9. November 1989, (Ton-Abschrift), p. 2. aus: Transkription des Kamerabandes von Hans-Hermann Hertle, in Auszügen wiedergegeben in: Hans Hermann Hertle, *Die Berliner Mauer. Biografie eines Bauwerks*, 2. durchgesehene und aktualisierte Aufl., (Ch. Links Verlag: Berlin, 2015), S. 194/195.

an end, we will all go to Mecklenburg where everything happens 100 years later".[28] Honecker's Berlin Wall prediction of the Berlin Wall's 100 years dissolved when days after Leipzig the revolution reached Mecklenburg. Suddenly, we did the math: One hundred years equaled just a few days. The rush to unification began.

On November 18, East German Premier Hans Modrow offered a new relationship with West Germany in a community of agreements (*Vertragsgemeinschaft*). On November 28, 1989, West German Chancellor Helmut Kohl offered his Ten Point Plan for a Confederation[29] leading to unification as the alternative to chaos or civil war that threatened the revolution. Germany shifted stability from the four Allied Powers of the Second World War – the United States, France, the United Kingdom, and the Soviet Union. The Four Powers had exercised their rights and responsibilities for Berlin and Germany to help stabilize the process of change and unification through negotiations for German unification.

After the fall of the Berlin Wall, fear that a vacuum of power in East Germany might leave uncontrolled weapons and threaten East Germany with internal violence. Declassified reports show that George H.W. Bush and Gorbachev shared their concerns – and resolve – about three developments: The disintegration of the East German SED regime, Gorbachev's decision that united Germany could remain in NATO, and uncertainty about the status of the 380,000 Soviet soldiers in the GDR. Soviet Foreign Minister Eduard Shevardnadze in 1989 and 1990 fought against a catastrophic Soviet military intervention that would have denied East Germans the right to decide their own fate, as Gorbachev promised. The Soviet Military Forces that would remain in Germany after unification until 1994 led to an understanding not to station NATO forces on the territory of the former GDR after unification and that only a national army of the *Bundeswehr* – Bundeswehr Ost – would be in Eastern Germany.[30]

The pace of the revolution was breathtaking, and in Kavelstorf, near Rostock on December 3, 1989, citizens stormed an East German State Security (*Stasi*) arms warehouse and discovered a massive stockpile of weapons with few guards.[31] That act fed rumors of uncontrolled weapons in East Germany and led

---

28 Bismarck, Otto von, (attributed to Bismarck), If the world would one day come to an end, he would go to Mecklenburg because there everything happens decades later. wf.hagenow.de, can be found in Karl Kraus, Kraus Online, Ludwig Boltzmann Institut für Geschichte und Theorie der Biographie, Online: https://www.kraus.wienbibliothek.at/content/wenn-die-welt-untergeht-dann-gehe-ich-nach-wien-dort-passiert-alles-zehn-jahre-spaeter, (Wien, 2019).
29 Deutscher Bundestag, StenographischerBericht, 177. Sitzung, Plenarprotokoll 11/177, (Bonn, 1989).
30 James D. Bindenagel, Countering disinformation on German reunification and NATO enlargement, in *Europe's World*, Citizens' Europe, Online: https://www.friendsofeurope.org/insights/countering-disinformation-on-german-reunification-and-nato-enlargement/, (Brussles, 2019).
31 USBerlin NIACT Immediate cable 3430, 051213Z December, "Momper's Grim Analysis of GDR Situation".

to talks at the highest level to keep calm. Secretary of State James A. Baker III sought stability in the upheaval and to promote elections to help control the breakdown of order in East Germany. He visited West Berlin on December 11–12, 1989, to explain President Bush's policy that as "Europe changes, the instruments for Western cooperation must adapt."[32] Although he spoke of a new security architecture that included the Soviet Union, Baker also made clear that the emerging architecture must have a place for NATO, even if also serving new collective purposes.[33] Baker also met with Chancellor Kohl, who was concerned about the deteriorating political situation in East Germany. Providing security and stability in Europe was at the heart of Baker's West Berlin speech as he spoke of designing and gradually putting into place a new architecture for a new era.[34]

Baker's motorcade drove from West Berlin across the Glienicke Bridge, known for spy-swapping – Gary Powers, Natan Scharansky, and others. Baker crossed into Potsdam in East Germany and met GDR Prime Minister Hans Modrow and also separately with Manfred Stolpe, who represented the Lutheran Church. They discussed German unification, German NATO membership, GDR elections, and future economic cooperation, but Baker told Modrow to address economic cooperation after elections in East Germany. It was Modrow's promise to Baker of free and fair elections for a new *Volkskammer* that would move East Germany further down the path to unification.

In February 1990, Baker also met with Gorbachev in Moscow and secured his agreement that a united Germany could remain in NATO and that NATO would not station troops in the territory of former East Germany while Soviet Troops were still there. In February 1990, Chancellor Helmut Kohl also met Gorbachev, who confirmed his agreement to German unification with Germany in NATO. Critical decisions were occurring in East Germany. On December 1, 1989, the ruling East German communist party, the SED, removed their monopoly on power from their constitution, confirming the communist party no longer had constitutional legitimacy to govern.

East Germans wanted to be 'One German people' and decided to participate in West German parties, particularly the Christian Democratic Union (CDU) and the Christian Social Union (CSU), both of which were calling for German unification. East Germans had to establish legitimate parliamentary governance through free and fair elections held on March 18, 1990. East Germans voted in the first free and fair democratic election in the history of their country, and East

---

32 James A Baker in: The New York Times, *UPHEAVAL IN THE EAST; Excerpts From Baker's Speech on Berlin and U.S. Role in Europe's Future*, Online: http://www.nytimes.com/1989/12/13/world/upheaval-east-excerpts-baker-s-speech-berlin-us-role-europe-s-future.html?pagewanted=3, (West Berlin, 1989).
33 Ibid.
34 Ibid.

German citizens elected a government with a mandate to open the way for the unification of Germany. The West German Basic Law, with its commitment to democracy, the rule of law and respect for human dignity, offered East Germans a new, democratic identity compatible with West Germany. In Leipzig in January 1990, East Germans cheered "We are one people" or "*Wir sind ein Volk*" and demanded reunification.[35] They won the day, fulfilling the dissidents' demand that they were the people (*Wir sind das Volk*) when the *Volkskammer* chose Lothar de Maiziere as prime minister, who led the way for the East Germans mandate for unification. On August 23, 1990, the *Volkskammer* voted for accession to the West German constitution, and Germany unified.[36]

Other parties, notably the West German Social Democrats (SPD), were calling for more time. The West German Social Democratic Party called for unification through Article 146 negotiations and a new constitution to be ratified by referendum rather than accession under Article 23 of the Basic Law. German unification of the two parliamentary democracies was possible, but not all agreed to that path. The Green Party, *Bündnis-90,* was against annexation under this article of the Basic Law, arguing with a play on words from a telephone text recording played when no connection was possible – no connection translates to no annexation (*"Kein Anschluss unter dieser Nummer"*).

After the election, the East German Parliament (*Volkskammer*) voted to accede to the Basic Law under then-Article 23. Not only was Germany united, but it also became fully sovereign. Through the accession to the West German constitution, the newly reconstituted States that were East Germany united Germany with the self-determination that gave the country democratic legitimacy. However, not everyone was enamored with Germany's sudden unification. The prospect of German unification that followed the Peaceful Revolution had started an intense debate about a resurgent Germany. The fall of the Berlin Wall raised the idea of a united, sovereign Germany, which recalled a frightening 20th century filled with German domination, war, and destruction in Europe and throughout the world. What would a sovereign Germany mean to Europe? The end of the Cold War was coming. What would happen to the closing of the German Question at unification? Would Germany keep its membership in NATO?

France, Britain, and other countries feared a united Germany would become a European hegemon and that unification might lead to domination or even war as experienced in the 20th century. The German Question is about its role in Europe. During the Cold War confrontation, Germany remained divided, and its sover-

---

35 Mary Fulbook, Wir sind ein Volk? Reflections on German Unification in: *Parliamentary Affairs*, Volume 44, Issue 3, (Oxford University Press: Oxford, 1991), p. 389.
36 Mitteldeutscher Rundfunk, Die Volkskammer beschließt den Beitritt zur Bundesrepublik, Online: https://www.mdr.de/zeitreise/beschluss-beitritt-brd100.html, (MDR 1990, zuletzt aktualisiert 2018).

eignty was in the hands of the Four Allied Powers from the Second World War – the U.S., France, Great Britain, and the Soviet Union. The Four Powers had held the sovereignty of any future, united Germany – Berlin and Germany as a whole. They now had agreed to unite Germany. Unification meant Germany's extraordinary economic strength, increasing the military role, and move from geo-economic to a geopolitical role was forthcoming. Europeans raised concerns. The debate opened notably in France and the United Kingdom on Germany's peaceful rise. Keeping it peaceful required tapping Germany's commitment to democracy, the rule of law, a deeper EU, and the revitalized transatlantic partnership.

Helmut Kohl, Mikhail Gorbachev, and George H.W. Bush in cooperation with James Baker, Eduard Shevardnadze, and Hans-Dietrich Genscher passed the baton for negotiations of Treaty on the Final Settlement with Respect to Germany *(Two + Four Agreement)* for unification with the Four Powers with both German states, but primarily among themselves. Although they brought East Germans along, the negotiators reached critical decisions on German sovereignty with minimal consultations with East German Prime Minister de Maiziere and Foreign Minister Markus Meckel. Gorbachev's agreement to drop the Brezhnev Doctrine and allow Germany, as well as other countries, to make their own decisions on military alliances was confirmed with Chancellor Kohl in February and with President Bush in May 1990.

In May 1990, Bush and Gorbachev met in Washington, and Gorbachev reconfirmed the Soviet Union's acceptance of U.S. policy to keep Germany in NATO after unification. Gorbachev repeated his renunciation of the Brezhnev Doctrine during his Washington meetings with President Bush. The U.S. offered a concession to ease the end of the Cold War: to reduce U.S. forces in a united Germany. The victorious Four Powers from World War II retained rights and responsibility for Berlin and Germany as a whole, which would determine what Germany's sovereignty would be after unification. At unification, the Four Powers relinquished their limits on German sovereignty. The restoration of German sovereignty through the *2+4 Negotiations* created a unified, sovereign Germany in October 1990.

Ending the Cold War was more than the Four Powers giving up their World War II-era rights; the Cold War determined the lives of two generations, symbolized by the face-off of American and Soviet tanks at Checkpoint Charlie. During this period leading up to the East German election, the small American Embassy in East Germany was deluged with visits by Congressmen and Senators seeking to get a first-hand look at the revolution, the March 18, 1990 election, and the progress toward unification. One of them was Senator Chris Dodd from Connecticut, who came to observe the East German election campaign in March 1990 as a guest of Elmar Brok from the West German Christian Democratic Party.

Unification negotiations between the two Germanys and the Four Powers from World War II were well underway, and the campaign for the East German parliamentary election on March 18, 1990, was in full swing. The West German CDU helped the East CDU in the election campaign, and European Parliament Member Elmar Brok invited Connecticut Senator Chris Dodd to visit East Germany to experience the parliamentary (*Volkskammer*) election campaign. American Embassies offer support to visiting Congress Members and Senators, which led me to come from East Berlin to meet and greet Senator Dodd at Tempelhof Airport in West Berlin on his way to East Germany. While waiting for Senator Dodd to arrive, the US Berlin Military Brigade protocol officer informed me that Major General Raymond E. Haddock, the U.S. military commandant in West Berlin, had made arrangements to dismantle Checkpoint Charlie. That Checkpoint was the symbol of Berlin's and Europe's division and dismantling it was a significant political statement.

After sharing the news of Checkpoint Charlie's planned demise with Ambassador Richard C. Barkley in East Berlin, he informed State Department Central European Office Director Pierre Shostal. When Secretary of State James Baker learned of the general's, plans he stopped them. Baker saw decommissioning of Checkpoint Charlie as a highly symbolic event, which could demonstrate to the world, especially to skeptical publics in several countries via the global media, that the Four Powers were determined to end the confrontation of the Cold War peacefully. Baker ordered the Checkpoint Charlie decommissioning ceremony be on June 22, 1990, to set the stage for the same day's *2+4 Negotiations* in Berlin.

Symbolically, the Cold War ended on June 22, 1990, with the decommissioning of Checkpoint Charlie in Berlin. The six foreign ministers made promises and positions for the coming peace. For decommissioning to work, Soviet Foreign Minister Eduard Shevardnadze needed to accept Baker's invitation. The State Department sent orders for our embassy to make every effort to win the support of the Soviet Embassy for Shevardnadze to attend the decommissioning. My Soviet counterpart, Minister Igor Maximetchev, took much effort to convince him that the June 22, 1990, Checkpoint Charlie decommissioning ceremony was critical for his Foreign Minister. Decommissioning took on the added importance not only as a symbol of divided Berlin, Germany, and Europe but was also a sign of the beginning of cooperation with the Soviet Union.

Secretary Baker had invited the foreign ministers from East and West Germany, the four World War II "Victorious Powers" foreign ministers of France, Britain, the Soviet Union, and the United States as well as the mayors from East and West Berlin and the military commanders from divided Berlin's four sectors. However, the Russian public and Gorbachev's opponents were still sensitive about the implication of German unification and the *2+4 Negotiations*. Gorbachev could slow down the negotiations to assuage skeptical Russian people, but if he did, he risked giving time to his opponents to act against a unification treaty.

Shortly before the date of the decommissioning, Soviet Foreign Minister Shevardnadze finally decided to participate and used the occasion to lay out the Soviet position. *Stars & Stripes*, the U.S. military newspaper, described the decommissioning as an elaborate, well-rehearsed ceremony attended by

> the foreign ministers of the two Germanys, France, Britain, the Soviet Union, and the United States ... *Stars & Stripes* reported that Soviet Foreign Minister Eduard A. Shevardnadze, in a surprise announcement, proposed the withdrawal of the victorious World War II Allies' troops from Berlin six months after German unification.[37]

All who were watching could see the change that was coming to the Cold War conflict.

Secretary of State James A. Baker III, in his remarks, said:

> At this checkpoint, the United States stood with its allies and with the German people, resolved to resist aggression and determined to overcome the division .of the Cold War. And now, with the help of a new generation of Soviet leaders, that time has come.[38]

There was even a bit of triumphalism when British Foreign Minister Douglas Hurd said: "We should not forget and our children should not forget the reasons for which Checkpoint Charlie stood here for so many years… At long last, we are bringing Charlie in from the cold."[39] Following the decommissioning of Checkpoint Charlie, the foreign ministers went back to their *2+4 Negotiations* in Berlin at Schloss Niederschönhausen.

Agreement on German unification was reached and at midnight on October 2, 1990, walking for the last time from the U.S. Embassy to the German Democratic Republic at Neustädtischekirchstrasse in East Berlin, through the Brandenburg Gate to West Berlin, my wife and I witnessed Berlin's and Germany's unification at the Reichstag. East and West German dignitaries, including West German Chancellor Kohl and East German Prime Minister de Maizière, stood on the dais of the Reichstag as fireworks exploded in celebration.

The story of the Peaceful Revolution, and the courage, hopes, and politics that shaped events and confirmed established values, principles, and laws that govern Germany today, will be retold many times. American continued interest in united

---

37 Ken Clauson, "Berlin's Checkpoint Charlie closes", Stars and Stripes, Online: https://www.stripes.com/news/berlin-s-checkpoint-charlie-closes-1.12086, (Washington D.C., 1990).
38 James A. Baker III, in: Ken Clauson, "Berlin's Checkpoint Charlie closes", Stars and Stripes, Online: https://www.stripes.com/news/berlin-s-checkpoint-charlie-closes-1.12086, (Washington D.C., 1990).
39 Douglas Hurd, in: Ken Clauson, "Berlin's Checkpoint Charlie closes", Stars and Stripes, Online: https://www.stripes.com/news/berlin-s-checkpoint-charlie-closes-1.12086, (Washington D.C., 1990).

Germany's membership in NATO after unification was essential to peace in Europe. The United States and the transatlantic partnership have been critical supporters of European integration. U.S. foreign policy objectives have worked to promote American and European commitment to shared values of freedom, human rights, democracy, and the rule of law.

Chapter 2: A Peaceful Revolution for Democracy: An Eyewitness Account

The Thirtieth Anniversary of the Peaceful Revolution and unification is an opportunity for an eyewitness report from the U.S. Embassy to the German Democratic Republic to re-tell some of the events seen in the revolution. I was there; here is my story.

In the autumn of 1989, East Germans took to the streets, defied their government, and demanded freedom. East German demonstrators were encouraged by the visit of then-Soviet President Mikhail Gorbachev on October 7, the eve of the 40th Anniversary of the GDR. To his eternal credit, he was pursuing new thinking that would transform and revitalize the Soviet Union through *perestroika* and *glasnost*. East Germany's First Secretary Erich Honecker himself was challenged to accept Gorbachev's reforms but rejected them. East German dissidents used Gorbachev as protection as they protested in the streets against Honecker without the intention to deny the legitimacy of the East German state. Even though Honecker himself rejected Gorbachev's message, Gorbachev determinedly championed the new path toward parliamentary democracy and market reforms to make the Soviet Union more competitive with the West.

The pace of the revolution was breathtaking and would determine the success in East Germany of more openness and economic restructuring. It threatened Erich Honecker's ruling party. Across East Germany, a democratic revolution would sweep away the communist government at a breathtaking pace. It takes courage to launch a revolution. After all, established governments brutally crushed attempts in the March 1848, Democratic, and in the November 1918, Socialist Republic revolutions. However, 1989 was different. Courage would be triumphant, and a Peaceful Revolution would bring down the East German government.

A conspiratorial group of dissidents organized one of the first acts in the 1989 revolution, a citizens' movement designed to catch the government in a lie about municipal elections on May 7, 1989. That defiance of the government would help launch a budding revolution. On May 6, 1989, Walter Andrusyszyn, an American diplomat, visited me in East Berlin and, in the fading light of day on the Weidendamm Bridge in East Berlin, introduced me to Thomas Krüger, an East German dissident. Krüger was meeting with a small group of opposition dissidents that night in a conspiratorial apartment in Berlin-Weissensee and invited me to join them. In a "conspiratorial" apartment in East Berlin, dissidents prepared to challenge the dictatorship of the Socialist Unity Party (SED) through poll watching. They planned to report the next day that the government had falsified the results in that election.

The group of mostly young German men and women were organizing a poll-watching effort for the May 7 Berlin municipal elections. It was the night before the election, and this budding rebellion against Honecker's communist dictatorship would soon challenge the SED dictatorship. Those gathered in that "conspiratorial" apartment in East Berlin were willing to risk their jobs, families, and even their lives to fan the flames of 'reforms' that would lead to the revolution. The next day they set out to tally all the results in every polling place. That morning after attending church, I took my family to the Blumenthalstraße voting booth in a Kindergarten to capture the spirit of those challenging the government. We learned that each polling place would announce its results. Soon we would witness the poll watchers as they collected those results and, with the count they had taken, exposed the lies of the government-announced municipal election results on May 7, 1989. The dissidents' act of rebellion resulted in government resistance with some dissidents' arrests and harassment. They planted the seeds of revolution.

Asylum seekers in the U.S. Embassy: Freedom

Throughout the summer of 1989, other East Germans voted with their feet in a seemingly unstoppable wave of East Germans fleeing through Hungary to freedom. In September, Germans fled to Prague and Budapest, to seize opportunities opened as Eastern Europe was in flux Tension was in the air as East Germans fled. In September alone, 33,255 GDR citizens escaped the country. Between September 30 and October 4, 1989, around 13,000 East German citizens in the West German Embassy in Czechoslovakia traveled by train from Prague to their new home in West Germany.[40]

The U.S. Embassy did not escape the trials and tribulations of those in upheaval seeking freedom. The Solidarity movement had swept through Poland and yet, surprisingly, had not been crushed by Soviet intervention. However, fleeing Poland under martial law of Prime Minister Wojciech Witold Jaruzelski

---

40 Chronik der Mauer, Chronicle 1989, Online: http://www.chronik-der-mauer.de/en/chronicle/_year1989/_month9/?moc=1, (Bundeszentrale für politische Bildung: Bonn, 2015).

was also tricky. Hungry was most interesting to us in East Berlin; Hungry was also going its own way and by the summer of 1989 had already signed the UN Convention on Refugees, putting them in conflict with requirements of the Warsaw Pact.[41] The Warsaw Pact required the Hungarian government to send any Warsaw Pact citizens back to the country they were trying to flee. But if they were refugees, designated as refugees under the UN Convention, they could be let free. Once the Hungarians symbolically cut the fence – the iron curtain – in May, numbers of refugees began to increase.

Ambassador Richard Barkley and I visited Honecker's lawyer, Wolfgang Vogel, at his modest home on Lake Schwerinsee in August, and he told us that the Hungarians would likely allow several hundred East Germans in Hungary escape to the West. After the Hungarians had dramatically cut down the barbed wire fence along their border in May, their border was as an escape hatch from the communist bloc. Cutting down the fence launched a flood of German refugees fleeing in late summer. The Hungarians were about to honor their new commitment to a UN Refugee Convention and to ignore their obligations under the Warsaw Pact to return East Germans to the GDR.

East Germans traveled to Czechoslovakia and to Hungary to flee to West Germany. Communist governments were under tremendous and growing pressure to maintain control. And that pressure was felt acutely in East Germany as it approached its 40th Anniversary.

Our concern was whether the Soviet Union would act militarily to protect its interests and maintain control in East Germany. Would they protect the Berlin Wall the East Germans built, or not? We recalled that James Markham of the New York Times, who at a meeting in Vienna in January 1989 had asked Georgy Arbatov, Director of the Soviet Union's Institute of United States and Canada Studies from 1967 to 1995, whether the Berlin Wall would stand. Arbatov told Markham to ask in Berlin, not Moscow, which surprised us since we believed the Soviets stood behind the Wall. Erich Honecker had an answer: The Berlin Wall would stand for a hundred years.

Honecker, at this point, was an anachronistic leader within the Soviet Bloc; he was the worst figure for reforms that Gorbachev had proposed. He certainly was not accessible. He and the Czech leader were the two pro-Stalinist-leaders still resisting glasnost. They were the two stalwarts to Stalinism, and Gorbachev had to encourage them to step down from their offices. The Hungarians had led the way by accepting glasnost. The Poles launched the revolution in 1980 with the Solidarity movement. East Germans, a million who had sought to immigrate, started to poor over the Hungarian and Czechoslovakian borders.

---

41 Barkley-Bindenagel visit with Wolfgang Vogel at Schwerinsee.

Honecker and SED leaders were much embarrassed by the trainload of East German "refugees," who had been released from the West German Embassy in Prague in September and allowed to travel to West Germany. The Honecker-Regime demanded that the train travel through East-Germany, and the Germans get papers from the GDR as they went to Hof in West Germany. Jeff Biron, an American embassy driver, on October 5, witnessed the second train of refugees transported from the West German Embassy in Prague to Hof. Demonstrators blocked the trains in Dresden, and Jeff called us in Berlin from his hotel overlooking the confrontation in Dresden at the train station. Police used tear gas and clubs to clear the tracks to move away from other East Germans wanting to get on the train. After Jeff continued on his private travel, Mary Agnes McAleenan, an economic section secretary who was also an eyewitness, continued to report to the political section in Berlin.[42] All sides were very much on the verge of a violent confrontation. Honecker was determined not to have another incident like the Prague Embassy before the anniversary celebration on October 7.

Suddenly and without warning, on October 3rd, just before the 40th-anniversary celebration, the GDR closed its border for East German travel to Hungary and Czechoslovakia and imposed an exit visa requirement for travel to both countries. The U.S. Embassy in East Berlin was immediately affected late in the afternoon of October 3rd. Official word of the border closing reached us during the day. That afternoon 18 people leaving the GDR were forced by border police to return from at the border because they didn't have exit visas. They didn't go home, however. They arrived in Berlin and went to the Permanent Representation Office of West Germany, seeking to emigrate. The West German Mission had been closed since July 1989 because over in July, more than 130 refugees had attempted the same route to freedom through the West German Mission. It took the West German mission, led by Franz Bertele and Jörg von Studnitz, months to win exit visas for them. Ambassador Barkley wanted to avoid the fate of the West Germans, who had to close their office; the American Embassy was to stay open. We also had learned the lessons from an earlier East German attempt to seek asylum in the under then-Ambassador Rozanne Ridgway, when the U.S. Embassy Berlin (East) asked the asylum seekers to leave. We would not repeat that act in 1989.

Fleeing to the West on October 3, this group of nervous East Germans turned to the American Embassy for help. They arrived at the American Embassy late in the day, and the Marine Guard called for political counselor Jon Greenwald as several children entered the embassy with their parents knocking on the door seeking asylum. One of our consuls came out to meet them and asked what they

---

42 G. Jonathan Greenwald, *Berlin Witness: An American Diplomat's Chronicles of East German's Revolution*, (Pennsylvania State University Press: Pennsylvania 1993), pp. 166–167.

were doing. As he opened the front door of the embassy, they rushed in, and that moment, captured by live international television, was their opening for freedom.

Once they inside the embassy, five children under the age of five, and 13 adults fearful of leaving and not knowing what to do next entered the U.S. Embassy. They told us that they wanted safe passage out of the GDR to the Federal Republic of Germany because they knew that after the 40th Anniversary, the security forces would crack down on citizens fleeing the country, which was a crime of fleeing the GDR, *Republikflucht.* They feared they would never get out of East Germany and would face prison. They hoped that the American Embassy would offer that a chance to flee after East German border officials had refused to let them cross the border into Czechoslovakia.

Political Counselor Jon Greenwald and Consul General Mary Rose Brandt settled the fleeing Germans into the public areas of the entrance; they were frightened and agitated. Ambassador Barkley immediately called Wolfgang Vogel, Honecker's lawyer, to inform him that we had people in the U.S. Embassy seeking to flee. Barkley asked for some assistance and told Vogel that he thought it appropriate that they leave. U.S. Consul General Mary Rose Brandt obtained their names and identification and took their names to Vogel's office in Reiler Strasse.

Wolfgang Vogel went through the process of getting approval from State Security (Stasi) and Erich Honecker, clearing the conflict with refugees on international television before the 40th Anniversary was upon the SED. The wish to avoid adverse television coverage during the celebration was an incentive to resolve the asylum seekers' problem. The East Germans stayed overnight in the front hall of the embassy chancellery outside the "hardline" blocking internal entrance that we used for security. We waited for an answer from the Honecker government on permission for them to emigrate. Embassy staff members went shopping to get them some food and then took care of them overnight. Jon Greenwald reported that closing the border closing was an act of desperation by Honecker accentuated by the arrival of Soviet President Gorbachev for the anniversary. East German leaders prepared to use violence to prevent disruption of the 40th Anniversary celebration that coming weekend. It appeared that the Honecker era was ending, and some reforms, at least easing travel restrictions, were coming.[43]

At the same time outside the Embassy and around in East Berlin were dozens of International TV crews preparing for the 40th Anniversary. The TV crews, milling about with no live pictures, found our embassy, with its asylum seekers, a prime-time story to report. We did not think that television could peer into the embassy building, but we also did not know whether they would report on the asylum seekers in the embassy. Not unexpectedly in the morning, there was a

---

43 Ibid., pp. 162–163.

German news report that there were asylum-seeking Germans in the U.S. Embassy. The news service was German, which turned the embassy into a Mecca for others seeking to flee East Germany. A West Berlin news service reported on the asylum seekers. The evening the East Germans arrived, there was a journalist inside the lobby. I recalled seeing a visitor when visiting the refugees and that he was a journalist who did not say anything and left. In any case, the next day, the world's spotlight turned on us, and suddenly, some 200 people gathered outside the Embassy and tried to get in.

Tension rose as the people outside pushed up against the 1880s constructed embassy building. After the Second World War, the building had been the home of the East German Craftsmans' Guild when the U.S. rented it in 1974 soon after the United States established diplomatic relations with East Germany. A wooden frame held to the stone arch and secured with wooden wedges held the door to the embassy, leaving the center archway very unstable. Although we had asked the State Department for money to replace it with something more stable, we had to live with the shaky portal. The asylum seekers were between this wobbly door and the hardline security parameter, which they obviously could not pass. We had no choice but to keep them in the front entry where this door could fall on them if it came to a confrontation at the front door.

In the late morning, I went to Vogel's office to receive his slips of paper with his signature and name of each of the fleeing East Germans. These papers were the exit visa passes to get them out of East Germany. When I returned to the Embassy to give out the passes, the asylum seekers questioned whether we could guarantee that this slip of paper was real and would work for them. Vogel had to talk to them on the phone to convince them of the passes' validity.

At the same time, about 3 p.m., the 200 people outside where getting restless and demanded entry as they pressed up against the building. As *Deputy Chief of Mission* (DCM /Deputy ambassador), I made one of the most challenging calls in my assignment when I requested help to secure the embassy entrance from the East German Ministry of Foreign Affairs (MFAA). I told them that we needed to maintain access to the building according to the Geneva Convention to allow unimpeded access to the embassy and asked if they would have the demonstrators move on the other side of the street but not disperse them. We had no problem that they demonstrated, but we needed to access the embassy.

I knew the danger of that decision when the East German government officials were pleased the Americans asked for the *Volkspolizei* (*Vopos*/People's Police) move against East Germans. Sure enough, the Volkspolizei came and forced the 200 people back across the street, but still in front of the embassy. Then the worst scenario unfolded as rumors of protests grew, and the press assembled to cover the Communist party celebration. In the late afternoon, several people came to the shaky front door, rang the bell, and demanded entry. A consul, Steven Slick, opened the door, and the crowd surged. Immediately the East German police moved to restrain them.

As the *Vopos* moved the crowd back across the street, a woman sat down on the sidewalk with her children. *Vopos* returned, picked her with her children, and loaded them on the back of a police truck, eerily reminiscent of the Nazis and the transports during the Holocaust. TV Crews in East Berlin for the 40th Anniversary filmed the entire scene. The event was broadcast immediately on television, including CNN in the U.S. I was inside the chancery building and could not see what was going on outside, nor was I watching television, and therefore did not see the broadcast, but the TV crews covered all angles.

We still had the eighteen fleeing Germans to set free with their Vogel exit passes and could not open the doors without expecting a rush from the assembled demonstrators across the street. About 4 o'clock, I recommended we close the embassy for the day to allow the refugees to leave without being stormed by others. It was an anxious moment. I told Ambassador Barkley that what we need to do is close the Embassy, and hopefully, people would go home and allow us to let these 18 people out.

The word that we were closing reached the demonstrators outside of the building and also the television crews, which reported immediately and surprised the State Department. Jim Dobbins, the European Bureau Deputy Assistant Secretary, called before I could get from the front door to my office. He was outraged and enraged. He had just heard from the Secretary's office, and they were yelling at him, and he was yelling at me not to close the embassy. From the TV reports, the press office of the State Department had assumed that we were closing the embassy permanently, as the West Germans had done earlier. Dobbins made clear that only the State Department could order an embassy closed. I explained the danger of the insecure door, the crowd of demonstrators seeking to force their way into the embassy and tried to reassure him that we were closed only for the day. I told Jim Dobbins that it was 4 o'clock and that we will be open the next morning. We were not closing like the West German mission. We just needed to provide for the safety of these people we were helping to flee East Germany. He was still not happy, but given assurance that we were closing early for the day and not permanently shutting, and he reluctantly accepted my report. We maintained an open Embassy.

Ambassador Barkley also went back to Vogel and asked him to take into consideration and treat favorably any of the demonstrators who also applied for exit visas. Vogel gave us assurances that the message would be delivered and told Barkley that he had already identified the woman and children who were transported on the police truck to get them exit visas. After we closed for the day, we were able to let the East German asylum seekers out without incident as they made their way to West Berlin and freedom. That excitement was typical of the kind of role an embassy played in this revolution.

The Germans had agreed to leave the embassy, and we just opened the door. They decided for themselves whether they would walk out on their own. We were not going to force anybody out. We had to convince them that what we had done was legitimate. It had taken Wolfgang Vogel's personal calls directly to them, explaining that they had to believe in this piece of paper, which in his phone call Vogel had negotiated free passage for themselves and their husbands and wives.

We had no immediate feedback after they left. Later, Wolfgang Vogel confirmed that they emigrated. However, for us, the issue was not to repeat a years-earlier incident in the same embassy when a fleeing East German was turned away and immediately arrested by the East German police. Not to repeat that nightmare was always the question for us. We would not expel people from the Embassy, nor could we give them asylum, nor could we guarantee their emigration. We could only act as a facilitator between them and the GDR government, in this case with Wolfgang Vogel. We had found Wolfgang Vogel, whom we over the many years had dealt with him as an honest, straightforward negotiator as Erich Honecker's lawyer. The fleeing Germans from the U.S. Embassy that October 1989 fled to West Germany before the East Germans celebrated their 40th anniversary.

East Germany's 40th Anniversary and Crackdown on Counterrevolutionaries

Days after the asylum seekers left for West Berlin, the 40th anniversary of East Germany, the confrontation between East German Street demonstrations and the East German police reached a critical point. Honecker's regime or the street demonstrators would prevail. On Saturday, October 7, 1989, just over a month before the collapse of the Berlin Wall, East Germany celebrated its 40th anniversary. A massive torchlight parade marched down Berlin's main boulevard, *Unter den Linden*; a gala dinner followed in the *Palast der Republik* with leaders from the Communist world and included the U.S. Ambassador Richard Barkley. President Gorbachev attended the celebration but returned immediately afterward to Moscow. Gorbachev, after warning that those who came too late, would be punished by history.[44]

---

44 Bindenagel, James, Eyewitness Report; Mikahail Gorbachev, in: Claus Menzel, Wer zu spat kommt, den bestraft das Leben. Vor 20 Jahren sagte Gorbatschow das Ende der DDR voraus, Online: https://www.deutschlandfunk.de/wer-zu-spaet-kommt-den-bestraft-das-leben.871.de.html?dram:article_id=126749, (Deutschland Funk, 2009).

As soon as the festivities had ended, the Honecker regime launched its crackdown on demonstrators supporting Gorbachev's reforms in East Germany. In Berlin, demonstrators had gathered for months at the Evangelical Lutheran Gethsemane Church to appeal for the release of political prisoners, the freedom to travel, and adherence to the *Helsinki Final Act* guaranteeing human rights. On October 7, 1989, I joined them for a time before 10 p.m., when hundreds of police swooped down with violence, bludgeoning and arresting more than 3,000 people. Similar crackdowns took place elsewhere in Berlin and other cities in East Germany. In Leipzig, on October 9, peaceful demonstrators courageously faced off a massive armed force from the regime, and that showed the revolution could be non-violent.

A small group of dissidents gathered in the village of Schwante and dared to challenge the legitimacy of the ruling Socialist Unity Party. Their act was to threaten its existence by creating a new Social Democratic Party (SDP). The communist party in 1946 had forced the once-proud Social Democratic Party in East Germany to merge with it to forge the Socialist Unity Party (SED). The SED would govern East Germany with a monopoly on power set down in the East German constitution. These dissidents hit the legitimacy of the ruling party in the hopes it would lead to the collapse of the SED, and that took courage. If the SED lost its political legitimacy, it might signal the end of East Germany. Honecker could only fall back on the Soviet military to sustain his legitimacy over East Germany. If his planned SED crackdown on 'counterrevolutionaries' failed, Honecker would stand alone.

Two Lutheran Ministers, Martin Gutzeit from Oranienburg, und Markus Meckel from Magdeburg, started this personally dangerous initiative to create an SDP political party early in the year. On August 26, 1989, at a public seminar about the French Revolution and human rights in the Berlin Golgotha church, they advocated publicly for the breakup of the SED by founding a new Social Democratic Party. By September, a core opposition group was growing. Greifswald Pastor Arndt Noack and the Berlin historian Ibrahim Böhme joined in the movement.[45]

Honecker's showdown with 'counterrevolutionaries' was to come on October 7, 1989, as East Germany's celebration of its 40th anniversary was underway. In East Berlin, the National Peoples' Army marched down Leipziger Straße in a show of military might. After Mikhail Gorbachev left East Berlin, Honecker's crackdown began that night with the police rounding up demonstrator throughout the coun-

---

45 Wolfgang Grof, In der frischen Tradition des Herbstes 1989, in: Sozialdemokratische Partei, 7. Oktober 1989. Morgenröte in Schwante, Online: https://www.spd.de/aktuelles/30-jahre-sdp/morgenroete-in-schwante/, (Archiv der sozialen Demokratie (AdsD) der Friedrich-Ebert-Stiftung: Bonn, 2020).

try. That same day outside of Berlin, in the small village of Schwante, a group of men and women gathered to found the SDP as a political party in defiance of the SED. Led by Pastors Meckel and Gutzeit, this group of 40 courageous Germans, signed the charter establishing a new Social Democratic Party. Among the group of some 40 activists, with Ibrahim Böhme, Angelika Barbe, Arndt Noack, Thomas Krüger, and Stephan Hilsberg.[46]

Those who had already arrived waited for others to come to the Lutheran Church parsonage in Schwante. No one knew how violently the regime would react to the growing protests. Markus Meckel recalled that the tension was so high that he went underground on October 2, 1989.[47] The tension was widespread from the June 17, 1953, Soviet tanks crushing the demonstrators in East Berlin, and China's massacre of students on Tiananmen Square in June 1989, which raised the specter of an East German "Chinese Solution" threat to democratic dissidents. Some wondered and hoped Gorbachev's perestroika and openness might prevail peacefully. They were painfully aware that launching a charter of a new Social Democratic Party carried with it personal risk.

Thomas Krüger had a mission to get to Schwante. He was bringing a draft letter requesting West German SPD leader Willy Brandt's support the new SDP. A Western endorsement by Socialists International would boost the East SDP and help the dissidents defy the Honecker regime. He recalled the dramatic chase by the *Stasi* as he set off. The *Stasi* (*Ministry for State Security*/Ministerium für Staatssicherheit/MfS/*Stasi*) was close on his tail. Still, Krüger was determined to fulfill his mission despite the Stasi secret police chase in their Lada automobiles, which were faster than the Wartburg cars used by the Peoples Police. Krüger had to ensure he made it to the meeting. That meant shaking off the Stasi following him. He headed directly to a church in Oranienburg. Slipping out of his car, Krüger proceeded directly inside, exited through the back door, and took a footbridge over a stream. Waiting on the other side was another car to take him with his letter for Brandt to Schwante. Krüger sped away, and for a short time, the Stasi stood at their vehicles stuck on the other side of the stream. Krüger was relieved when he arrived with the smuggled draft letter to Brandt ready for the signatures of the assembled dissidents.[48]

The SDP Charter was signed, creating a new political party, and the move toward democracy took a tentative step forward. Those gathered in the church

---

46 Claudai van Laak, Es geschah in Schwante: Die Gründung der SDP der DDR vor 20 Jahren, in: Deutschlandfunk Kultur, Online: https://www.deutschlandfunkkultur.de/es-geschah-in-schwante.1001.de.html?dram:article_id=156898, (Berlin, 2009) and author's observation 1989.
47 Yvonne Jennerjahn, Wendejahr 1989. Es begann in Brandenburg: Vor 30 Jahren wurde die SPD gegründet, in: Märkische Zeitung, Online: https://www.maz-online.de/Brandenburg/Es-begann-in-Brandenburg-Vor-30-Jahren-wurde-die-SPD-gegruendet, (Brandenburg, 2019).
48 Thomas Krüger, as told to the author 1990.

residence celebrated the founding of the Social Democratic Party of the German Democratic Republic. The letter to Willy Brandt, chairman of Socialists International to support the founding of the Social Democratic Party, was also signed. International recognition was crucial. Once Krueger had the Brandt letter, he had again to evade the *Stasi* and get the signed message to his contact in the West, Frank Reuter of the West German Permanent Mission. While Krüger sped in one direction, Steffen Reiche sped off to Berlin to meet with Western journalists to announce the founding of the SDP. Most of the dissidents risked prison but were undeterred.[49]

All the while, Stasi agents were determined to thwart the efforts to found a new political party. The *Stasi Office for Church Questions* (Kirchenabteilung des Ministerium für Staatssicherheit) had long identified the threat a new Social Democratic Party posed to the SED. The *Stasi* made an operations plan (Maßnahmeplan) to send *Stasi*-agents to crash the Schwante meeting. Their orders were to interrupt the proceedings, to intervene with arguments opposing the founding of the SDP, to create doubt on its effectiveness, to disrupt debates, to tear apart issues, and to create distrust among those gathered. The Stasi plan failed to stop the founding of the SDP.[50]

All dissidents knew the Stasi were spying on them, listening to their conversations, and following them, although no one knew the Stasi was also at the table. Only after the March 1990 election was the SDP president, Ibrahim Böhme, revealed as an informant for the *Ministry for State Security*.[51] He was the most prominent agent, Stasi-Spitzel. Later, on June 9, 1990, the East German SDP elected Wolfgang Thierse as the new party chairman and Willy Brandt, former Chancellor of West Germany and honorary chairman of the West German SPD, as honorary chairman of the East German SPD as well.

The crises moved from the streets of many cities to the East German communist party, SED, itself. The peace vigil and demonstrations in Leipzig found a resonance throughout the country. Herbert Wagner, later mayor of Dresden, along with leaders of the Dresden "Group of 20" protesters, met with others also opposed to the ruling SED party. Wagner had found a novel way to count supporters by establishing a bank account (*Giro Konto*) where East Germans could send donations of East-Marks. The contributions rose quickly, indicating an-

---

49 Ibid.
50 Yvonne Jennerjahn, Wendejahr 1989. Es begann in Brandenburg: Vor 30 Jahren wurde die SPD gegründet, in: Märkische Zeitung, Online: https://www.maz-online.de/Brandenburg/Es-begann-in-Brandenburg-Vor-30-Jahren-wurde-die-SDP-gegruendet, (Brandenburg, 2019).
51 Wolfgang Grof, In der frischen Tradition des Herbstes 1989, in: Sozialdemokratische Partei, 7. Oktober 1989. Morgenröte in Schwante, Online: https://www.spd.de/aktuelles/30-jahre-sdp/morgenroete-in-schwante/, (Archiv der sozialen Demokratie (AdsD) der Friedrich-Ebert-Stiftung: Bonn, 2020).

other wave of protest, and soon, some 100,000 East-Marks were raised to promote change. Shortly afterward, the political movement *Neues Forum* was founded.[52]

A Miracle of Peace in Leipzig: Courage for Freedom

Meanwhile, in Leipzig, residents took to the streets weekly to face down courageously a regime that had killed fellow citizens, whose only crime had been to seek freedom. Many East Germans have been killed as they attempted to escape over the Berlin Wall with 140 in Berlin alone. But freedom was a strong force, and on Monday, October 9, the crackdown just after the Berlin 40th Anniversary, demonstrators in Leipzig prepared for their march. Street demonstrations followed the usual Monday peace vigil at the *Nikolaikirche* That night, however, Honecker also made plans to end the counterrevolution in the streets. The East German secret State Security Service, *Stasi*, Companies' Shock Forces (*Betriebskampfgruppen*), and the Army were stationed in Leipzig to end the protests. Honecker had banned the press from the city, and the stage was set for violent confrontation and bloodshed.

Nikolaikirche in Leipzig

For years, the East German authorities had allowed Leipzig's peace vigils in protests for peace. The movement was initially sanctioned by the GDR in the early 1980s to fight against the announced deployment of a U.S. neutron bomb back in 1979, and because they had been anti-Western protests against NATO missile deployments. These demonstrations had been a part of growing anti-nuclear, anti-missile deployment protests in the 1980s, and were similar to those in West Germany.

Throughout the nuclear missile debate over deployment of U.S. Pershing missiles in West Germany, this church group transformed into a regular peace vigil that also began to question the SS-4 and SS-23 Soviet short-range and SS-20 intermediate-range nuclear missiles in East Germany. As the debates against nuclear missile deployments grew, Honecker's GDR differed with Gorbachev's reform in the Soviet Union, *glasnost* and *perestroika*. The East German protest

---

52 Herbert Wagner comment to author, of the Committee of 20 in Dresden, October 28, 2019.

movement used Gorbachev's *glasnost* policy to justify openness, allowing protest without contesting the legitimacy of the East German state.[53]

Monday demonstrations, led by Pastor Christian Führer at St. Nicholas Church (*Nikolaikirche*) in Leipzig, became the focal point of protest as a way to speak out for peace and freedom of travel guaranteed by the CSCE Helsinki Final Act in 1975. Every Monday at 6 p.m. after a peace vigil in the church, demonstrators would march. Then small numbers of people would leave the church, walk past the Police Station/Stasi office, and marched on to the Leipzig City Ring (*Innenstadtring*). The marchers carefully crafted the message to talk about a renewal of the GDR for freedom to travel and better socialism, not revolution. The vigils became a way to speak out for peace and freedom of travel. Street demonstrations followed after the Monday night peace vigil. The demonstrators did not want to face violence and death. The peace vigils would move outside the church and would grow in intensity as the GDR arrested some of the protesters. The vigil added prayers and pleas for the release of imprisoned protestors that drove people to march along the circle of downtown Leipzig.

While Leipzig citizens were organizing their opposition to the Honecker government, American embassy officers were talking with as many people as possible. They were reporting to Washington about the face-off that came nearer. On Monday, October 9, 1989, all eyes turned and focused on Leipzig. Families had split up so one parent could stay with the children if the other parent died in the demonstration. Some 70,000 courageous people would demonstrate.

Leipzig citizens feared for themselves, for friends, and those around them. They feared those in uniforms standing against them. They feared for their country. In Leipzig, as elsewhere in the GDR, the expectation of a Chinese Solution fed the fear of violence and was palpable. Would a "shoot-to-kill" order be carried out? In September, the number of demonstrators went from a few thousand to tens of thousands to hundreds of thousands throughout the country. Pastor Führer was allowed to host his peace vigil that night, but no longer with the encouragement or tacit allowance by the GDR. October 9 was the showdown date.

In the U.S. Embassy in East Berlin, we expected and feared a violent clash between the demonstrators and the police would end in bloodshed. In East Berlin, the U.S. Embassy spent the night on watch. Would the Soviet Army follow the Chinese example and intervene in East Germany to save it from an uprising? The Soviets had done so before in East Berlin in 1953. An embassy diplomat, Imre Lipping, was in Leipzig, ready to report to the U.S. Embassy.

---

53 Martina Waiblinger, Dass die DDR ausgerechnet an der Kirche scheitern sollte. Christian Führer und die Nikolaikirche. Bericht aus einer Tagung in Bad Boll von 6.–9. Januar 2009, Online: http://www.kirche-fuer-alle-web.de/christianfuehrer-nikolaikirche.pdf (Bad Boll, 2009).

On that fateful Monday, Leipzig's demonstrators met at the *Nikolaikirche* and other churches for the regular peace vigil. Afterward, 70,000 took to the streets, marching the city "ring" in protest against their government. It is here they shouted for the first time: "We are the People." The 70,000 people demonstrators made it the most massive demonstration at the time, and confrontation between the police and the demonstrators was feared and seemed inevitable.

Could the October 9 demonstration be kept from turning bloody? Renowned Gewandhaus Orchestra Conductor Kurt Masur was worried. He, too, knew of reports on protests in many cities that had seen stones thrown, windows smashed, cars burned, and police with rubber truncheons and water cannons beating back protestors. Even the previous Monday demonstration in Leipzig ended in violence. Masur would later see the events as revolutionary and recalled what he thought that afternoon: "When 17- and 18-year-olds said goodbye to their parents that day, it was like they were heading off to war. But everyone had had enough. All of them – all 70,000 of them – were able to overcome their fear and with civil courage marched."[54] There was a good reason to fear the "Chinese Solution," as seen on Tiananmen Square in Beijing.

All signs pointed to Honecker's willingness to use violence. Honecker had banned the press and was willing maybe even eager, to draw blood. Hospitals restocked blood supplies, and doctors' leaves were canceled.[55] The police, backed by the military, indeed were prepared to stop the counterrevolutionaries with the 'Chinese Solution.' If necessary, the protest that night would be broken up by the force of arms. Yet the people were desperate for their freedom.

Although the police and their reinforcements and the army were on alert, a strange twist happened on the way to a potentially violent confrontation. Gorbachev's East German supporters, notably Hans Modrow, later the last communist prime minister in East Germany, saw the dilemma. If the use of force crushed the demonstrators, it would also end *glasnost* and *perestroika*. If necessary, the protest that night would be broken up by force. The people were desperate for their freedom. One of the dissident movement groups, *Neues Forum*, heard that military units were deployed all around Leipzig. They called Masur for help. And for that day, the *Gewandhaus* turned into a communications center.[56]

---

54 Kurt Masur, in: Spiegel Online, Interview With Conductor Kurt Masur – The Spirit of 1989 Has Been Exhausted, Online: https://www.spiegel.de/international/germany/interview-with-conductor-kurt-masur-the-spirit-of-1989-has-been-exhausted-a-721851.html, (Hamburg, 2010).
55 James D. Bindenagel, The Miracle of Leipzig, Online: https://www.aicgs.org/2014/11/the-miracle-of-leipzig/, American Institute for Contemporary German Studies, (American Institute for Contemporary German Studies: Bonn, 2014).
56 Ibid.

Late that Monday afternoon, Masur called to join with the regional SED cultural representative party secretary, Kurt Meier, to seek a peaceful solution to the upcoming evening confrontation. Meier returned Masur's call two hours before the march and gathered a small group of six people at his house. Masur described the group as a miniature version of all the people – a theologian, a cabaret performer, three district secretaries from the ruling SED, and Masur himself. The three communist party representatives had not received specific instructions from Berlin and were constantly telephoning Berlin for instructions but to no avail.[57]

Relying on Gorbachev's decision not to intervene in the GDR by keeping Soviet soldiers on their military bases, the local SED leaders decided if the protestors avoided violence, the Leipzig police, the *Stasi*, and the Army would not attack them. They drafted and rushed to sign an appeal for non-violence (*Keine Gewalt*). When they agreed, Masur recorded the call for no violence. As the situation was threatening to escalate, loudspeakers in Leipzig broadcast his appeal, in which he asked the city's inhabitants: "We urgently request that you remain calm so as to make peaceful dialogue possible."[58] It was re-broadcast for hours, and the text was read at church vigils throughout the city. Outside, as the demonstrators faced the police, the situation threatened to escalate. Miraculously, violence was avoided, except for a few isolated confrontations on the fringes. The marchers took to the *Innenstadtring* and had remained peaceful.[59]

In the U.S. Embassy, we speculated later that there were likely other motivations to call for non-violence. In essence, perhaps Gorbachev didn't want violence but would allow the demonstrations to pressure Honecker to step down. Maybe the discussants wanted to support Gorbachev's politics, rather than make a kind gesture toward the demonstrators. What is still not clear because we were not in the Leipzig decision circle was whether or not police and senior leaders in Berlin agreed to tolerate or ignored the plan to broadcast the Masur message calling for no violence. Egon Krenz did not act on the reports from Leipzig. Orders never came, and no one carried out the shoot-to-kill order. No shots were fired. That was the *Miracle of Peace in Leipzig*. That night, Leipzig set the 1989 Peaceful Revolution in motion.

But how did the peace hold in Leipzig? Could peaceful protests be held elsewhere? The U.S. Embassy reported that Gorbachev's *glasnost* and *perestroika* were at risk had there been violence. Masur's communist collaborators played

---

57 Ibid.
58 Kurt Masur, in: Spiegel Online, Interview With Conductor Kurt Masur – The Spirit of 1989 Has Been Exhausted, Online: https://www.spiegel.de/international/germany/interview-with-conductor-kurt-masur-the-spirit-of-1989-has-been-exhausted-a-721851.html, (Hamburg, 2010).
59 Ibid.

politics supporting Gorbachev, rather Honecker, not making altruistic gestures toward the demonstrators.

Leipzig Aftermath: The Politburo Ousts Honecker

The Central Committee of the Politburo was in disarray over whether to continue to crackdown on the demonstrators. The Politburo meeting following the October 9 reluctance of the police and the party secretary to end the counter-revolutionary demonstrations was tense. Honecker gave a direct order to stop counterrevolutionary activities. The following week in Leipzig on October 16, the demonstration numbers doubled to 150,000 but remained non-violent. Two days later, on October 18, the Politburo met again, and Egon Krenz led the ouster of Erich Honecker, an action also led by key Politburo Members Willi Stoph and Günther Schabowski. Egon Krenz was named as his successor, and two days later, on Wednesday the 18th, Honecker was deposed.

At that point, the political focus was totally on the Politburo. A few days later, after Honecker was ousted, Egon Krenz took his seat at the table but did not fire all members of the Honecker Politburo; he got rid of only half of them. I took a call announcing Honecker's downfall while in my office meeting with a Wall Street journalist, who also had heard the news. I called the State Department Operations Center to alert Secretary Baker and promised an embassy analysis, which the embassy political counselor Jon Greenwald delivered within two hours. Ambassador Richard Barkley was on his way to Washington and could give a first-hand report.

The U.S. Embassy quickly determined that Krenz would not have any credibility with the man in the street. Egon Krenz announced a turnaround (*Wende*) of the communist party, and the Politburo sought to establish legitimacy and to get the people behind them. The leaders were nervous about the demonstrations, dissident activity, and so many youths escaping their paradise. We in the U.S. Embassy focused on how the SED party would address the concerns of the people out on the street who wanted the freedom to travel. The Politburo was planning to revise the travel law allowing more travel with the hope that these changes would take care of the question of the refugees.

Under Krenz, Prime Minister Willi Stoph had also resigned and remained as acting Premier, leaving the administration of the government in limbo. The good news for the ruling party was that Honecker was deposed (*Entbindung* or cutting his ties to his office), as described in *Neues Deutschland*. The bad news for the SED was that they didn't have Gorbachev's favorite candidate, Hans Modrow, in office. Krenz, who kept half of the Honecker's Politburo, was soon losing all of his credibility. Although there was a change, it was half-heartedly executed, and people were not reassured.

Krenz had a real problem; he had to establish his credentials as a leader. He needed to address the debate about allowing East Germans the freedom to travel without damaging the country. Krenz sought to change the travel law for East Germans and make it possible for him to win their hearts and minds. Maybe it was possible if the East Germans were only seeking the renewal of the GDR, not to overthrow the government.

Egon Krenz's Failed Wende (Turnaround of the communist party)

Therefore, Krenz did two things. First, on November 4th in Berlin, the government organized a vast gathering to show willingness for dialogue. A million people came and showed their solidarity with the GDR. Appearing were Marcus Wolf, the head of the foreign intelligence arm of the Stasi, and others such as Stephan Heym, a well-known East German author, who was an American citizen, former U.S. soldier, and communist. Jens Reich of *Neues Forum* and many other speakers spent all day telling the East Germans that they were all working together to renew the GDR in socialism.[60] That demonstration was probably the last principal act of a dying government.

On November 6, the GDR announced a revised travel law in their newspaper, *Neues Deutschland*. One could travel for 30 days, and there were only five or six reasons why one could not travel. In our morning embassy staff meeting, Ambassador Barkley arrived at the embassy late and asked why so many people were on the streets. It seemed that he could not arrive on time because demonstrations protesting the new travel law blocked the streets. That staff meeting was one of the more fascinating ones we had had. Jon Greenwald and I were already chatting when Jon reported that the SED had changed the travel law and that they had liberalized the travel regime. Jon was certain Krenz was trying to make travel a reality.

East Germans did not see the revised travel law as sufficient to meet their demands. They went again to the streets to protest and demand free travel. Egon Krenz's effort was rejected as too little, too late. During the day, we determined it wasn't just the people in Berlin that the ambassador had seen; there were hundreds of thousands throughout the country rejecting the proposed liberalized

---

60 Jens Reich in an Interview with Charlotte Janus, Der Staat war dem Untergang geweiht, Online: https://www.t-online.de/nachrichten/wissen/geschichte/id_86775462/jens-reich-im-interview-wie-das-neue-forum-die-ddr-veraendern-wollte.html, (Frankfurt am Main, 2019); GHDT, Mass Rally on Alexanderplatz in East Berlin (Novemver 4, 1989), Online: http://ghdi.ghi-dc.org/sub_image.cfm?image_id=124, (East-Berlin, 1989).

travel law. Krenz's gambit did not work; he was under more pressure. It seemed to us that Krenz still did not have the support of the Soviet Union. The Soviet Union's choice, Hans Modrow, was not yet in charge. At the same time, the dissidents were emboldened by what they had achieved. They had rid the GDR of Honecker; however, they now had a weak, old-guard SED leader Krenz, whose government had moved too slowly to change the travel law. The people didn't like it; they wanted freedom, freedom to travel. This rejection of Krenz's leadership, of course, caused panic in the SED, which led the Politburo to meet again on November 9. The meeting was to consider, among other things, more changes to the travel law. Jon Greenwald wrote in his report to the State Department that the Berlin Wall was becoming irrelevant in preventing travel from East Germany. President George H.W. Bush was briefed about that comment on the irrelevance of the Berlin Wall through travel law changes the next morning.

The intensity of the rejection in the following days grew very, very quickly, leading to the night of the fall of the Berlin Wall just three days after the first Krenz attempt to revise the travel law. As revolutions go, no one can predict them, and if they do, they're probably commenting about the past from insights gained afterward. No one had an inkling the Berlin Wall was about to fall on that 9th of November and turn the world upside down.

The Berlin Wall Falls, November 9, 1989: Self-Determination

The summer of 1989 in East Germany had seen the rise of demonstrations against the communist manipulated elections and demanded freedom to travel. On June 4, two events signaled a coming confrontation. While in Poland, voters elected non-communists for the first time to their parliament, in China, the Beijing Tiananmen Square student demonstration for democracy was brutally crushed by the People's Liberation Army. The rebellion in Leipzig was a miracle of non-violence in pursuit of freedom. The October 9th demonstration left open the possibility of a violent revolution but also might not lead to Soviet repression descending upon East Germany despite conventional wisdom.

East German leader Erich Honecker predicted that the Berlin Wall would last 100 years. But would it? At the American Embassy in East Berlin on November 9, 1989, the day began as any normal one could in a so-far peaceful revolution that already had hundreds of thousands of Germans in East Germany demonstrating in the streets. However, the threat of violence still hung in the air. On that warm November evening, all was peaceful and calm.

Events were already moving quickly. A few months earlier, Ambassador Barkley and I visited Wolfgang Vogel at his modest home on Lake Schwerinsee. There we learned that the Hungarians, who had dramatically cut down the barbed wire fence along their border in May and opened the gates for East Germans fleeing their country through Hungary. Vogel knew the Hungarians would likely allow several hundred more East Germans to escape to the West. Vogel told us that fleeing Germans would be named refugees and allowed to stay in Hungary. Under the UN Convention Relating to the Status of Refugees, which the Hungarians had recently signed, Hungary would recognize the fleeing East Germans as refugees and ignore its obligation under the Warsaw Pact to return East Germans to the GDR. The Hungarian border became an escape hatch from the communist bloc.

History was about to overtake us. On the afternoon of November 9, I attended an Aspen Institute reception in West Berlin in honor of Hildegard Boucsein, Director David Anderson's new deputy. David was a former U.S. Ambassador to Yugoslavia, and when he hosted Aspen Institute receptions, everyone came. That night the mayors of East Berlin and West Berlin, Allied military commanders from the West, Honecker's East German spy-swapping lawyer Wolfgang Vogel and many other Eastern and Western political leaders were in attendance at that lovely Wannsee-Schwanenwerder lakeside house. Not one of us had an inkling of the excitement that would engulf the city, Germany, and the world that evening. We were an unsuspecting group of insiders. The fall of the Berlin Wall on November 9, 1989, would be a surprise to us all.

At the end of the Aspen Institute reception, Vogel asked if I could give him a ride downtown to his car, which was in Central-Berlin. As Erich Honecker's lawyer with whom we worked to exchange spies, I was pleased to offer him a ride to get his assessment of the East German reaction to the changes in the GDR travel law. Thousands of demonstrators throughout the country rejected the government's easing of some travel restrictions because they fell short of expectations.

Vogel was most likely to know the GDR's next steps. On the way back to East Berlin, we excitedly discussed how politics were developing in the GDR. I could not miss the chance to ask Vogel to clue us in on what the Politburo, was thinking about the revolutionaries' demands for free travel rights that were driving the revolution. We discussed the future of East Germany as we drove through West Berlin's High Street, the Ku'Damm, which was as bright as always, in contrast to the darkened East Berlin that could not afford such bright lights. Vogel told me that the GDR attorney's collegium had met November 7–8 and had proposed additional lifting of most travel restrictions in the GDR travel law. Vogel thought the new changes, not yet announced, would satisfy East Germans' demand for more freedom of travel. I dropped Vogel off near his car and headed toward the *Invalidenstrasse* Checkpoint to cross back into East Berlin; the same crossing Vogel had made in 1961 when he saw Soviet tanks as the East German Shock

Troops built the Berlin Wall. Vogel said that Egon Krenz would implement the changes soon.

Travel Law Eclipsed by Schabowski's Announcement

I sped back into East Berlin around 7:30 p.m. and went directly to the embassy political section, where I found a much-excited team of diplomats along with Jon Greenwald. They were stunned by East German government spokesman Günther Schabowski's statement on television. He had just moments earlier told the world that the Politburo had agreed to lift the restriction in the travel law. East Germans could get visitor visas quickly (*in kurzem*) for travel to the West from their local *Volkspolizei,* and the GDR would open a new processing center to handle emigration cases immediately.

Jon Greenwald concluded that the East German announcement by Schabowski would set the world on fire. Jon believed the announcement itself was unbelievable, as well as the were the changes to the travel law from the last couple of days. Jon sent Imre Lipping from the political section to find out the text of the Schabowski announcement at the press center. He sent Heather Troutman, another political officer, out to Checkpoint Charlie to see what was happening. While Lipping was hunting down the text of the travel law, the first East Germans attempting to cross without visas were sent packing by the guards at Checkpoint Charlie, who told them first to get visas. It seemed to us that the GDR guards could keep things under control, while the new procedures were being written.

Washington was energized, and Marlin Fitzwater, the President's press spokesman, was pushing President George H.W. Bush to make a statement. In the next hour, we watched the second broadcast of Schabowski's announcement on the nightly West German news program, *Tagesschau.* Imre Lipping quickly gathered the official statement, and Heather Troutman wrote an on-the-ground report about the guards at Checkpoint Charlie. Jon cabled the text of Schabowski's announcement: the freedom to travel and emigrate. That cable arrived immediately in the White House and State Department. I telephoned the White House Situation Room and State Department Operations Center to make sure they had the report and to alert them to the latest developments.

I then called the American Minister in West Berlin, Harry Gilmore, and we diplomats shared our quick assessment of the Politburo announcement. We thought the East Germans would wait to get their visas before crossing into West Berlin. Little did we know how quickly the East Germans would test the will of the border police to let them leave and return. I told Gilmore: "Harry, it looks like you are going to have a lot of visitors soon, but we are not sure. In any case, a flood of visitors to West Berlin appears headed west. We think that the next day when the government starts issuing visas, the gates will open." No one expected the dramatic upheaval on the night of November 9, 1989, even after the announcement. After all, these were Germans and were known for following the rules. After Schabowski set the visa rules, which we expected in short order, visitors would cross into West Berlin the next day. That seemed reasonable. After all, although Schabowski's oral statement was beyond anything we could have imagined, it was open to widely varying interpretations.

Tom Brokaw, the anchorman at NBC Television, who attended the press briefing, had asked Schabowski if this meant the Berlin Wall was open. Schabowski reportedly said yes. An Italian journalist asked when the new rules would go into effect and was told – immediately – (*sofort, unverzüglich*).[61]

Brokaw left the press conference and called Garrick Utley at NBC in New York on his cell phone. The oversized cellular phone was called a "brick" because it was shaped like one, but it worked. Utley gave Brokaw, who was an eyewitness to the announcement, the approval to broadcast the story. Then, for the next one and a half hours, Brokaw stood before the Brandenburg Gate and announced on American television that the Berlin Wall was open[62], even though none of us had the official announcement or knew how the East Germans planned to implement the new rules, after all, the guards had standing orders to defend the border at their checkpoints.

East Germans heard the German television coverage and decided that it meant that travel to the West was possible immediately. They decided to take the government at its word and stormed the checkpoints. This revolution was spinning out of control.

The Berlin Wall at Bornholmerstraße

We assured ourselves that embassy reporting officers were in place to follow events. We had reported the latest news, and I headed home to the East Berlin suburb of Pankow-Niederschönhausen around 10 p.m. On the way, that East German iconic car – the *Trabant* – filled the ordinarily empty streets leading to

---

61 Schwaboski, Günter, Internationale Pressekonferenz von Günter Schabowski (in Begleitung der SED-ZKMitglieder Helga Labs, Gerhard Beil und Manfred Banaschak), 9. November 1989, (Ton-Abschrift), p. 2. aus: Transkription des Kamerabandes von Hans-Hermann Hertle, in Auszügen wiedergegeben in: Hans Hermann Hertle, *Die Berliner Mauer. Biografie eines Bauwerks*, 2. durchgesehene und aktualisierte Aufl., (Ch. Links Verlag: Berlin, 2015), p. 194/195.
62 Tom Brokaw, in: ZDF, US-Reporter beim Mauerfall. Mein Gott, der hat gerade gesagt, dass die Mauer fällt, Online: https://www.zdf.de/nachrichten/heute/interview-us-reporter-tom-brokaw-nbc-news-berichtete-1989-aus-berlin-live-vom-mauerfall-100.html, (Berlin, 2019).

the checkpoints. They lined up by the dozens. *Trabbis,* as they were derisively and also lovingly called, were parked haphazardly around the streets and abandoned near the *Bornholmerstrasse* checkpoint that crossed over the light rail train (*S-Bahn*) into West Berlin. The *Trabant* automobile was small with a two-cycle engine, and a body made of plasticized pressed wood designed and manufactured in East Germany. You could hear its little lawn-mower-sounding engine spewing out a mixture of gasoline and oil smoke as it traversed the city. The *Trabant* was the symbol of the East German economy; that is, it worked, but you wouldn't want to have one.

While driving home on *Schönhauserallee* in East Berlin around 10:00 p.m., I was surprised to see so many *Trabbis.* Across the checkpoint at *Bornholmerstraße,* safely ensconced in the West, was a TV camera crew from *Der Spiegel* poised with blazing lights on the bridge ready to send pictures of this confrontation around the world instantaneously. I recognized the guards, who were still under orders to protect the Wall. I had often been at *Bornholmerstraße*. It had two or three police barracks aligned within it. Driving across the checkpoint, I had seen these barracks with soldiers carrying rifles. I had seen fire-hoses laid out next to these barracks in preparation to spray water against people pressing on the crossing. Similar hoses were used that night at the Brandenburg Gate.

Germans gathered at the *Bornholmerstraße* checkpoint around 10:15 p.m. and shouted at the guards defending the crossing. Although they were told to come back the next day with visas, these anxious East Germans, hoping to have a glimpse of West Berlin, challenged the guards to see West Berlin that night. Opening the Wall might allow them to return home to East Berlin afterward. Those brave souls grew in numbers, and confidently demonstrated civil courage. I heard them yelling something. From the vantage point of my car, I could not determine precisely what was happening during the confrontation at *Bornholmerstraße* and decided to follow the action at home on television. I needed to get to a telephone, too, and raced home through the last few blocks to get home quickly. Inside, I turned on the television to see pictures from the TV crew I had seen beaming East Germans breaching the Wall to the world. I reached for the telephone. The latest events were turning into excitement; any concerns we had as we witnessed the fall of the Berlin Wall, and events soon enveloped us.

I knew the checkpoint at *Bornholmerstraße* well and crossed it regularly; my children crossed there daily to attend the German-American John F. Kennedy School in Zehlendorf, West Berlin. Fire hoses, like those used later at the Brandenburg Gate, were carefully laid out in readiness to repel any wall jumpers. Inside the crossing, armed border guards filled the barracks with a standing order to shoot-to-kill to defend the border.

There looming in the background, were the guards I saw in that confrontation, I had the nagging question whether the guards would carry out the shoot-to-kill order. Would conventional wisdom predict what Gorbachev was going to do? Frankly, we believed in the conventional wisdom that with 380,000 Soviet forces in the country with nuclear weapons, any confrontation would not end quickly. Until that night, there were few signs that the military superpower, the Soviet Union, would give up East Germany without a struggle. At *Bornholmerstraße*, demonstrators confronted the guards who opened the barrier that had divided East and West Berlin ever since Ulbricht erected this Berlin Wall, the hated symbol of communism and division some 28 years earlier. There the Germans in East Germany soon breached the Berlin Wall, where East German Border Guard Lieutenant-Colonel Harald Jäger defended it.

Foreign Minister Hans-Dietrich Genscher had long argued that the West should take Gorbachev at his word about new thinking. We were skeptical, although we, of course, had followed Gorbachev's policy since he took office in 1985. His new thinking expressed through *perestroika* and *glasnost* and his speech at the UN in September 1988, ending the Brezhnev Doctrine that kept foreign policy decisions in Moscow's hands, were stunning policy shifts. However, history in the making in Poland and Hungary weighed heavily on our view of possible outcomes. On November 9, we didn't believe that freedom would come to East Germany until the communist leadership ended.

Yes, the SED leadership was changing. Erich Honecker, who was ousted days earlier, had been a throwback supporter of the Stalinist period. He had confronted Gorbachev expressing determination never to loosen any controls, nor to make life easy for the Soviet President. Gorbachev wanted to have change in East Germany, but certainly not to lose it. The new leader, Egon Krenz, was not Gorbachev's favorite. Hans Modrow, who was the still party chief in Dresden, was favored. However, these communist leadership changes were side-tracked by the breach of the Berlin Wall.

The Berlin Wall Breached

As soon as I arrived home shortly after 10:15 p.m., I telephoned the State Department in Washington. I called Ambassador Barkley, Jon Greenwald, and Harry Gilmore in West Berlin. The television sound was loud, but I turned it on and started making calls. My wife Jean came in and joined me in witnessing the confrontation at *Bornholmerstraße*. Within minutes, East Berliners breached the Berlin Wall, just where I had been minutes earlier. First, a wave of East Berliners came through the *Bornholmerstraße* checkpoint signaling freedom for all East Germans. East Germans streamed across to the West, and TV flashed their images around the world.

Into the night, we had to find out what was going on after Schabowski's announcement and to report to Washington that demonstrators had besieged the Berlin Wall at the *Bornholmerstraße* checkpoint and the Brandenburg Gate. Jon Greenwald had just arrived home and called me to say he saw numerous *Trabbis* on *Bornholmerstraße* on his drive home as well. I called Ambassador Barkley and told him to turn on his television. He was incredulous as I told him he would not believe what was happening.

I again called the U.S. Minister in West Berlin, Harry Gilmore, and had to revise my earlier statements. I told Harry that although I said you would see plenty of East German visitors in the next few days, they might be coming that night. It looked like things were going to break loose, and we did not know how events will unfold.

We continued for hours to watch the television coverage and kept in touch with Washington. After we saw those first people go through the Wall, lights came on in the neighborhood. We spent several hours talking, coordinating; the revolution seemed to be going peacefully. Who let them break through the Wall? At first, no one cared. They were free. I was just happy to see the peaceful opening – no violence, greeted with the East German "Little Red Riding Hood" – *Rotkäppchen* – champagne.[63] I was relieved and glad to see the demand for freedom fulfilled. The East Germans deserved their freedom, their liberty.

There were unanswered questions about those first wall jumpers at the *Bornholmerstraße* checkpoint. Just what did those guards with the hoses and rifles do to defend the Berlin Wall on November 9, 1989? Only later, Lieutenant-Colonel Harald Jäger, speaking in a *Der Spiegel* magazine interview on the 20th anniversary, explained what the guards at the border had decided that night: I gave my people the order – raise the barrier. Jäger told in his own words in 2009 that he had:

> Repeatedly spoke to all officers in charge that evening, on the street, but also in his office. They demanded: "Harald, you've got to do something!" I said: "What am I supposed to do?" I wanted to hear what they thought. They stood together in my office, and I wanted them to tell me what I should do. "It's up to you, you're the boss," they said. I said: "Should I let the GDR citizens leave? Or should I give the order to open fire?"[64]

---

63 Germany's favorite sparkling wine Rotkäppchen (meaning "Red Hood" in German) doesn't just share a name with a folk story, its history of struggle and success is also not unlike a Little Red Ridinghood fairytale. Like the vast majority of private enterprises under the Soviet Union-affiliated German Democratic Republic (GDR, East Germany), Rotkäppchen was nationalized, in: Sofia Lotto Persio, This Sparkling Wine Survived Nationalization And Privatization To Become Germany's Favorite, in: Forbes, Online: https://www.forbes.com/sites/sofialottopersio/2019/11/11/this-sparkling-wine-survived-nationalization-and-privatization-to-become-germanys-favorite/, (New York City, 2019).
64 Lieutenant-Colonel Harald Jäger, in: Spiegel Online, The Guard Who Opend the Berlin Wall. I Gave my People the Order – Raise the Barrier, Online: https://www.spiegel.de/international/

Jäger recalled that people could have been injured or killed even without a shot fired. If there had been scuffles, panic could have ensued among the thousands gathered at the border crossing. He gave his people the order: "Open the barrier!" That's how Jäger's order to his guards ended.[65]

I saw Colonel Jäger at the *Bornholmerstraße* checkpoint on television lift the gate and open the way for East Germans to freedom. Although he had called for orders to carry out the shoot-to-kill order, the answer he heard was that someone would get back to him. Orders never came. That was the critical moment in the revolution when the Soviet Union did not mobilize its forces, a fateful decision.

A few months after the fall of the Berlin Wall, my wife Jean and I had coffee with the Uwe Gerson family, friends from our local East German church. Among the guests were East Germans who had been among those people at *Bornholmerstraße* that night when they breached the Berlin Wall. As we recounted this story, one of them asked if we knew what happened to the first freedom-seekers who burst into the lights of the Spiegel TV cameras and changed the course of history. Of course, we did not and were intrigued to hear a first-hand account. Uwe Gerson's brother-in-law took out his GDR identification card, a paper passport-like document with a photograph on one side and his name typed on the other.

Across the picture was a GDR exit visa stamp. Lieutenant-Colonel Harald Jäger stamped the photo and mutilated the identification card, which invalidated it. It hit us. The first people crossing into the lights of the TV cameras had been expelled! The guards ejected the first hundred or so people who I had seen standing there that night. They threw them out and were intending to close the gate area to avoid a confrontation. Getting rid of; that is, expelling the first group of demonstrators, was a desirable solution. The guards had tried to save East Germany from its discontented citizens by throwing the rascals out of the country. But it wasn't those guards who had the last laugh.

The rest of the story played out on television. Tom Brokaw broadcast the opening of the Berlin Wall on American television. With Spiegel Television, the story was spread quickly by the West Germans to the East Germans and the world. This media-dominated world was and is the one in which we live. The story told in the public domain was: the East Germans are free; the Berlin Wall had fallen. That story turned on all the lights in my neighborhood. People saw on television the open Berlin Wall and hundreds fleeing west.

Some worried that the GDR would not give them visas if they waited. Now that was the time to decide to go on their own while the newly announced visa

---

germany/the-guard-who-opened-the-berlin-wall-i-gave-my-people-the-order-raise-the-barrier-a-660128.html, (Hamburg, 2009b).

65 Ibid.

requirement still gave them the window of opportunity. Many thought they had only one chance at freedom. They poured into West Berlin, considering the opportunity would not last; this was the only chance they would get to taste freedom. Other Germans in the GDR drove miles from outside of Berlin to get there in time to cross and not possibly miss the only chance that they might have in their life to go to Berlin. Television broadcasters had only reported what they had seen and not the new rules. TV created facts on the ground, and it was good that they did.

End Game East Germany

At this moment, it was clear that East Germany's days were limited. Only a military intervention by the Soviets could prolong its agony. However, President Gorbachev risked *perestroika* and *glasnost* in Russia. If he had chosen to intervene militarily in the GDR, he would lose East Germany if he did not. Nevertheless, we had no idea of the next steps or how the revolution would play out.

While the world was caught up in the euphoria of the pictures at the Brandenburg Gate, President George H.W. Bush instructed us that there would be no dancing on the Wall. The East Germans had won some freedom, but the revolution had unleashed the forces of history contained by the cold war.

The Soviet Embassy in East Berlin, Minister Igor Maximetchev, chose to let Moscow follow the story rather than seeking to intervene. It was still possible that the night shift, mid-level Soviet officers might overreact and unleash a military response.[66] Gorbachev's political advisor Andrey Grachev confirmed the Maximetchev story at a Georgetown University conference on the 20th anniversary of the fall of the Berlin Wall. Maximetchev's response showed that occasionally, great things happen when good men do nothing.[67]

We in the U.S. Embassy were also concerned about Soviet military forces remaining in their barracks. We had no idea whether Gorbachev would intervene. He certainly had the troops to do so, but he had ordered them to stay in their barracks during the 40th-anniversary celebrations. On November 9, they also did just that. We waited for the guards to act on the standing shoot-to-kill order with the hope that they would not carry it out.

Non-intervention in East Germany meant Gorbachev was giving up the trophy of Soviet victory in World War II to protect his domestic policies in the Soviet

---

66 Igor Maximetchev in an interview with the author, Potsdam East West Forum, 2009.
67 Andrey Grachev, Europe and Russia 30 years after the fall of the Berlin Wall: Hopes, chances, failures with Andrey Grachev, Online: https://doc-research.org/2019/10/europe-russia-30-years-fall-berlin-wall/, (DOC Research Institute: Berlin, 2019).

Union. Gorbachev saved his chance to pursue *glasnost* and *perestroika* at home. If he had intervened militarily or tried to stop East Germans, then he would have returned to the Brezhnev Doctrine; that is when Moscow decided all vital issues, not the sovereign satellite country. That is how we saw him resolve his dilemma to keep *glasnost* and *perestroika* in the Soviet Union, even though it meant he would have to negotiate the fate of East Germany. Of course, the decision did not occur overnight, and it is more with hindsight that we saw the dilemma Gorbachev faced. On November 9, 1989, suddenly he was faced with the loss of legitimacy in the German Democratic Republic. While the pace of the revolution was breathtaking, German unification was not on the active political agenda of either East or West Germany when the Berlin Wall fell. Also, not in the 100 years that Honecker had declared the Berlin Wall would stand to divide Germany.

Uncontrolled Weapons in East Germany

The revolution did not end on that fateful night. West Berlin's governing mayor Walter Momper reported on developments in East Germany, and the U.S. Mission titled its report: "Momper's Grim Analysis of GDR (East German) Situation." Momper's comments on December 4, 1989, stirred Washington to action. He gave the American government a wake-up call about a collapsing East Germany and suggested the country was on the verge of civil war. If that was the case, then there might have been no alternative to the 380,000-strong Soviet Army intervening to restore order.[68]

Disintegration had already begun. On November 13, the parliament voted into the office an interim government that would last until free elections took place. These elections were scheduled for May 1990 by Hans Modrow as Prime Minister (SED) and Lothar de Maiziere (CDU) as deputy prime minister. De Maiziere had set conditions for forming a government with Prime Minister Modrow, including the elimination of the constitutional provision guaranteeing a leading role for the SED.[69] Modrow had reluctantly agreed to de Maiziere's demand. On December 1, the *Volkskammer* met in an emergency session and voted to remove from the constitution the SED's monopoly on power, shifting legitimacy to the people. The end of the SED's constitutional monopoly on power was a critical victory for the people who had demanded sovereignty for the people. Having achieved freedom,

---

68 USBerlin NIACT Immediate cable 3430, 051213Z December, "Momper's Grim Analysis of GDR Situation".
69 Lothar de Maiziere, *Ich will, dass meine Kinder nicht mehr lügen müssen*, (Verlag Herder GmbH: Freiburg im Breisgau, 2010), p. 86.

the people would exercise their right to self-determination in the upcoming parliamentary elections.

A special SED party convention convened shortly afterward at the *Palast der Republik*, but without clear leadership. The entire SED Politburo and the Central Committee had resigned. Egon Krenz lost all leadership positions. There were revelations of lavish living in the private, leadership compound at Wandlitz and corruption by SED leaders. Among those communist leaders sacked and stripped of their party membership were Chairman Erich Honecker, former Prime Minister Willi Stoph, and Stasi chief Erich Mielke. As Momper had reported, economic leader Günter Mittag and labor leader Harry Tisch were arrested on corruption charges. Even the party newspaper, *Neues Deutschland*, no longer represented the Central Committee and dropped the term from its masthead.[70]

A delegation of U.S. Senators, the Senate Arms Control Observer Group led by Senators Claiborne Pell and Richard Lugar, visited Berlin December 1–3 amid the collapse of the communist party. Ambassador Richard Barkley hosted them for dinner on Friday, December 1st, in his *Nordenstrasse* residence in *Niederschönhausen*. Barkley's dinner included several dissident leaders and leaders of the SED for an on-the-ground look at the evolving revolution. East German government attendance fell sharply, and news of the expulsions and leadership vacuum in the party resulted in exchanges occurring only between the dissidents and the American senators.

After meetings in West Berlin on Saturday, the senators returned to East Berlin for a visit to the Soviet museum of Nazi capitulation in *Karlshorst*. The on-going revolution quickly overshadowed the senators' visit to this World War II site. The group stopped at the Lust Garden across from the office of the chairman of the Communist party, site of candlelight sit-in protests, and *Alexanderplatz*, where demonstrators confronted the *Volkspolizei* regularly.

On the way to *Karlshorst*, the senators saw the Gethsemane Church, site of the October 7, 1989, *Volkspolizei* crackdown on peaceful demonstrators. While continuing to the World War II museum, suddenly, the bus stopped, and the *Volkspolizei* stood in the street but were surprisingly un-confrontational. The police claimed they were not responsible for what was occurring. Then hundreds of Germans silently erupted from underground passages to form part of a human chain that stretched across the country a plan that Pankow pastor Ruth Misselwitz had explained earlier to me. It made clear the revolution had won the support of the people. The senators gathered with the demonstrators whose silent, candlelit human chain stretched from *Sassnitz* in the North to *Eisleben* and the border of Bavaria. Suddenly, just fifteen minutes later, those same hundreds

---

70 Ibid.

of thousands of people who had formed a human chain across the entire country calling for radical democratic change vanished.

The senators' museum tour paled in comparison to the living history the senators witnessed that afternoon. The force of freedom embodied in the courage of the demonstrators in the face of state violence was imposing.

Kohl, Gorbachev and Bush Leadership

At the same time the GDR was falling apart, President George H.W. Bush was in Brussels at a meeting of NATO. In a conversation with Chancellor Kohl at a private dinner in Brussels on December 3, Bush discussed the U.S. – Soviet Summit in Malta that had concluded that day. There, Presidents Bush and Gorbachev established a stable working relationship. President Bush told Chancellor Kohl about his conversations with President Gorbachev, who worried that West Germany was in too much of a hurry with the German question. Gorbachev's chief problem with the unfolding events in East Germany was uncertainty. Bush told Gorbachev that it was not in America's interest to let the revolution get out of control. He also expected GDR Prime Minister Modrow, known to be close to Gorbachev, to become the leader of the communist party in East Germany.[71]

Kohl responded to Bush with a description of on-going events in East Germany, noting that the communist leadership had resigned, and there was a crisis in running the government. The people were outraged by the privileges that their leaders had for themselves. Concerns arose when reports circulated about the chaos in East German cities. Kohl then reported that people had broken into a warehouse near Rostock and found weapons and that the residents had demanded to know where the GDR sent arms.[72]

Uncontrolled weapons would, of course, disturb Kohl's efforts at stabilizing East Germany in the aftermath of the fall of the Berlin Wall. West Germany granted "welcome money" of DM100 to each East German, which had already amounted to $1.8 billion at the beginning of December. Although West Germany would eventually end such grants, other programs would be initiated, such as sending doctors to cover an urgent shortage, environmental protection measures, and building a telephone system. Kohl also reported that Gorbachev had assured him he would not stand in the way of free, open elections. Bush called for

---

71 George H.W. Bush Memorandum of Conversations with Helmut Kohl, Brent Scowcroft, John Sununu, December 3, 1989, in: Svetlana Savranskaya, Thomas Blaton and Vladislav Zubok (Eds.), *Masterpieces of History*, Online: https://books.openedition.org/ceup/2895?lang=de, (Central European University Press: Budapest, 2010), pp. 647–650.
72 Ibid.

an approach that did not scare Gorbachev but instead moved the political process forward. Kohl recalled the CSCE process that had allowed for the peaceful change of borders and then argued that the West should not force Gorbachev into a corner.[73]

Kohl also sought to reassure President Bush of his Ten-Point Plan on the German-German Confederation, announced on November 28, delivered just ten days after Modrow's similar governmental statement to the *Volkskammer* calling for a Community of Contracts (*Vertragsgemeinschaft*) between the two Germanys. Kohl's speech, he informed the president, was not an alternative to what the West was doing.

Kohl also assured Bush that he had carefully coordinated the Ten-Point Plan announcement with French President Francois Mitterrand. However, Mitterand and his team complained that Kohl had not informed them about the plan. Kohl reiterated Germany's commitment to France for the integration of Europe, which would include the European Monetary Union. Only after the GDR had a genuinely free and democratic government could confederative structures be established. Kohl was uncertain it would ever happen. In any case, he promised not to do anything reckless and thanked President Bush for his response to the ideas in the Ten-Point Plan. Now, it was essential to give the East Germans time to determine what they wanted. Only a year ago, such talk of unification would have been considered crazy. President Bush agreed that self-determination was the answer to a peaceful solution. Kohl called for a period of peaceful development.[74] Their exchange reflected the reporting from East Germany's revolution.

Kavelstorf December 1989: An Arms Dealer's Uncontrolled Weapons

Local citizens' protests focused on the secret *Stasi* warehouse at Kavelstorf near Rostock.[75] They demanded an end to East German arms sales and called on the government to close the facility. *Stasi* Colonel Dressler, already in November 1989 had ordered the *Stasi* to move quickly to destroy the paper trail linking the arms sales company IMES to the *Stasi* and to turn over parts of the warehouse to the Interior Ministry. The destruction of documents was successful, and a later investigation by the *Bundestag* could not discover them.[76]

---

[73] Ibid.
[74] Ibid.
[75] James D. Bindenagel, The Role of the United States in German Unification, Online: http://www.bpb.de/geschichte/zeitgeschichte/deutschlandarchiv/213549/the-role-of-the-united-states-in-german-unification, (Bundeszentrale für politische Bildung: Bonn, 2015).
[76] Deutscher Bundestag, Beschlußempfehlung und Bericht des 1. Untersuchungsausschusses nach Art. 44 des Grundgesetzes, 12.Wahlperiode, Drucksache 12/7600, (Bonn, 1994), p. 180.

There was, however, a cache of weapons held in the *Stasi* warehouse (*Objekt*) in Kavelstorf near Rostock. On Saturday, December 2, 1989, Wolfram Vormelker, founder of the local chapter of the opposition group, *Neues Forum*, along with some 100 citizens of the village of Kavelstorf, stormed the offices of IMES. The manager of the firm sought to block the entrance. He rejected accusations IMES was engaged in illegal *Stasi* activity, stating that the firm was manufacturing metal fabrications and defensive weapons for the Soviet Union.

Protesters struggled with the guards to gain access but avoided violence as the door opened. The 100 local citizens stormed in and were met face-to-face with stacks of weapons ten meters high – assault weapons, machine guns, Kalashnikovs, pistols, and palettes of ammunition. Vormelker walked around with a Geiger counter, calling the Stasi "*Ihr Schweine*" – pigs – but found no radioactive material. The Kavelstorfer were shocked to learn they had been living for years next to explosives hidden from them.[77]

The City Council Assembly met and demanded testimony from IMES officials such as Erhard Wiecher, Kurt Hillmann, and Johannes Walter, managers who had remained at the facility. The city council wanted information as to its operations, goods stored in the warehouse, and the importation of military material. They were outraged at the immorality and the illegality of the arms trade. The managers denied any connection with the *Stasi*.[78]

The denial was not credible. *Stasi* super-spy, Marcus Wolf knew Alexander Schalck-Golodkowski's division was responsible for earning hard currency (*Abteilung zur Beschaffung von Auslandsdevisen*). Schalck-Golodkowski, who reported directly to Erich Honecker and whose deputies were from the *Stasi*, fought and won against efforts to curb plans to reduce weapons production because arms sales earned extraordinary amounts of hard currency.

Even the KGB respected the military effectiveness of the East German Army (*Nationale Volksarmee*) and allowed the GDR to engage in arms deals. The Minister for National Defense Heinz Hoffmann operated under orders (*Befehl Nummer 2/75*) that allowed military assistance in foreign countries.[79]

The SED expelled some leaders from the party and arrested others for corruption. GDR State Secretary for Commerce and Foreign Currency Alexander Schalck-Golodkowski, who was in charge of foreign arms sales to raise hard cur-

---

77 Viktoria Urmersbach, Glasnost in Kavelstorf, in: Nord Deutscher Rundfunk, (Hamburg, 2009).
78 Deutscher Bundestag, Beschlußempfehlung und Bericht des 1. Untersuchungsausschusses nach Art. 44 des Grundgesetzes, 12.Wahlperiode, Drucksache 12/7600, (Bonn, 1994), p. 181.
79 Heide Alyu, Aktenverzeichnis zum "Selbständigen Referat Bewaffnung und Chemischer Dienst" (SR BCD) in der Bezirksverwaltung Rostock des Ministeriums fuer Staatssicherheit der DDR, Der Bundesbeauftragte fuer die Unterlagen des Staatssicherheitsdienstes der ehemaligen Deutschen Demokratischen Republik, (Rostock, 2012).

rency, feared lynch justice would be his fate.[80] He fled to West Berlin on December 2 and was held in a West Berlin prison. According to *Bild*, Schalck-Golodkowski had collected enough information to expose the entire GDR leadership.[81]

Schalck-Golodkowski may have had reason to fear arrest in the GDR. On December 4, 1989, after the discovery of the arms cache, the GDR Military States Attorney opened an investigation on suspicion of the illegal arms trade. The Kavelstorf warehouse in the port of Rostock operated with the export firm IMES, and its arms shipment turnover was significant. The weapons inventory for shipment in November 1989, shortly before the time Kohl spoke with Bush, was extensive. It included more than 60,686,520 rounds of ammunition and small arms; 26,370 handguns, 48,960 hand grenades, and 9429 armor-piercing anti-tank weapons (*Schützenpanzer, Kampfpanzer, Kanonen, Haubitzen, Fla-Geschütze, Raketen, Flugzeuge, Handfeuerwaffen, Ersatzteile, Instandsetzungsleistungen,* and *Technologietransfer know-how*).[82] The warehouse export inventory list completed on December 12, 1989, was worth some 20 million East Marks.

At the same time in Brussels, Chancellor Kohl and President Bush discussed the U.S.-Soviet Summit in Malta that had just ended as the uprising in East Germany accelerated. Kohl described the crisis facing East Germany, its crumbling government, and expressed concern about uncontrolled weapons. The East German government was collapsing, leading figures had resigned, and the people were demanding to know about their leaders' special privileges.

Kohl told President Bush about an incident in Rostock where people had broken into a warehouse and found arms. They would now demand to know where these arms were going.[83] After Schalck-Golodkowski fled, his team of Stasi-led guards managing the weapons at Kavelstorf quietly disappeared. Could weapons here or elsewhere have fallen into the hands of the Stasi, militia, or others?

Concerted efforts were needed to calm the waters and smooth out the transition. On December 3 and 4, Bärbel Bohley met with SED leader Gregor Gysi and *Stasi* Foreign Intelligence chief Markus Wolf. Other opposition leaders met with *Stasi* Minister Schwanitz on December 4 to express concerns about the danger of

---

80 Ralf Schuler, Nachruf auf Alexander Schalck-Golodkowski († 82). Er war die graue Eminenz der DDR!, in: BILD Zeitung, Online: https://www.bild.de/politik/inland/devisenhandel/schalck-golodkowski-die-graue-eminenz-der-ddr-41457982.bild.html, (Axel Springer Verlag: Berlin, 2015).

81 Ibid.

82 Heide Alyu, Aktenverzeichnis zum "Selbständigen Referat Bewaffnung und Chemischer Dienst" (SR BCD) in der Bezirksverwaltung Rostock des Ministeriums fuer Staatssicherheit der DDR, Der Bundesbeauftragte fuer die Unterlagen des Staatssicherheitsdienstes der ehemaligen Deutschen Demokratischen Republik, (Rostock, 2012).

83 William. R. Smyser, *From Yalta to Berlin: The Cold War Struggle over Germany*, (St. Martin's Press: New York, 1999), p. 356.

violent outbreaks after the citizens broke into the Kavelstorf Stasi warehouse. SED calls against opposition leaders threatened violence against individuals. Such requests made the temperature and anger rise. *Neues Forum* also released a statement that the communists were moving money out of the country, destroying files, and fleeing. In Erfurt, 4000 flyers were distributed, and a small group mobilized just before the Monday demonstration, which brought 50,000 people to the streets.

On December 4, Erfurt would be the first to begin attacks, occupation, blocking action and oversight of its *Stasi* office. Rumors flew that the *Stasi* was destroying files, and flying officers to Romania. Violence was in the air. In Leipzig, the Monday demonstration on December 6th would pass by the *Stasi* headquarters there. Gysi pledged to Bohley that he would do all that he could to avoid violence. Bohley organized a small group to occupy the *Stasi* offices during the demonstration to ensure files were not destroyed and made an announcement to that effect. The *Stasi* officers feared they would be identified and later be held to account. Both sides channeled fear into newly founded citizens committees that would work with the police and the public prosecutors.[84]

These incidents over December 2 and 3, 1989, showed how high anxiety had risen among SED members that the volatile situation would slide into violence and civil war. U.S. embassy diplomats in East Berlin kept Washington informed of the dizzying pace of revolutionary events throughout the autumn of 1989, reporting several times a day on developments.

Then, early in the morning on December 6, 1989, the U.S. Embassy in East Berlin was alerted by an alarming "Night Action" cable report from the U.S. Mission in West Berlin about the political disintegration of East Germany. The U.S. Mission in West Berlin reported on West Berlin Governing Mayor Walter Momper's briefing to the Western Allies about the crisis in East Germany. Most disturbing was Momper's speculation that if the growing unrest continued and reports of uncontrolled weapons in Rostock were confirmed, it would be a worst-case scenario. Then there may be no alternative to the 380,000-strong Soviet Army intervening to restore order. U.S. Minister in West Berlin, Harry Gilmore, whose report on Momper's briefing was sent shortly after that presidential discussion with Kohl, fit into the story of disintegration in the GDR.[85]

In his press conference on December 4, West Berlin Mayor Momper had urged Germans in the GDR to remain calm and to maintain an orderly process of change and renewal. Demonstrations were growing in size and number. Anger was rising. Momper called for those with authority in the GDR to attend a Roundtable discussion of political parties and political opposition, as well as

---

84 Ibid., p. 353.
85 Ibid.

church and civic leaders. They convened to set up a mechanism overseeing preparations for the upcoming *Volkskammer* elections planned for May 6, 1990. The Roundtables were soon also acting as local governments. Momper saw the Roundtables as legitimate political bodies to control the transition regime and the election. The National Roundtable was to convene in Berlin on December 7. Stability was not guaranteed.

On December 4, Momper had briefed the American, British, and French allies that the previous weekend's developments in East Germany had created a wholly new, unstable situation in the GDR. He feared a rapid, further loss of authority and destabilization of the communist system and a total breakdown of governance, triggering a tidal wave of East German refugees into Berlin. Momper concluded that he could not rule out the prospect that the GDR would slide, perhaps rapidly, into something like a civil war.

Momper told the Allies in Berlin that an aggressive crowd at the Central Committee meeting, leading up to the party congress on December 15-17, had given an ominous warning of what might come in East Germany. *The Berliner Zeitung* captured the urgency of Momper's report in its headline: "Chaos in the GDR."[86]

The U.S. Embassy in East Berlin was under pressure to report its on-the-ground views of the stability of an East Germany governed by an interim national government and Roundtable. Governance at the local level was slipping into the Roundtable as the communist party gave up power, and the *Stasi* collapsed. By the evening of December 6, we sent our cable report to Washington:

> Despite the disorder born of change, the East German government still runs, the people work, and the economy functions. The forces of democratic change are organizing for elections. Demonstrations continue peacefully amidst rumors of political violence. The pace of this revolution is breathtaking.[87]

Nevertheless, we saw that virtually all East German state institutions had lost political authority. However, individuals such as Prime Minister Hans Modrow, Dresden Mayor Wolfgang Berghofer, and SED leader Gregor Gysi retained personal respect. However, even they did not represent a political structure capable of assuring stability. Opposition groups, disparate and disorganized, lacked programs and any real governmental authority. Modrow's interim government included Deputy Prime Minister Lothar de Maizière, who connected best with the

---

86 Walter Momper, *Berlin, Nun Freue Dich! Mein Herbst 1989*, (Das Neue Berlin: Berlin, 2014), p. 221.
87 My US Embassy Cable. my USEmbassy cable; USBerlin NIACT Immediate cable 3430, 051213Z December, "Momper's Grim Analysis of GDR Situation", see also: Neues Deutschland, Baker informierte über die Lage in der DDR: Tempo der Entwicklung atemberaubend", 9-10.12.1989, (East-Berlin, 1989b), p. 5.

churches and its ministers who were leading the uprising. At the same time, their populist slogan, "We are the People," was spreading throughout the land and challenging the ruling communist party's state sovereignty.

Revelations of scandal among the country's leadership had shattered illusions of trust in the government and created great public anger and frustration. Numerous officials of the ruling SED, the so-called "Bloc" political parties that had aligned themselves with the communist party and the communist trade union federation, resigned. SED party leaders were nervous seeing the arrests of Politburo members Günter Mittag and Harry Tisch. Mayor Momper saw danger in the prospect that if a single SED functionary or *Stasi* gnome were lynched, many others would meet the same fate.

Momper planned to meet with GDR opposition members Bärbel Bohley and Rainer Eppelmann to tell them to move full bore into politics aimed at the election. Although Prime Minister Hans Modrow's authority was crumbling under the disintegration of East Germany, the U.S. Embassy in East Berlin was not informed of the Bush-Kohl discussion and the concern about uncontrolled weapons discovered in Rostock. Momper's briefing about a GDR teetering on the edge of the civil war included this concern about uncontrolled weapons in Rostock. Momper also sought to meet with Modrow to urge him to take decisive steps to regain popular confidence – disarming the militia and company shock troops (*Betriebskampfgruppen*) and calling in uncontrolled weapons to restore stability. If violence began, it would quickly spread.[88]

Reports of uncontrolled weapons with sightings of the dissolving Stasi and the city governments perhaps in collapse worried the GDR leadership. However, the Round Table governance of civic leaders replaced the government. West Berlin's U.S. Mission reported that the descent of the GDR into civil war had legs.[89] In Washington, concerns arose when reports circulated about the chaos in East German cities.

Before fleeing West on December 2, Schalck-Golodkowski left a letter for Prime Minister Modrow proposing three courses of action to control the weapons.[90] First, immediately, but temporarily, put the warehouse, firearms, and ammunition under the control of the Minister of the Interior; second, fulfill the weapons export contracts of IMES, and third, sell the warehouse to VEB *Kombinat Deutrans*. When the Roundtable heard of the recommendations Schalck-Golodkowski made, it demanded the VEB Agrotechnic-Rostock Kavelstorf warehouse be sold after the 1990 election.

---

88 Walter Momper, *Berlin, Nun Freue Dich! Mein Herbst 1989*, (Das Neue Berlin: Berlin, 2014), p. 221.
89 USBerlin NIACT Immediate cable 3430, 051213Z December, "Momper's Grim Analysis of GDR Situation," U.S. Department of State, December 5, 1989.
90 Conversation with Lothar deMaiziere in 2016 in Berlin.

Deputy Prime Minister de Maizière at first worried how the GDR would be faced with demands to return the money for the paid arms contracts. Instead, he moved decisively and ordered Minister for National Defense Heinz Hoffmann to take control of the Kavelstorf warehouse, and to disarm the special police forces, militia and company shock troops (*Betriebskampfgruppen*). Calling in uncontrolled weapons to restore stability moved East Germany back from the brink of armed violence. De Maizière knew that if violence began, it would quickly spread. The National People's Army (NVA) carried out the order, and the military took the weapons under control.[91]

At the same time, the revolution continued with a December 6 massive Monday night street demonstration in Leipzig. After the peace vigil in the *Nikolaikirche*, the rally began on *Karl-Marx-Platz* and threatened to turn violent. Although protests had been non-violent, pent-up anger made ugly incidents a permanent danger, and the Embassy reported to Washington that an attack on the *Stasi* building in the path of the marchers was a troublesome possibility.

On this night, unsubstantiated rumors circulated among the 150,000 protestors that the *Stasi* had stashed billions of Marks in Swiss accounts and were destroying their files. The Leipzig *Stasi* regional headquarters, known as the Round Corner (*Rundeck*), was targeted for an attack. Luckily, *Neues Forum* was ahead of the crowd and had peacefully taken over the *Stasi* office by the time the demonstrators arrived. The takeover remained non-violent, this time.

Civil Unrest

On December 4th, other incidents of public unrest occurred. Civilians stormed *Stasi* buildings in Erfurt and then later in Leipzig. Protestant Bishop Dr. Martin Kruse warned the population not to take justice into their own hands. GDR officials considered the possibility of imposing a state of emergency. Momper saw no way for the communists to improve their position; its political cadre failed; the police had no leadership. East Germany was coming apart.

Momper had reached out to his counterpart in East Berlin, Lord Mayor Erhard Krack, to push for a regional committee that would urge Modrow to implement practical improvements. The Allies questioned the mayor's choices of East Germans to lead the effort, but Momper replied that there were few choices since Günter Schabowski and other close contacts were gone as the whole store was disintegrating. He hoped free elections could lead to stability. However, his darker script of progressive loss of authority in which the military (*Nationale Volksarmee*)

---

91 Lothar de Maiziere, personal interview in Berlin, September 2014.

and other East German institutions could not be relied on to maintain or restore order.[92]

In a descent toward anarchy and potentially civil war, the Russians might seek to restore order. In the U.S. Embassy, we worried about any movement by Soviet soldiers from their barracks would be a dangerous escalation of violence. Momper urged the Allies to sensitize Moscow to the disintegration of the GDR and to make them realize that marking time and doing nothing might not be feasible if the GDR continued to unravel. Momper and his State Secretary Dieter Schroeder planned to raise their concerns with Soviet Embassy Minister Igor Maximetchev. Maximetchev, who had served the Soviet Foreign Ministry in German affairs since the 1950s, was perhaps overly optimistic about the GDR and was not inclined to consider the unthinkable developments that Momper had laid out to the Allies.

The British also were concerned about a power vacuum in East Germany, and British Foreign Secretary Douglas Hurd was hopeful that the government could restore some measure of authority.[93] West German Foreign Minister Hans-Dietrich Genscher noted that Hans Modrow had emerged as a symbol of authority. He and Dresden Mayor Wolfgang Berghofer were seemingly the only SED leaders with credibility. The SED, as a party, had lost all confidence of the people.

It would take some time to fill the power vacuum. The National Roundtable convened in Berlin on December 7 as planned, demanded the dissolution of the *Stasi*, and prepared for upcoming free elections. The locally created Roundtable governing bodies had uncertain powers to decide local matters, and at least for this short time of uncertainty, to stabilize local governance. The East German people were taking charge and taking over the SED party, but tentatively. The Modrow government endorsed this move, and already on December 7th, the Roundtable process spread across East Germany.

These and other acts of courage and self-determination echo today. Can Germany find the courage found at unification to reinvent itself in unraveling world order?

---

92 Walter Momper, *Berlin, Nun Freue Dich! Mein Herbst 1989*, (Das Neue Berlin: Berlin, 2014), pp. 219–220.
93 Carsten Volkery, Maggie Thatcher und die Wiedervereinigung. Die Deutschen sind wieder da, in: Spiegel Online: https://www.spiegel.de/geschichte/maggie-thatcher-und-die-wiederverei nigung-a-948498.html, (Hamburg, 2009).

Secretary of State James A. Baker III Visits Prime Minister Hans Modrow in East Germany

International diplomacy played a role as well. The U.S. Embassy in East Berlin also suggested U.S. Secretary of State James A. Baker III meet with the East German leadership while in West Berlin on December 12, 1989. Ambassador Barkley convinced him late that evening to visit East Berlin the next day, after his West Berlin speech.

U.S. Secretary of State James A. Baker III was concerned about the reports of a deteriorating situation in East Germany and sought to refute statements that East Germany was spinning out of control. The day after the U.S. Embassy in East Berlin reported on its views of on-the-ground developments in light of the disintegrating GDR, and Baker met with the Washington Post editorial board. When asked about whether East Germany was on the verge of civil war, he read the summary of Embassy East Berlin's report to the reporters that the pace of the revolution was breathtaking. East Germany in December 1989 was descending into disorder, and Kohl, Gorbachev, and Bush understood that after the initial euphoria of the fall of the Berlin Wall, uncertainty was filling the air. Their leadership would prove critical to stability amid chaos.

The Monday demonstrations continued peacefully and had spread to nearly every town and city in the country. However, the threat of violence was always present. The pace of the revolution was breathtaking; events were happening fast for us at the U.S. Embassy in East Berlin. We could live through and report to Washington on many, but not all of the events. Others around us were reporting on incidents that seemed to lead to violence or seemed to indicate that the Soviet troops would leave their barracks. We in the U.S. Embassy were concerned confrontations between Soviets and East Germans would be violent and set a chain reaction of events of escalating violence.

After the fall of the Berlin Wall on November 9, 1989, New York Times columnist Thomas Friedman captured the Bush administration's concerns. East Germany's collapse could have forced a disorganized, de facto unification with West Germany before Germany's neighbors or the Soviet Union were prepared to accept it.[94] Washington was wary of a weak East German government that was on the verge of collapse. The Bush-Gorbachev and Bush-Kohl relationships would become increasingly important as reports circulated in Washington in early

---

94 Thomas L. Friedman, Baker, in Berlin, Outlines a Plan To Make NATO a Political Group., in: The New York Times, Online: http://www.nytimes.com/1989/12/13/world/upheaval-east-baker-berlin-outlines-plan-make-nato-political-group.html?pagewanted=all, (The New York Times: New York, 1989).

December that the chaos of the East German revolution had led to the appearance of a troubling specter – one of civil war in East Germany.

Baker was also concerned about keeping the reform movement peaceful and changes flowing from the fall of the Berlin Wall in East Germany manageable. Baker was keenly aware of American responsibility for Berlin and Germany as a whole from World War II that remained a legal condition for unification. Consequently, he considered visiting East Germany while in Berlin to send the message that the United States was serious about its role and its rights in Germany.

However, when he arrived in West Berlin, Baker first called in the two American ambassadors – Richard C. Barkley in East Germany and Vernon Walters in West Germany – and sought their advice on whether he should visit East Germany while on the current trip. Such a visit would be the first trip by a U.S. Secretary of State to East Germany. It was a difficult decision to make since the U.S. considered East Germany to be an illegitimate, unrepresentative regime, even though the U.S. had established diplomatic relations with East Germany since 1974.

Barkley assured him that his visit would not provoke further instability and argued that fair elections would likely end communist rule as had happened in Poland in June 1989. The Secretary's visit would reinforce the call for an East German election at the time planned for May 6, 1990. A Secretary of State visit would also offer a chance to encourage peaceful political change and also to explain U.S. policies on unification and NATO.

Walters argued that such a high-level visit could strengthen the communist government by giving it legitimacy. After deliberating with the ambassadors, Baker called President Bush's National Security Advisor Brent Scowcroft to discuss the possible visit. Then after consulting the president, Baker decided later that night to visit East Germany the next day. Baker also discussed his planned visit with German Foreign Minister Hans-Dietrich Genscher and Soviet Foreign Minister Eduard A. Shevardnadze.

Baker decided to come to East Germany the next day, and Ambassador Barkley returned to his dinner in East Berlin in time to ask Deputy Prime Minister Christa Luft to call Prime Minister Modrow and arrange the meeting. I called Imre Lipping and asked that he contact Bishop Dr. Werner Leich, chair of the *Bund der Evangelische Kirche* (BUND), to see if he also could meet Secretary Baker. Such a high-level visit prepared in a few hours was painful to arrange but critical to our policy discussions.

East German stability and German unification were indeed on Secretary Baker's mind when he traveled the next day to East Germany following his speech in West Berlin. His top priorities included calling for elections as well as a non-violent peaceful reform movement. He also enunciated U.S. policy that President Bush proposed that unification should occur in the context of Germany's continued commitment to NATO and an increasingly integrated European Community, and with due regard for the legal role and responsibilities of the Allied powers.[95]

Providing security and stability in Europe would be at the heart of his speech in West Berlin, and he spoke of designing and gradually putting into place a new architecture for a new era. Although he spoke of modern Euro-Atlantic security architecture, Baker also made clear that Europe must have a place for NATO, even if also serving new collective purposes. Baker first met with Chancellor Kohl and delivered his speech about U.S. views on a changing Europe, in which he explained that as "Europe changes, the instruments for Western cooperation must adapt."[96]

After Baker delivered his speech in West Berlin, he traveled across town to Potsdam, on the outskirts of East Berlin. The visit was dramatic and Tom Friedman, writing in the New York Times on December 13, 1989, reported that Baker

> [d]irectly after his [West Berlin] speech, slipped into a Mercedes limousine and traveled to East Germany to deliver another message in a previously unannounced round of talks with East Germany's Communist Premier Hans Modrow, as well as with several East German opposition leaders.[97]

The motorcade was, indeed, quite a sight. On Baker's drive from West Berlin, a bevy of West German Mercedes police cars and police vans with sirens blaring and blue lights flashing led his way. Then he came to the border, to the famous place of spy-exchange, the Glienicke Bridge where Americans and Russians exchanged downed American U-2 pilot Gary Powers and Russian human rights dissident Natan Scharansky.

Baker recalled that the motorcade left the West Berlin escort behind, and emerged like a caterpillar shedding its husk. Once past the Soviet guard on the Glienicke Bridge, a lone East German policeman on a motorcycle and a single East German *Volkspolizei* in his tiny Wartburg car with a dimly lit blue light led Baker into Potsdam in East Germany. There he met East German Premier Modrow at the Interhotel Potsdam. The images diminished the people meeting in a tourist hotel and showed the declining power of East Germany. The end of East Germany was discernible.

In his meeting with Modrow, Baker achieved his primary purpose of reaffirming plans for a free and fair election in East Germany in May and withheld

---

95 U.S. President Georg Herbert Walker Bush's Conditions for Unification (December 4, 1989), Online: http://ghdi.ghi-dc.org/sub_document.cfm?document_id=2874, (Brussels, 1989b).
96 Thomas L. Friedman, Baker, in Berlin, Outlines a Plan To Make NATO a Political Group., in: The New York Times, Online: http://www.nytimes.com/1989/12/13/world/upheaval-east-baker-berlin-outlines-plan-make-nato-political-group.html?pagewanted=all, (The New York Times: New York, 1989).
97 Ibid.

any economic cooperation for Modrow's proposed joint ventures until after the election was held (later set for March 18, 1990). The U.S. policy supported East German self-determination, which President Bush had proposed to Chancellor Kohl in early December. As for unification, Baker explained American policy on German unification and encouraged Modrow to start on a peaceful path to reform. Speaking to reporters after his one-hour meeting with Prime Minister Modrow, Secretary Baker said:

> I felt it was important that we have an opportunity to let the Premier and the people of the German Democratic Republic know our support for the reforms that are taking place in this country. We also wanted to make it very clear that we support the process of reform peacefully, and we are very anxious to see the process move forward.[98]

Baker did hold out some future hope in response to Modrow's discussion of U.S. investment in East German joint ventures. Baker told Modrow that if East Germany followed in the footsteps of *glasnost and perestroika* like in Poland and Hungary, it could expect to receive a sympathetic hearing from the West.[99]

Premier Modrow, who was also concerned about stability in East Germany, said at the same press encounter following the meeting at Potsdam's Interhotel that East Germany "tries in its relations with the United States to be a stable element."[100] Modrow added that East Germany was also "a building block" in the "common European home" that Gorbachev sought. However dramatic the unannounced visit to East Germany was in helping to stabilize the chaos, it was German unification that would soon become the leading foreign policy issue.[101]

Baker also met separately with the Lutheran Church legal representative Manfred Stolpe and Lutheran ministers in the *Nikolaikirche*. Those leaders of the peaceful reform movement heard the U.S. urge them to keep the movement nonviolent and to approach the issue of German reunification with sober restraint. Perhaps to the surprise of the American delegation, the East German opposition leaders in Potsdam on December 12 made clear that they had no intention of abandoning their quest for the renewal of East Germany in exchange for promoting German unification. German unification was still too provocative to challenge the East German Government. Such an opportunity would come shortly.[102]

Later we learned that the interim government ordered Minister for National Defense Heinz Hoffmann to control those weapons in Kavelstorf near Rostock

---

98 Norman Kempster, Baker Vows Support for E. Germany : Diplomacy: Regime calls dramatic visit the start of a 'dialogue.' Reforms praised by secretary of state, in: Los Angeles Times, Online: https://www.latimes.com/archives/la-xpm-1989-12-13-mn-106-story.html, (Los Angeles 1989).
99 Ibid.
100 Ibid.
101 Ibid.
102 Ibid.

that Chancellor Kohl had raised with President Bush on December 3. The takeover by the military of armaments from the Kavelstorf arms warehouse, company militias, Sport und Technik clubs, and select police units. Admiral Hoffmann carried out the order quickly, which had stabilizing effects.[103]

Free and Fair Elections

Modrow governed well his interim government from November 18 until he made a fateful decision in January to reconstitute the *Stasi* as the office of National Security (*Amt für National Sicherheit*). Immediately, the public understood the new intelligence police role and angrily dismissed it. Modrow had labeled the new secret police the *Office for National Security*, which led to a simple acronym – *NASI*. NASI sounded so close to the Nazis Gestapo that a Roundtable, a government of unity, was the only option to govern. They also advanced the date of elections from May 6, 1990, to March 18, 1990. These elections would democratize East Germany and give a mandate to the parliament to unify Germany. A consensus quickly emerged to channel all political energy into the campaign for the March 18 election, drawing the people together for democracy and the unification of the two Germanys.

Baker's mission to East Germany placed him with Kohl, Gorbachev, and Bush as the leadership team that would successfully manage the international diplomacy of the political transfer of power from the East German communist party to that of a freely elected *Volkskammer* and Prime Minister De Maizière. The threat of civil war passed, and a parliamentary mandate for German unity would fulfill the call: "We are one people." The 1990 Charter of Paris established the new world order.

As Germany regained its sovereignty with democratic legitimacy in its constitution, the West did not disappoint Gorbachev for his support of German unification. He did not come away empty-handed. He achieved agreements for:
1. A new German-Soviet treaty.
2. A CSCE Conventional Forces in Europe Treaty reducing the number of military forces in Europe.
3. A German-Polish treaty settled the Oder-Neisse border and established stability on the Russian border.
4. NATO also assured Russia repeatedly that it was not a threat to the Soviet Union.
5. NATO changed its strategy to make nuclear weapons indeed of last resort, minimizing the principle of "first use."

---

103 De Maiziere interview with author, 2016.

6. The Allies changed both "forward defense" and "flexible response" concepts that had been against east European and Soviet territory.
7. NATO also extended a hand of friendship to establish diplomatic liaison with NATO and later signed the NATO-Russia Founding Act.

Germany is no longer West Germany

Germany changed at unification. Its territory increased, its population grew, and its economic power confirmed it as the continental power it has become. Over the past thirty years, its reluctance to accept corresponding responsibility and leadership hid behind the country's imperial and National Socialist history to avoid accusations it would return to a hegemonical past. The Peaceful Revolution that brought down a dictatorship for the first time in German history also dissolved the consensus Democracy (*Konsensdemokratie*) in West Germany. Although a new, more contentious domestic political style emerged, Germany has held to its West German democratic traditions. The radical change from East Germany to united Germany united the East Germans' fight for freedom with West Germans democracy. Germany today risks more mistrust from denying its leadership role as the economic engine of Europe in the global economy, its role as the backbone of the European pillar, and sustaining partner in the values-based transatlantic relationship.[104]

Other changes brought through the unification process included the dramatic change in the political parties as the Western Christian Democrats absorbed the East-CDU, Democratic Aufbruch, and the German Social Union (Deutsche Soziale Union). The Social Democratic Party of West Germany joined with the East German SDP. Later SPD chairman Oscar LaFontaine would split off from the SPD to found the Leftist Party (Die Linke) with the East German Party of Democratic Socialism (PDS). The Greens, established in the 1980s, joined with Bündnis-90. The FDP merged with the East German LDPD. Eventually, these changes would fragment the political framework set by the centrist parties, CDU and SPD, into a fluidity of five or six parties in the Bundestag. The constellation of political parties complicates building coalitions to form governments. Even the Grand Coalitions that earlier represented 90 percent of the voters today reach a slim majority.[105]

The dissolution of the East German economy and the introduction of the Trust Agency, which introduced the market economy resulted in massive costs,

---

104 Edgar Wolfrum, *Der Aufsteiger Eine Geschichte Deutschlands von 1990 bis heute*, (Klett-Cotta Verlag: Stuttgart , 2020), pp. 23–27.
105 Ibid, pp. 32–53.

high unemployment, and the rise in populism. Unification delayed reforms in the social system, high wage costs, and an international recession, while racism, fear of foreigners (Xenophobia), and right-wing extremism grew. After much delay, Chancellor Gerhard Schroeder's 'Agenda 2010' was surely the most extensive labor market reform in German history and helped make the German economy fit for the 21st century. The abandonment of the D-Mark for the euro embedded Germany more deeply in the European Union.

Germany's role in international security also changed with unification. The Balkan Wars, the terror attack in the US on 9/11/2001, as well as conflict and wars in Afghanistan, Iraq, North Africa, and Syria, drew united Germany into a series of conflicts and wars. The decision of the Constitutional Court on July 12, 1994, allowed Germany to deploy its Armed Forces out of the NATO area, albeit with an alliance and a mandate from the Bundestag. Although Chancellor Gerhard Schroder said 'no' to the Iraq War, Germany's security role has changed.[106]

Today, a mere 30 years later, democracy is at risk of failing in the breakdown of the liberal order. At its core lies the issue here is whether a democratic Germany should and can lead Europe without dominating the continent. Can Germany, as a leader in partnership, remain a responsible geopolitical power and a leader of Europe? In an unraveling world order, will Germany accept responsibility beyond crisis management and become more strategic while keeping its obligation to Europe through Leadership in Partnership and restraint?

But going a different route, which would end delegating decision-making to Washington, would also lead to Germany's discomfort. It would also lead to threats of violence and crises coming closer to Germany. Still, the EU needs leadership, not just multilateralism. Germany's role is essential towards Russia, the post-Soviet space, the West Balkans, and diplomacy in the Middle East and North Africa. Germany's unique historical sense of responsibility and its present position of power and opportunity present its leaders with a window of opportunity to accept international responsibility. Germany is moving past its strategic cultural deficit developed from its comfortable position of being safe in NATO and prosperous in Europe. Reactive crisis management is not sufficient for a stronger European pillar of the transatlantic partnership.

Alina Polyakova and Benjamin Haddad, writing in the July/August 2019 Foreign Affairs, posed the question of the future of the Transatlantic Alliance by titling their article: "Europe Alone. What comes After the Transatlantic Alliance."[107] Germany and the United States are challenged to reshape the future of

---

106 Ibid, p. 77.
107 Alina Polyakova and Benjamin Haddad, Europe Alone, What comes After the Transatlantic Alliance, in: Foreign Affairs, Online: https://www.foreignaffairs.com/articles/europe/2019-06-11/europe-alone, (New York City, 2019).

the Transatlantic Alliance. Europe has a choice to make. It cannot claim the mantle of independent global leadership and continue to rely on the United States for its security, including in its immediate neighborhood.

> Reversing the trend toward European irrelevance and disunity is the responsibility of European policymakers. In the long run, a strong continent that is able to defend its interests and fight its own battles will benefit Washington more than a divided and weak one. The transatlantic alliance can and should remain the bedrock of the Western model of liberal democratic values and principles. But it will have to transform to meet the growing economic, security, and political challenges from China and Russia. Rather than pining for the return of a transatlantic partnership that will surely continue to fray, the United States and Europe must now invest in and accept the consequences of autonomy.[108]

They add that U.S. policymakers also have to choose whether

> they prefer to maintain a weak and divided European continent that is aligned with their interests and dependent on U.S. power? Or are they ready to deal with a more forceful and autonomous partner that will sometimes go against their favored policies?[109]

Germany, for its part, needs greater cross-departmental cooperation, a shared vision for greater German international engagement, and strategic foresight are necessary for it to become a convincing global actor – both to its domestic public and to its international partners. The country can pursue its national interests through the overarching principle of *Leadership in Partnership*, although but it cannot preserve the liberal order on its own. Multilateral cooperation, after all, calls on Germany to defend its interests, while sharing leadership. Leading in partnership is a cornerstone of the current world order and is the key to Germany's goals in a changing world.

---

108 Ibid.
109 Ibid.

Part Two: The German Problem: National sovereignty or sovereign obligation to Europe

> I fear German power less than I am beginning to fear its inactivity. You have become Europe's indispensable nation. You may not fail to lead: not dominate, but to lead in reform.
> – Radosław Sikorski[110]

The book's second part addresses Germany's leadership dilemma: the need to balance national sovereignty and interests with its constitutional commitment to Europe. President Steinmeier said at the Munich Security Conference 2020: Europe "is our strongest, most elementary national interest."[111]

The *"German Problem"* is one of a reluctant leader caught between its national interests and its sovereign obligation, notably to Europe.

Having been defeated in World War II, Germany was not allowed to assume a position of political leadership for much of the 20th century, and indeed, it lacked full sovereignty to do so before 1990. The positive pole of this situation was that Germany had the luxury of neither having to plan alone strategically nor having to assume the total cost of providing for its security. It could instead focus on economic growth and development under the umbrella of US security guarantees. In the decades after unification, the Federal Republic has pursued its civilian role, while it relied on the NATO Alliance's strategic deterrent defense to ensure peace and prosperity. Indeed, the policy succeeded in unification that answered the "German Question" of the country's place in Europe with its power bound by European integration and the transatlantic relationship. Chancellor Helmut Kohl declared with distinct pleasure that friendly nations surround the country for the

---

110 Radoslaw Sikorski, I fear Germany's power less than her inactitity. Eurozone break-up would be apocalyptic, writes Radoslaw Sikorski, in: Financial Times, https://www.ft.com/content/b753cb42-19b3-11e1-ba5d-00144feabdc0, (London, 2011a).
111 Frank-Walter Steinmeier, Eröffnung der Münchner Sicherheitskonferenz, Online: https://www.bundespraesident.de/SharedDocs/Reden/DE/Frank-Walter-Steinmeier/Reden/2020/02/200214-MueSiKo.html, (München, 2020).

first time.[112] Germany set out to be "Model Deutschland," the most peaceful and most perfect version of itself that it could be. Since unification, the country has sought to help shape a democratic Europe as well as to promote global peace as a "Civilian Power." For three decades, Germans continued to defer to NATO for strategic security planning.

Today, the country remains determined to avoid returning to its history of a special German Way *(Sonderweg)* and rejects claims to hegemony or dominance. Since unification, Germany's size, growing economic weight, and geographic position in the middle of the continent have nevertheless inevitably pushed the country towards a more active role in European affairs. Germany was and is too big and an economic heavyweight to keep on the sidelines of European politics. Its European neighbors, just as much as the Germans themselves continue to view the idea of German leadership skeptically, especially when a more proactive German stance was deemed unavoidable and desired.

Germany's leadership dilemma of how to assume its responsibilities, including an international leadership role without dominating the continent, is unresolved. Scholars have commented on Germany's changing role. Herfried Münkler has argued that after German unification, the European center shifted from its institutions, the EU Commission, European Parliament, and the European Court as well as the European Central Bank, to States. Gregor Schöllgen and Hans-Peter Schwarz agreed with this historic shift. By 1994 Schwarz[113] argued that Germany had become the central power in Europe, although it had not sought it. Münkler described Germany's political position in Europe as the power in the middle of Europe.[114]

A review of some moments in German foreign and security policy since unification illustrates where there is a German Problem of leadership. Choosing between national sovereignty and sovereign obligation, as well as how decisions such as those taken in the creation of the European Monetary Union and various security operations, can reveal the dilemmas in Germany's unilateral or partnered foreign policy decisions.

These dilemmas define the contrast between the German Problem of its unresolved leadership role in Europe and the resolved German Question, which was about Germany's place in Europe. Going back to the 1870s, the German Question revolved around the issue of integrating a strong Germany in the middle of

---

112 Deutscher Bundestag, Rede von Dr. Helmut Kohl, Bundeskanzler a.D., Online: https://www.bundestag.de/parlament/geschichte/gastredner/gorbatschow/kohl-247410 (Berlin, 1997).
113 Hans-Peter Schwarz and Deborah Lucas Schneider, Germany's National and European Interests. In: *Daedalus*, Vol. 123, No. 2 (Cambridge, 1994), pp. 81–105.
114 Herfried Münkler, *Macht der Mitte. Die neuen Aufgaben Deutschlands in Europa*, (Koerber Stiftung: Hamburg, 2015), pp. 37 to 45.

Europe.[115] In 1990, unification reinstated this territorially and the demographically relevant country into the international community of nations. The clear answer to the German Question reassured allies and Europeans to support a united Germany. By virtually sacrificing military, nuclear weapons, and hard power in general as well as focusing more on soft power, Germany was integrated into the European Model. But answering the German Question did not solve the German Problem.

The question here is one of whether the Federal Republic, as Brendan Simms asks, "which is prosperous and secure as never before, can be persuaded to take the political initiative and make the necessary economic sacrifices to complete the work of European Unity?"[116] That is the "German Problem" of a reluctant leader caught between its national interests and its sovereign obligation, notably to Europe. The German Problem, according to Stephen Fröhlich, is the need to end self-restraint. The German choice of not getting involved cannot sustain in the times of uncertain leadership, especially by a country that has the political weight and influence to be a benevolent European hegemon, which is a responsibility the leadership in Berlin is not ready to take on. Rather than being proactive, Fröhlich argues, Germany's foreign policy is opportunistic and reactive, characterized by volatility, national interest, unpredictability, and dominance in exercising power. The issue remains: power politics and power positions have changed in Europe. Also, the perception of power and Germany have changed. There are expectations about Germany other than its past. The problem now is: what happens if Germany does not recognize and act on German interests that are European interests and European interests that are German. [117]

Today, as external circumstances are changing, the German Problem becomes increasingly relevant. At a time where Europe's security architecture is coming under distress, the question remains open whether Germany can assume a more proactive role and meet the responsibility that falls upon its shoulders in European affairs without dominating the continent. At the same time, it is uncertain whether Europeans can accept German leadership based on a partnership approach, institutionalized cooperation, the rule of law, and Germany's respect for human dignity. The European choice between a values-based systematic partner, the United States, and an interests-based systemic competitor, China, has global consequences.

---

115 Andreas Rödder, *Wer hat Angst vor Deutschland? Geschichte eines europäischen Problems*, (S. Fischer Verlag: Frankfurt am Main, 2018), p. 199.
116 Brendan Simms, Cracked heart of the old World, in: The New Statesman, Online: https://www.newstatesman.com/world-affairs/europe/2013/03/cracked-heart-old-world, (London, 2013).
117 Stephan Fröhlich, *Das Ende der Selbstentfesselung*, (Springer Verlag S.V.: Frankfurt am Main, 2019), p.11.

As the United States increasingly turns to Europe to take charge of its own security interests, Europe has to make a choice in the rising global power shift between the transatlantic partnership and China or seek to balance its interests between the two great powers. In a climate of growing economic, political, and security challenges, Europe needs to decide whether it continues its dependence on the United States, which at this point is no longer as dependable a partner it once was. But Europe can also not lay claim to independent global leadership while relying on the US for security. Europe's freeriding in defense and its concentration on economic prosperity in the good old days – "Europa's Banality of Good" – have come to a close.

Will this reluctant leader Germany succeed in balancing its national interests with the demands from its sovereign obligation to Europe to make Europe relevant again? Will Germany conclude that Europe's interests are in the national interest of Germany?

Chapter 3: The German Problem

> Germany has more neighbors than any other country so that for Deutschland, it is a great challenge to reinvent itself epeatedly. However, that is also a great chance because that means if Germany can solve this problem, then it supports stability in Europe.
> – Henry Kissinger [118]

> [...] in November 1990, the month after the reunification of Germany, the heads of the states and governments of the Conference on Security and Co-operation in Europe met in Paris. The highlight was the signing of the Charter of Paris on the 21st of November. All 34 member states committed "to build, consolidate and strengthen democracy as the only system of government of our nations."
> – Heinrich August Winkler[119]

Rethinking German Unification

The ethos of Germany is the Basic Law of the Federal Republic of Germany, which becomes the foundation of the Berlin Republic. The Peaceful Revolution in the German Democratic Republic, through an act of self-determination, and with a free and democratic election in the German Democratic Republic gave it lasting legitimacy. Germany has taken these constitutional principles and applied them to its foreign policy, emphasizing peacebuilding and encouraging other states to build institutions based on individual dignity and human rights.

Historically, German sovereignty has not belonged to them alone since the 1648 Treaty of Westphalia, except during the rule of the Kaiser Wilhelm, 1871–1918, and during the Nazi-Regime, 1933–1945. The struggle for leadership in Europe explicitly links the internal order of Germany with peace in Europe. The 1648 Treaty of Westphalia established the sanctity of sovereignty of states, although Germany was a set of territories, not a nation-state. France and Sweden held sovereignty over the territories during and after the Thirty Years War. The broad impact of European wars was centered on Germany and ravaged Europe.

---

118 See interview with Henry Kissinger and Karl Kaiser, in: Center for International Security and Governance, *International Security Forum 2018 Report*, (Rheinische Friedrich Wilhelms Universität: Bonn, 2019).

119 Heinrich-August Winkler, Denk ich an Deutschland : Was den Westen zusammenhält, in: Frankfurter Allgemeine Zeitung, Online: https://www.faz.net/aktuell/politik/inland/heinrich-august-winkler-was-den-westen-zusammenhaelt-13815991.html?printPagedArticle=true#pageIndex_0, (Frankfurt am Main, 2015)., 22.09.2015.

After Napoleon, the Concert of Europe balanced European powers, and after the Second World War, the European Union pooled national sovereignty. International institutions were designed, in part, to contain Germany or mobilize it for the common good, Krasner included the League of Nations, the United Nations, the European Union, the Non-Proliferation Treaty (NPT), and NATO.[120]

What then is this Germany, united in 1990, with its full sovereignty legitimated through a Peaceful Revolution of self-determination? Historically, sovereignty for Germany packs today's policy choices with dilemmas. The Peace of Westphalia Produced the Modern Sovereign State and territory, not individual identity (as in tribes, trading leagues, and empires are the critical features of the Westphalian system's authority).[121] However, for most of the nineteenth century, Germany struggled to find its place in Europe and the world. Wars and revolution in that century led to German unification in 1871 and an Imperial Germany, which dominated the troubled twentieth century by first casting the form for the tumultuous century at its opening. The National Socialists dictatorship followed Imperial Germany, and both of those Germanys projected global power through two world wars from 1914 to 1945.

After the Second World War, West Germany's limited sovereignty and the Soviet-dominated German Democratic Republic still left open the German Question of "whither Germany" in the center of the struggle for security and democracy in Europe and the Central Front of the Cold War as part of the worldwide confrontation between communism and democracy. The days of suppressing Germany, like those in 1949 when the first North Atlantic Treaty Organization Secretary-General, Lord Ismay, said NATO's goal was "to keep the Russians out, the Americans in, and the Germans down"[122] are long over.

Germany, with its regained national sovereignty, is a respected nation-state with a place in Europe and the world. Now Germany must decide whether to accept the country's international leadership and exercise its sovereign obligation to its allies and partners. Whether the German polity, along with Germany's friends, allies, and neighbors, will agree, is uncertain.

After the fall of the Berlin Wall, the debate over German unification ignited anew. The mere idea of a united, sovereign Germany recalled a frightening history of a century filled with German militarism, domination, war, and destruction in Europe and the world. International observers saw the end of a militaristic foreign policy that began in 1871 and ended with the defeat of Nazi Germany in

---

120 Brendan Simms, *Europe The Struggle for Supremacy from 1453 to the Present*, (Basic Book: New York City, 2014).
121 Stephen D. Krasner, Think Again: Sovereignty, in: Foreign Policy, Online: https://foreignpolicy.com/2009/11/20/think-again-sovereignty/, (Washington D.C., 2009).
122 North-American Treaty Organisation, Ismay in NATO, Online: https://www.nato.int/cps/en/natohq/declassified_137930.htm, (Brussels, 2020).

1945. Nevertheless, returning full sovereignty to Germany was a shock to European leaders. The Westphalian Peace Order created the principle of the sanctity of sovereignty forged in 1648 from the conflicts of the Thirty Years War. But it didn't prevent wars; they simply changed the character to become wars among states, no more feudal conflicts. German sovereignty after the 1871 unification was a heavy burden that became more difficult after the National Socialists dictatorship. After the Second World War, Germany became a civilian power (*Zivilmacht*), the phrase Hanns Maull coined to describe the country. *Zivilmacht* became comfortable and universally accepted in a Germany conscious of its growing power. Still today, the country carefully balances between avoiding power projection while exercising economic power and promoting human rights.[123]

In any case, Germany's power surged following unification and the restoration of German sovereignty. Since then, democracy has continued to grow and thrive, although characterized by reluctant leadership in foreign and security policies. If German sovereignty is founded on an ethos of united Germany, then the country has adopted a reinvented German political culture that is guided by principles applied to its foreign policy. Peacebuilding premised on encouraging other states to build institutions premised on individual dignity, and human rights have served Germany and Europe well. The constitutional principles, anchored in Germany's understanding of its past and in its commitment to seeking a better future, have been crucial to establishing Germany's international role as a leader in partnership with other countries.

Germans are reluctant to look to their future as it reflects on its troubled history, which its allies use to block leadership. While Germany is committed to the European Union, the lack of European unity calls for German leadership. Still, it brings back the specter of both the Thirty Years War and World War II, European conflagrations lasting three decades each. After the Second World War, Europeans to avoid wars in Europe were seeking deeper integration and found a vision of a new governmental structure that could form a political union. Europeans, and especially Germans, are traumatized by the history of war. That historical experience weighs heavily.

---

123 Knut Kirste and Hanns Maull, Zivilmacht und Rollentheorie, in: Zeitschrift für Internationale Beziehungen, 3. Jhrg. (Nomos Verlagsgesellschaft: Wuppertal, 1996), pp. 283–312.

Germany's International Responsibility Doctrine

German foreign policy is an expression of the country's identity borne out of its history. The past seventy years brought a historical Hegelian shift from Prussian militarism to pacifism and a shift from a classic nation-state to Model Germany. Germany has exercised its sovereignty in defense of the rules-based international liberal order and has become Europe's leader in partnership with other countries. Stability and security are better served by the rule of law, than from a balance of power politics or hegemony.

There is a strong belief that the rule of law and democracy offer reliable diplomacy tools for conflict resolution through international courts and the United Nations. Skepticism against the military as an instrument of diplomacy is a mark of German politics. The use of force should only be used as a last resort and in alliance with the United Nations or NATO. This consensus is often seen as German idealism and is criticized as failing to recognize realism.[124]

The challenge for Germany is not new. King of Prussia Frederick the Great understood the realist dilemma with his well-known proverb: "Diplomacy without arms is like music without instruments."[125] German leadership embedded the country's defense and security in the German-American partnership, which has shaped transatlantic policy in security, economics, human rights, post-conflict justice, and constitutionalism.

Nevertheless, for the past three decades, the Berlin Republic has pursued its civilian role as model Germany, while it relied on the NATO Alliance's strategic deterrence and defense to ensure peace and prosperity along with Europe.

In his reassessment of 1989, Thomas Bagger described Germany's conclusion that it could remain as it was and wait for others to transform themselves as they converged to become an open market, liberal democracies. In a country surrounded by only friends and allies, as Chancellor Helmut Kohl often repeated, the country lost any perception of a military threat to the country. Military power no longer mattered; civilian power did. Germany's pursuit of multilateralism was one of the codifications of rules and multilateral solutions. European integration

---

[124] Harald Müller, Diplomatie als Instrument deutscher Außenpolitik, Online: http://m.bpb.de/apuz/230577/diplomatie-als-instrument-deutscher-aussenpolitik?p=all, (Bundeszentrale für politische Bildung: Bonn, 2016).

[125] Dictum was coined by Frederick the Great, one does not know in which setting, but it has been widely referenced, among others from Sir Malcolm Rifkind on the role of Great Britain in world affairs, in: The Times, Diplomacy without Arms, Online: https://www.thetimes.co.uk/article/diplomacy-without-arms-39flhbg09jz, (London, 2010).

was inevitable and irreversible. This linear thinking led to the Economic and Monetary Union of the European Union and the introduction of the Euro.[126]

However, a sovereign Germany deals not only with its history and also an unraveling world order. The combined challenges of multi-polarity, rising unilateralism, and global risks call the transatlantic partnership into question in a perfect storm of threats and trouble. The Russian invasion of Ukraine and the annexation of Crimea shattered the peaceful worldview that dominated German thinking. Soon the Chinese dismissed on July 12, 2016 the ruling of an independent arbitral tribunal of the UN Convention on the Law of the Sea (UNCLOS) on sovereignty as "nothing more than a piece of waste paper."[127] Then the brutal war in Syria, the collapse of the Arab Spring, and other conflicts ended the peaceful security order enshrined in the Charter of Paris from the end of the Cold War.[128] Culminating the changes in the world were two critical decisions, one of which was the American president's decision to step back from international leadership, and the other was Britain's decision to leave the European Union. Competition to fill the American leadership gap has followed.

Germany's unique historical sense of responsibilities and its present position of power and opportunity; however, present its leaders with a window of opportunity for accepting international responsibility. Indeed, unification answered the German Question and left the country surrounded by friendly nations as Chancellor Helmut Kohl declared. Germany has found its place in Europe. Model Germany has since unification sought to help shape a democratic Europe as well as to promote global peace as a *Zivilmacht*. Germans outsourced to NATO its strategic security planning, and the use of military force.

Can this sovereign Germany lead but not dominate Europe? Germany respects human dignity, has full sovereignty legitimized by self-determination for democracy, adheres to the rule of law, and exercises its sovereign obligation to Europe. Can Germany contribute its leadership to the strategic debate for Eu-

---

126 Thomas Bagger, The World According to Germany: Reassessing 1989, [Originally publsished: "The Washington Quarterly",(Milton: Taylor and Francis, 2019)], in: Atlantik Brücke, Online: https://www.atlantik-bruecke.org/the-world-according-to-germany-reassessing-1989/, (Berlin, 2020).
127 Catherine Wong, Nothing more than a piece of paper': former Chinese envoy dismisses upcoming ruling on South China Sea claims. China will not be intimated even if US sends 10 aircraft carriers to region, says Dai Bingguo amid rising tensions over rival territorial claims to disputed waters, in: South China Morning Post, Online: https://www.scmp.com/news/china/diplomacy-defence/article/1986029/nothing-more-piece-paper-former-chinese-envoy-dismisses, (Hong Kong, 2016).
128 Bill Hayton, Two Years On, South China Sea Ruling Remains a Battleground for the Rules-Based Order, in: Chatham House, Online: https://www.chathamhouse.org/expert/comment/two-years-south-china-sea-ruling-remains-battleground-rules-based-order, (London, 2018).

rope's future as a pillar in the transatlantic relationship? Can it be done without NATO? Is that the 'German Problem'?

The German Problem is one of how Germany resolves its dilemmas as it exercises sovereignty and balances its national interests against its sovereign obligation to Europe, reaffirmed in the Aachen Treaty. France and Germany agreed to "address the challenges of the 21st century together – with close co-ordination of European policy, robust common foreign and security policy, and an economic area with standard regulations."[129] Germany has begun in earnest to accept more international responsibility since calls from President Joachim Gauck[130] and Ministers Frank-Walter Steinmeier[131] and Ursula von der Leyen[132] at the 2014 Munich Security Conference. Since then, a 2016 Defense White Book has been published stating that Germany has to act more proactively.[133] Germany has agreed, tentatively and in theory, to accept responsibility, and is poised to take a leadership role in Europe.

Can the country resolve the dilemma of its sovereign obligations and national interests in pursuit of Leadership in Partnership? Or will it seek to dominate Europe? United Germany's constitutional *Staatsräson* is exercised in a leadership style of *Leaders in Partnership* in Europe consistent with German commitments to avoid hegemony (*Nie Wieder Allein*) and to embed its security in the transatlantic relationship (*Nie Wieder Krieg*). Leadership in Partnership is a structure of partners with sovereign obligations and responsibility to Europe, which guides how Germany leads. Sovereign obligation retains sovereignty while fulfilling responsibilities to Europe. Germany also remains bound by a "Culture of Self-Restraint" (*Kultur der Zurückhaltung*) or reluctant leadership. This remembrance culture (*Errinerungskultur*) acts as a restraint on policy excesses.

Germany can step up to leadership. Meanwhile, the international leadership chair is vacant. U.S. President Donald Trump has absented America from international leadership of global affairs. Europe and Germany have to take on

---

129 *Treaty between the Federal Republic of Germany and the French Republic on Franco-German Cooperation and Integration,* Online: https://www.diplomatie.gouv.fr/en/country-files/germany/france-and-germany/franco-german-treaty-of-aachen/, (Aachen, 2019).

130 Joachim Gauck, Eröffnung der 50. Münchner Sicherheitskonferenz, Online: https://www.bundespraesident.de/SharedDocs/Reden/DE/Joachim-Gauck/Reden/2014/01/140131-Muenchner-Sicherheitskonf-erenz.html, (München, 2014).

131 Frank-Walter Steinmeier, Rede von Außenminister Frank-Walter Steinmeier anlässlich der 50. Münchner Sicherheitskonferenz, Online: https://www.auswaertiges-amt.de/de/newsroom/140201-bm-muesiko/259554, (München, 2014).

132 Ursula von der Leyen, Rede der Bundesministerin der Verteidigung Dr. Ursula von der Leyen auf der 54. Münchner Sicherheitskonferenz, Online: https://www.bmvg.de/resource/blob/22178/909a56e9af7501819eba0563f9724109/20180216-download-eroeffnungsrede-deutsch-data.pdf, (München, 2018), p. 2.

133 Deutsche Bundesregierung, *Weissbuch zur Sicherheitspolitik und zur Zukunft der Bundeswehr, 2016.*,Online: https://www.bmvg.de/de/themen/weissbuch, (Berlin, 2020).

more responsibility and to step up to a new transatlantic leadership role. Frank-Walter Steinmeier also made this clear during his tenure as Minister for Foreign Affairs. This leadership style articulated in new German responsibility through consensus in Munich in 2014 allows Germany to step up to leadership.[134] Decisions taken in the creation of the European Monetary Union and security operations reveal the dilemmas in unilateral or partnered decisions.

The combined challenges of multi-polarity, rising unilateralism, and global risks and threats have come together in a perfect storm at a time when the transatlantic partnership is drifting.[135] Europe is facing the internal challenges of populism and nationalism. Competition to fill the international leadership vacuum has begun. Under these conditions, Germany's self-elected position in the backseat of international leadership is starting to feel uncomfortable, but the path forward remains uncertain. Germany's unique historical sense of responsibility and its present position of power and opportunity, however, present its leaders with a window of opportunity for accepting international responsibility.

Germany is caught in a dilemma of refusing to lead, but reluctantly leading, despite the country's ongoing and studied determination to avoid the appearance of leadership. One choice leaves Europe without direction, and the other leads to attacks on Germany for dominating Europe. The dilemma is the reality that Europe cannot make decisions without Germany.

Unilateralism or Leadership in Partnership

Germany has pledged "Never Alone," not to follow a unilateral approach (*Sonderweg*). Instead, it has created a German model of leaders in partnership (*als Partner führen*). It is a group leadership approach that is opposite to the solo style of Trump that he has promised. In the European Union, leadership is based on pooled sovereignty and exercised by the Council of Ministers. In this recognition of a sovereign obligation to each other, EU members govern as leaders in partnership.

The dilemma faced was in Germany's dominant role in Europe exercised in the financial crisis with bailout resistance, austerity policy, and in the refugee crisis with its unilateral migration policy. While leading in partnership, some of these unilateral actions were active unilateralism others were unilateral veto power

---

134 Frank-Walter Steinmeier, Germany's New Global Role, Berlin Steps Up, In: Foreign Affairs, July/August 2016, Online: https://www.auswaertiges-amt.de/de/newsroom/160615-bm-foreignaffairs/281216, (New York, 2016).
135 James D. Bindenagel, *Germany's International Responsibility*, No. 5, July 2017 Commentary – Cisg-bonn.com, https://cisg-bonn.com/wp-content/uploads/2017/07/210717-Commentary-Paper.pdf, (Bonn, 2017).

exercises to render common solutions impossible. The current refusal to compromise with French President Emmanuel Macron on his vision for the Eurozone illustrates the dilemma.

In the twin crises – Brexit and the transatlantic partnership – Europe has decided to step up, and Germany with partners could show the political will to create a Eurozone budget and move toward political union. How can Germany proceed to make the most of the upheaval in European politics, while overcoming historical roles of dominance that render a strategic pursuit of its interests so tricky?[136] What is a domestically and globally feasible approach to containing the threats of an ongoing disintegration of European and international order as well as the various dangers imposed by unilateral actors?[137]

After the Second World War, the United States was determined not to let Germany and Western Europe fall to the Soviet Union and established itself as part of the European state system and is central to it today.[138] Germany now faces an increasing number of new or re-emerging powerful global actors as the U.S. withdraws from its NATO commitments and cooperation with the transatlantic community. After taking office, President Trump questioned whether the U.S. would fulfill its NATO defense commitments to Europe. Trump has even confronted Europe as a "foe" of the United States and subsequently imposed trade tariffs to address Germany's trade surplus with the United States. These and similar actions test European unity. Trump has defenders who would compare him to British Prime Minister Palmerston, whose tactical maneuvers operated as though a country has no permanent allies nor permanent enemies, but only national interests that the leader is obligated to follow. However, Trump's nationalist, interest-based policies are not in the 19th century but exist in the interconnected, interdependent, multilateral world of the 21st century. It is now essential for Europeans to fill the leadership gap Trump created.

Germany, as the dominant economy in the European Union, is moving, however slowly, into this power vacuum that calls for a new role in strategic planning. The German Problem is how to solve the dilemma of dominant but reluctant power. In a world of growing great power competition based on national interests, Germany stands with Europe. The European Union is debating an EU Global Strategy (EUGS) and is aiming at some European strategic autonomy. The 2016–2017 EU Security and Defense Package creates tools and demonstrates EU cohesion, but still lacks the shared strategic vision. Political will is still needed to step into European autonomy with military capabilities, defense procurement, budget, and strategic planning. The concept should not result in a

---

136 Ibid.
137 Ibid
138 Ibid.

European Army. NATO remains the only credible security guarantor that the EU can complement. The rhetoric of German officials suggests that Chancellor Angela Merkel can build on a solid base of political support for this EU effort; however, as Jörg Lau argues, "a vague consensus is not a strategy."[139]

Germany's foreign policy priorities include keeping France as an equal partner; managing Brexit without attempting to punish the United Kingdom; limiting the damage Trump can do to the West; decisively warding off Russian aggression; keeping Turkey aligned with Europe and reducing the "pull factors" drawing people from Africa to Europe.[140] Rather than managing these diverse issues on a case-by-case basis, Germany requires an overarching strategy that makes use of current opportunities to pursue its interests coherently and persuasively. A shift towards strategic thinking must first and foremost take place in the minds of German leaders and subsequently in its institutional structures. That suggests the exercise of sovereignty and acceptance of leadership will shape strategy.

Contained in German history is the driving force to implement sovereignty that results in an obligation to Europe as a whole. German exercise of sovereignty has, in addition to national interests, a Sovereign Obligation to Europe, as Richard Haass has written that states have sovereign rights but also have obligations to others.[141] Responsibility for a common good does not diminish national sovereignty. It stems from a need to expand and adapt the traditional principles of the international order for a highly interconnected world. The sovereign obligation thus retains respect for borders and opposition to change through coercion or force. It supports actions to enforce the norm against aggression, whether the incident involves Iraq invading Kuwait or Russia invading Crimea. And it retains respect for governments' rights to act as they wish within their borders, subject to the constraints of broadly accepted provisions of international law, such as the Universal Declaration of Human Rights and the Genocide Convention. The country's sovereign obligations do not reject or replace the traditional approach to order – one that remains necessary but is no longer sufficient – so much as it builds on sovereignty.[142]

In addition to Germany's role as a European Germany, the next step is to make its commitment to "Never Alone" leadership explicit and set down the funda-

---

139 Jörg Lau, Der kalte Krieg taut auf, Deutschland muss sich in einer Welt neuer Großmachtkonflikte behaupten. Berlins Außenpolitiker versuchen, sich dafür zu rüsten, in: Die Zeit, Nr. 7/ 2019, Online: https://www.zeit.de/2019/07/grossmachtkonflikte-deutschland-aussenpolitik-br exit-inf-vertrag, (Hamburg, 2019).
140 Ibid.
141 Richard N. Haass, World Order 2.0, The Case for Sovereign Obligation, in: Foreign Affairs, January/February 2017, Online: https://www.foreignaffairs.com/articles/2016-12-12/world-order-20, (Congers, 2017).
142 Ibid.

mental, historically-rooted principle of leaders in partnership as the guiding strategic approach for German engagement. The process toward the euro and European Monetary Union tests this thesis of German leadership.

Unraveling World Order

Javier Solana and Strobe Talbott saw the unraveling of the world order as an existential challenge to the transatlantic partnership:

> For most of the last 70 years, the United States, Canada and much of Europe have constituted a vast zone of peace, prosperity, and democracy. The trans-Atlantic community has grown to over 900 million inhabitants of more than 30 countries. The transatlantic partnership set an example for regional cooperation in Africa, Latin America, and Southeast Asia, and served as a mainstay of the liberal world order. That achievement is in jeopardy. The bonds within Europe have been fraying for some time, but this year has been the worst yet. [...] Jean-Claude Juncker, the European Union's highest official, said that the union faced 'an existential crisis.'[143]

There is a need for a strategy to reconcile Germany's national consciousness with a need for greater engagement in Europe – through cooperative leadership – leaders in partnership. The country needs greater cross-departmental cooperation and a shared vision for German participation in the international sphere. Germany can only become a convincing global actor – both to the national public and to its international partners – if it pursues national interests through the overarching principle of leaders in partnership.

Today, world order crises threaten the transatlantic partnership, one that has grown out of a shared commitment to freedom, democracy, the rule of law, and the respect for human dignity: these are the elements of peace and prosperity. German leaders currently pool national sovereignty in the EU and exercise their sovereign obligations in foreign policy. A new era of upheaval that has led to the unraveling of the world order is an existential challenge to the transatlantic partnership. Defense of these values needs the courage to preserve the benefits of peace upon which our world order now rests. Harold McMillan's quote about what is most likely to blow governments off course contains an essential element of reality. He said what drives policy is often "events, dear boy, events."[144] Events are now controlling the political debate.

---

[143] Strobe Talbott and Javier Solana, The Decline of the West, and How to Stop It, in: The New York Times, Online: https://www.nytimes.com/2016/10/20/opinion/the-decline-of-the-west-and-how-to-stop-it.html, (New York, 2016).

[144] Harold Macmillan quoted in: Ilana Bet-El, Events, dear boy, events, in: European Voice, Politico Europe, https://www.politico.eu/article/events-dear-boy-events/, (Brussels, 2016).

Chancellor Merkel's congratulatory statement to President Trump on his election as American president made it clear that the vast unraveling of the world order has taken an existential turn. Germany and America share a close partnership with shared values of democracy, freedom, the rule of law, and respect for human dignity. These values are the foundation of German and American foreign policy.[145] However, this system of international norms and shared policies is broken.

The political "event" of 2016 was Trump's election as president of the United States. His populist positions helped him win the presidency, but populism gives little guidance on a coherent set of policies. His transactional negotiating style has created uncertainty and ambiguity, particularly in alliance commitments. Donald Trump's previous and current campaign positions are deeply troubling. He has questioned NATO's Article 5 guarantee, demanded a ban on Muslim immigration, planned to erect a wall on the border with Mexico and rejected trade agreements – the Trans-Pacific Partnership (TPP), the North American Free Trade Agreement (NAFTA) and the Transatlantic Trade and Investment Partnership (TTIP). He has withdrawn the U.S. from the Iran nuclear weapons agreement and has canceled U.S. participation in the Paris Agreement on climate change. On the most critical international issue of non-proliferation, he has encouraged the Republic of Korea and Japan to acquire nuclear weapons, which is a call for nuclear proliferation.

In Europe, terrorist attacks like the horrific terrorist attack at the Christmas market at Kaiser Wilhelm Memorial Church on *Breitscheidtplatz* in Berlin are assaults on the international liberal order that has ensured peace and prosperity for seven decades. Terrorism in the Middle East, rooted in a century of the imperial and authoritarian rule that spawned the Arab Spring, has brought a flood of refugees to Europe. The 2003 Iraq War acted as a catalyst for the disintegration of stability in the region. Syrian Civil War refugees in Europe are feeding growing populist movements.

Nationalism, populism, and authoritarian governance offer alternatives to democracy and the rule of law. The West must resist this unraveling of the world order, or it will disappear. The perfect storm of these economic shifts has created an environment for the violent conflicts of Islamic State terrorism, the Syrian Civil War, and Russia's war of aggression in Ukraine. The South China Sea is a potential conflict zone between China and its neighbors. Governments seem to have lost control over events that threaten jobs and security. The populism that

---

145 David Frum, America's Friendship With Europe Has Been Horribly Damaged It's not all Donald Trump's fault. But he has in every way already made the situation gravely worse, in: The Atlantic, Online: https://www.theatlantic.com/international/archive/2016/11/trump-merkel-germany-europe/507773/, (Washington, D.C., 2016).

has unleashed illiberal forces in the U.S. and Europe sets a significant challenge to the transatlantic partnership. Internal and external events have shifted Germany's foreign policy paradigm.

Germany is called on to step up to leadership. By November 2011, Polish Foreign Minister Radek Sikorski seeing Germany as the dominant European power in Europe during the Euro Zone Sovereign Debt Crisis, challenged Germany's, Chancellor Merkel. He stated:

> I fear German power less than I am beginning to fear German inactivity. You have become Europe's indispensable nation. You may not fail to lead. Not dominate, but to lead in reform.[146]

Can German leadership in diplomacy sustain the multilateral liberal international order challenged by a multipolar world of populism, nationalism, globalization, and return to power politics/geopolitics?

In American Diplomacy, George F. Kennan captured the old fashioned challenge:

> The function of a system of international relationships is not to inhibit this process of change by imposing a legal straitjacket upon it but rather to facilitate it: to ease its transitions, to temper the asperities to which it often leads, to isolate and moderate the conflicts to which it gives rise, and to see that these conflicts do not assume forms too unsettling for international life in general. But this is a task for diplomacy, in the most old-fashioned sense of the term. For this, the law is too abstract, too inflexible, too hard to adjust to the demands of the unpredictable and the unexpected.[147]

Shared transatlantic values will remain the basis for the partnership as Europe and America tackle together the enormous challenges of terrorism, climate change, poverty, hunger, disease, and intervention for peace and security.

Changing Roles

Germany pools its sovereignty in sovereign obligation to exercise leadership with the EU in the European Union and NATO or the UN by deploying the *Bundeswehr*, with a parliamentary mandate. The country has rejected a German *Sonderweg* or unilateralism that, in the past, led to conflict. It has instead developed a "Never Alone" leadership model: Leaders in Partnership.

---

146 Radoslaw Sikorski, I fear Germany's power less than her inactivity. Eurozone break-up would be apocalyptic, writes Radoslaw Sikorski, in: Financial Times, https://www.ft.com/content/b753cb42-19b3-11e1-ba5d-00144feabdc0, (London, 2011a).
147 George Kennan quoted in: Barbara Koremenos, Escape clauses and withdrawal clauses. In *The Continent of International Law: Explaining Agreement Design* (Cambridge University Press: Cambridge. 2016), p. 124.

The global power shift of rising nationalism in China and Russia that is unraveling the international order has engulfed Germany and Europe. After Russia's military action in Ukraine and the annexation of Crimea, Europe imposed sanctions on Russia for violating Ukraine's border and annexing its territory. Then, in November 2016, Trump was elected president and questioned whether the US would fulfill its defense commitments to Europe. Trump's nationalist, interest-based policies have absented American international leadership in global affairs. China has moved to fill the power vacuum with its Belt and Road Initiative to project its rising power.

Trump's statements and policies raise the question of longer-term trends accentuated by this American retrenchment. Now that the United States has retreated even more from an international leadership role, Chancellor Merkel's remark "that we Europeans must really take our destiny into our own hands"[148] is prescient. Will Donald Trump act as a catalyst for deeper European integration and a stronger European Union that enhances the transatlantic pillar in the changing world order?

Can Europe help sustain and reshape the transatlantic relationship? If so, how? German foreign and security policy since the country's unification has shifted from a concentration on geo-economics to face a great power rivalry that calls for geopolitics. Chancellor Merkel said, "The times when we could fully rely on others have passed us by a little bit, that's what I've experienced in recent days."[149] Sigmar Gabriel, the former German foreign minister, echoed those remarks when he said the U.S. was "dropping out as an important nation."[150]

Nevertheless, Merkel added, "The trans-Atlantic partnership is of outstanding importance."[151] Germany, whether it wants the leadership job or not, is the best hope to defend the liberal international order. Rising powers shift world order. The Thucydides Trap, in which Sparta and Athens went to war over Athens' rising power, which destroyed both city-states. In this shift of power, can Germany continue its peaceful rise to European leadership? What fate then awaits Germany and Europe?

---

148 Krishnadev Calamur, Merkel Urges Europe to Take Our Fate Into Our Own Hands. The German chancellor's remarks come as President Trump doubled down on his criticism of Germany, in: The Atlantic, Online: https://www.theatlantic.com/news/archive/2017/05/merkel-europe-trump/528468/, (Washington D.C.: 2017).
149 Ibid.
150 Sigmar Gabriel quoted in: Deutsche Welle, More leading German politicians land into Trump, Online: https://www.dw.com/en/more-leading-german-politicians-land-into-trump/a-39038441, (Bonn, 2017).
151 Krishnadev Calamur, Merkel Urges 'Europe to Take Our Fate Into Our Own Hands.' The German chancellor's remarks come as President Trump doubled down on his criticism of Germany, in: The Atlantic, Online: https://www.theatlantic.com/news/archive/2017/05/merkel-europe-trump/528468/, (Washington D.C.: 2017).

As long as the U.S. questions the security guarantee for Europe, uncertainty, whether America will intervene on behalf of its NATO partners, sends an urgent call to Germany and Europe to strengthen their military capabilities as a deterrent against aggressive action and attacks on borders. The skepticism Trump has engendered should be channeled into ensuring the credibility of an American security commitment.

German Leadership in Partnership: A Sovereign Obligation

After having won full sovereignty, Germany governs in partnership and has maintained its commitment to Europe, its embedded security in NATO, and has developed a never-alone leadership model called Leaders in Partnership. As Germany accepts more responsibility, it has pursued two concepts that have served well its rise to leadership. Germany's sovereignty has included a sovereign obligation to Europe, where it has pooled its sovereignty in the EU, and at unification, when united, Germany chose to remain embedded in NATO.

There is a need for a strategic foresight to reconcile Germany's national consciousness with a need for greater engagement through cooperative leadership. Can the emergence of a German model of Leaders in Partnership address the need for international leadership and fill the vacuum left by Trump? What is this German model of Leadership in Partnership? Can a group leadership approach, one that is opposite to the solo style of Trump, lead Europe? Will the sovereign Berlin Republic lead Europe in sustaining the transatlantic leadership in an increasingly multipolar, nationalist, and populist world?

On the path to exercising military power, the Constitutional Court decided on July 12, 1994, that the *Bundeswehr* could only deploy outside of the NATO area if it was with an alliance and had a parliamentary mandate. The country has rejected a German *Sonderweg* or unilateralism that, as practiced in the past, led to conflict. In exercising sovereign obligation, Germany has deployed the *Bundeswehr* in NATO and UN military operations and taken more international responsibility for a neighborhood that includes the Middle East. Germany demonstrated leadership in ceasefire negotiations in Eastern Ukraine and the Minsk Agreements as well as in response to the refugee movements towards the European continent.

German armed forces have been deployed in numerous operations worldwide since the constitutional court's decision. In March 2017 alone, *Bundeswehr* personnel participated in 15 missions and similar deployments mandated by the UN, the EU, or NATO, as well as supporting Operation Inherent Resolve in Syria and Iraq. These missions range from training missions in Mali to UN peacekeeping in South Sudan, continued support for the NATO Kosovo Force peacekeeping mission, or contributions to NATO's standing maritime force in the Mediterranean. This evolving role of the Bundeswehr, as described in the 2016 Defense White Book, is one of leadership (*Führende Rolle der Bundeswehr*).

Political Union and the European Monetary Union

In the European Union, Germany has accepted the European Monetary Union and the Euro as a single currency. Germany, of course, served as the de facto leader in the 2010 Eurozone crisis and has taken on its responsibility for political integration in the EU. This understanding included completing a European Monetary Union, introducing the Euro and resolving Euro crises as agreed by French President Francois Mitterrand and Chancellor Helmut Kohl in a deal that led to the euro and consequently, to the Eurozone debt crisis negotiations. However, there is little doubt that Germany is constitutionally, historically, and morally obligated to support EU integration.

Some analysts in America, including Andrew Moravcsik, writing in Foreign Affairs, argue that Germany set the terms for nearly every agreement on monetary issues since the 1970s when Pierre Werner presented the original Werner Plan for European Monetary Union.[152] While the lingering Euro Crisis quite correctly centers on Germany and is an existential crisis for the Eurozone, the zone is fundamentally about European Union political integration. Chancellor Merkel explained to the *Bundestag* in 2011 that without exaggeration that "if the Euro fails, Europe fails."[153] ("Scheitert der Euro, scheitert Europa") She described the challenge as "the most difficult since the Second World War."[154] That is no exaggeration. Of course, there are economic issues at stake if the Euro collapses. Fred Bergsten described the projected chaos: "Germany's banks would collapse under the weight of their losses on loans in the periphery; a new Deutsche Mark would skyrocket [in value], undermining the entire German economy and Germany would once again be blamed for destroying Europe."[155] Can Germany's sovereign obligation provide Leadership in Partnership in Europe, carrying out

---

152 Andrew Moravcsik, Europe After the Crisis, How to Sustain a Common Currency, in: Foreign Affairs, Online: https://www.foreignaffairs.com/articles/europe/2012-05-01/europe-after-crisis, (Congers, 2012).
153 Angela Merkel quoted in: Spiegel Online, 'If the Euro Fails, Europe Fails' Merkel Says EU Must Be Bound Closer Together, in: Spiegel online, Online: https://www.spiegel.de/international/germany/if-the-euro-fails-europe-fails-merkel-says-eu-must-be-bound-closer-together-a-784953.html, (Hamburg, 2011).
154 Ibid.
155 C. Fred Bergsten, The Revenge of Helmut Schmidt, Speech at the American Academy in Berlin GmbH, Online: https://www.americanacademy.de/videoaudio/germany-euro-revenge-helmut-schmidt/, (Berlin, 2015).

its international responsibility to balance great powers and sustain a multipolar international order?

The Euro is at the heart of European Union governance. Progress toward European Monetary Union has moved slowly from crisis to crisis. German and French leaders throughout the 1970s and 1980s made their mark on the development of the European Monetary Union (EMU). The fundamental European Union driver that led to the Maastricht Treaty was a Franco-German power bargain that brought the EMU to the negotiation table after the fall of the Berlin Wall.

Solutions on the way to political union included the Maastricht Treaty that set down the plan for the Single Market and monetary union. The Treaty established criteria for economic convergence of inflation rates, interest rates, and budgetary and debt positions. The treaty also prohibited direct financing of public debt by central banks and established that neither the Community nor the EMU was liable for commitments of other governments. Solutions were hotly debated. Later, Chancellor Merkel developed a seven-point crisis management plan, disagreeing with French President Francois Hollande's proposal to create Eurobonds. Holland wanted to cut back on austerity measures and generate more economic stimulus, while Merkel's seven-point plan sought austerity.

Finally, prime ministers approved an intergovernmental treaty on December 8, 2011. EU leaders agreed to create fiscal unity parallel to the Monetary Union that already existed. It would enforce the budget restrictions of the Maastricht Treaty, reassure lenders that the EU would stand behind its members' sovereign debt, and allow the EU to act as a more integrated unit.

After improvised actions in the final year of the crisis saved the Euro, the Eurozone is far from regaining full health. Debt levels in Europe's south remained extreme. Unemployment remained near historic highs. Uncertainty raised the possibility of the EU turning into a "risk generator" within the global financial order or perhaps even worse – a "spoiler" of the very system itself. Forbes magazine commented that the "financial crisis of the European states has impacted the financial condition of European banks and all holders of European debt wherever they are located, and this negative reaction had impacted all of Europe and the global economy."[156] Eventually, a compromise worked out interim solutions.

President Macron has appealed to make the Eurozone the heart of Europe's economic and monetary power.[157] He has called for instruments to make Europe an area of growth and stability, including a budget allowing it to fund collective

---

156 Robert Lenzner, Europe In 2011 A Worse Crisis Than The U.S. In 2008, in: Forbes, Online: https://www.forbes.com/sites/robertlenzner/2011/09/30/europe-in-2011-a-worse-crisis-than-the-u-s-in-2008/#3963414a6958, (New York City, 2011).
157 Emmanuel Macron, Initiative for Europe, Online: http://international.blogs.ouest-france.fr/archive/2017/09/29/macron-sorbonne-verbatim-europe-18583.html, (Paris, 2017).

investments and to ensure stabilization in the event of economic shocks. However, complacency about the underlying state of the Euro area would be misplaced. The currency union continues to suffer from critical weaknesses, including financial fragility, suboptimal conditions for long-term growth, and profound economic and political divisions. The challenge lies in need to improve the Euro area's architecture to make it less vulnerable to crises and to deliver long-term prosperity to all of its members.

Despite what some pundits are saying, the political foundation of the EMU and the common currency keeps, as Helmut Kohl was correct to argue, the original intent to create the European Union. Despite the time passed since the end of the Second World War, the goal to unite the continent in peace remains as relevant as ever.

> "A look beyond one's nose into history shows: the evil spirits of the past are in no way banished, they can always return," he wrote in *Bild Zeitung* in February 2012, "that means: Europe remains a question of war and peace, and the idea of peace the motivation behind European integration."[158]

Kohl pleaded with political leaders: "[Don't] allow the current discussion and the crisis situation in Greece to lose sight of a unified Europe. The opposite is the case: we need – above all now – more and not less Europe."[159]

The political debate in Germany seeks a vision to build Europe, which President Macron has offered. Germany is called on to lead in Europe and to succeed; it needs a bold, strategic vision to sustain democracy, peace, and prosperity in Europe. That call is one to join with Macron, who reached out in leadership to Germany for a strengthened Europe. He made proposals on advancing the Eurozone.

The goal should be to make Europe a more robust transatlantic pillar and not to let America's uncertain path question the ideas and institutions of the International Liberal Order. European security and prosperity rest on this order. Germany has national legitimacy and exercises its sovereignty with a sovereign obligation to Europe and the international order. In keeping with German Leadership in Partnership, one of the German government's premier challenges will be to manage the transatlantic relationship during and after Donald Trump's presidency. Its success in this endeavor will be one way to measure its overall performance.

---

158 Helmut Kohl quoted in: Spiegel Online, Europe Remains a Question of War and Peace. Kohl Urges Germans to Stay Committed to Europe , in: Spiegel Online, Online: https://www.spiegel.de/international/europe/europe-remains-a-question-of-war-and-peace-kohl-urges-germans-to-stay-committed-to-europe-a-818095.html, (Hamburg, 2012).
159 Spiegel Online, Europe Remains a Question of War and Peace. Kohl Urges Germans to Stay Committed to Europe, in: Spiegel Online, Online: https://www.spiegel.de/international/europe/europe-remains-a-question-of-war-and-peace-kohl-urges-germans-to-stay-committed-to-europe-a-818095.html, (Hamburg, 2012).

Chapter 4: Geopolitical Power Shifts and Germany's Place in Europe: From a Geo-economic to a Geopolitical Power

> Never let a good crisis go to waste.
> – Winston Churchill [160]

> You never let a serious crisis go to waste. And what I mean by that it's an opportunity to do things you think you could not do before.
> – Rahm Emanuel [161]

> Only in the Post-war system, Germany felt that it could work explicitly to make itself a part of the international system. Germany has more neighbors than any other country, so it is a very difficult challenge for Germany to reinvent itself all the time. But it also presents a great opportunity because it means if Germany solves these problems it contributes to the stability of Europe.
> – Henry Kissinger [162]

Making Europe relevant in a world order dominated by the United States and China is an existential issue for Europe. But is Europe prepared to become a more influential partner in the transatlantic relationship that challenges United States leadership? Europe will not find global leadership as long as Europe is dependent on America for its security. A strong European Union is in American interests, even if Europe stands up for its interests and is a more difficult partner. As transatlantic history has shown, America and Europe, both anchored in democratic values, can argue over conflicting interests. But to become more relevant again, Europe will need to transform its relationship with the United States and, in reshaping the partnership, will need Germany to take a stance on security, economic, and political challenges from China, Russia, and the United States. As Alina Polyakova and Benjamin Haddad argue in Foreign Affairs, "in the long run, a strong continent that is able to defend its interests and fight its own battles will benefit Washington more than a weak and divided one."[163]

Germany's international responsibility in the crisis of an unraveling world order requires Germany to reinvent itself. Germany needs a security strategy for

---

160 Atributed to Winston Churchill on the eve of the Yalta Conference, 1944.
161 Emmanuel Rahm quoted in : Wall Street Journal, Rahm Emmanuel on the Opportunitie of Crisis, Online https://www.youtube.com/watch?v=_mzcbXi1Tkk, (Washington D.C.: 2008), min: 0:01–0:07.
162 see interview with Henry Kissinger and Karl Kaiser, in: Center for International Security and Governance, *International Security Forum 2018 Report*, (Rheinische Friedrich Wilhelms Universität: Bonn, 2019).
163 Alina Polyakova and Benjamin Haddad, Europe Alone, What comes After the Transatlantic Alliance, in: Foreign Affairs, Online: https://www.foreignaffairs.com/articles/europe/2019-06-11/europe-alone, (New York City, 2019).

itself and for Europe, one that elevates strategic planning above its policies for crisis management. A fully sovereign Germany, exercising its sovereign obligation to the EU and NATO with other leaders in partnership, while restrained by history, is the best hope to reshape the Multilateral Liberal International Order. Can Germany craft a security strategy that enables Europe to complete its global security strategy? Does German Leadership in Partnership or its unilateral decisions, as practiced in the quest for European Monetary Union and security in NATO, fulfill its pledge of *Never Alone* to avoid hegemony?

America's Withdrawal from International Leadership

Europe's challenge is how to manage its relationship with America under Donald Trump. That is a priority. His nationalist, interest-based policies increasingly absent America from international leadership, which has undermined its commitment to NATO and the U.S.-EU transatlantic values-based partnership. This development has challenged the Europeans to fill the leadership vacuum or to seek autonomy from the United States. Chancellor Angela Merkel accepted the Trump challenge and called on Europeans to take their fate into their own hands. Disruption in the world order raises the question of what kind of order could emerge and who would lead it. What kind of world order would China or Russia pursue? Is that a situation in which we would like to live? Can Europe lead such a world order in pursuance of values-based liberal world order? Even though the US has slowly but surely has taken a backseat in international politics, America is, nevertheless, a systemic partner of Europe.

Historically, Germany has played a vital role in America's global leadership. An isolationist America sent an expeditionary force to help end the First World War. On April 2, 1917, President Woodrow Wilson went before a joint session of Congress to seek a Declaration of War against Germany that "The world must be made safe for democracy."[164] With these words, President Wilson ended America's isolation. In 1919, Wilson sought peace with his Fourteen Points that "consisted of certain basic principles, such as freedom of the seas and open covenants, a variety of geographic arrangements carrying out the principle of self-determination, and above all, a League of Nations that would enforce the peace."[165] These principles challenged the balance of power within the world order that had been the basis of European politics since the Concert of Vienna.

---

164 Woodrow Wilson, Fourteen Points Spech, Making the World, Online: https://usa.usembassy.de/etexts/democrac/51.htm, also in: Arthur S. Link et al., eds., *The Papers of Woodrow Wilson*, vol. 45 (Princeton University Press: Princeton, 1984), p. 536.

165 Ibid.

After the Second World War, the U.S. chose to remain engaged in Europe and with Germany. In 1946, James F. Byrnes committed the United States to the well-being of Germany for the future of Europe. Americans accepted the indivisibility of peace and prosperity. As a result, the Germany of today is fully sovereign and the leader of Europe. After the "Long War" of the twentieth century fought over the future of parliamentary democracy defeated imperialism, fascism, National Socialism and communism, the world finally emerged from the shadow of war. The unification of Germany and Europe made clear that parliamentary democracy had prevailed over fascism and communism.[166] The Charter of Paris that confirmed European governance in democracy was to make the world safe for democracy seventy-six years after the outbreak of the Great War. Heinrich August Winkler captured the euphoria over the new European order at the end of the Cold War and unification of Germany and Europe when he said:

> [...] in November 1990, the month after the reunification of Germany, the heads of the states and governments of the Conference on Security and Co-operation in Europe met in Paris. The highlight was the signing of the Charter of Paris on the 21st of November. All 34 member states committed "to build, consolidate and strengthen democracy as the only system of government of our nations."[167]

Geopolitical Power Shifts

Geopolitical power shifts among the great powers – America, Russia, and China[168], as the leading players of the 20th century and the beginning of the 21st – are upsetting the balance of the world order. China and Russia, reflecting a global power shift of rising nationalism, are unraveling the old order. Territorial violations through the use of force led Europe and the United States to impose sanctions on Russia for violating Ukraine's border and annexing its territory. Two years later, in November 2016, Donald Trump was elected president of the United States and subsequently questioned whether the US would fulfill its commitments, including to the defense of Europe. Digitalization, globalization,

---

166 Philip Bobbitt, *The Shield of Achilles: War, Peace and the Course of History*, (Penguin Group: London 2002), p. 63.
167 Heinrich August Winkler, Denk ich an Deutschland. Was den Westen zusammenhält, in: Frankfurter Allgemeine Zeitung, Online: https://www.faz.net/aktuell/politik/inland/heinrich-august-winkler-was-den-westen-zusammenhaelt-13815991.html, (Frankfurt, 2015).
168 For further reading on global power shifts, please consider Enrico Fels, Shifting Powers in Asia-Pacific? The Rise of China, Sino-US Competition and Regional Middle Power Allegiance, (Springer Verlag VS: Wiesbaden, 2017), Xuewu Gu, Die weltpolitische Dreiecksbeziehung Beijing, Moskau, Washington, in: *Aus Politik und Zeitgeschehen*, Vol. 66, 23/2016 (Bonn, 2016), pp. 27–32 und Matthias Herdegen, Der Kampf um die Weltordnung, (C.H. Beck: München, 2018).

technology change, along with climate change, are creating a set of more complicated, complex, and dynamic security challenges. The list of conflicts is long and growing: the war in Syria, a failed state in Libya, the war in Yemen, radical Islam in the Sahel, an uncertain Iran nuclear weapons agreement, the frozen conflict in Ukraine, North Korean nuclear weapons, climate change, and populism. Crises in the European Union such as Brexit, cyberattacks, terrorism, and unstable financial markets pile on change.

Populist leaders fearing migration resulting from these issues and conflicts have used refugees to incite fear and promote authoritarian responses. Economic inequality is attributed to globalization as jobs move from developed economies to emerging ones, especially toward China. With resurgent nationalisms returning to Europe, the illusion of an ever-expanding EU bringing peace and prosperity to Europe is in doubt. The West should avoid policies, particularly migration policies that stoke fears and result in support for a growing list of populist leaders, including U.S. President Donald Trump. Influential leaders claim the national will. Trump has praised strong leadership – Russia's authoritarian President Vladimir Putin[169], Turkey's *AK Parti* leader President Recep Tayyip Erdoğan[170], National Rally's Marine Le Pen[171]. And worldwide other illiberal, populist leaders have gained or aspire to win office, including the leader of the Hungarian party *Fidesz*, President Viktor Mihály Orbán[172], and the leader of the Polish party PiS, President Jarosław Aleksander Kaczyński[173].

American leadership had sometimes failed to the detriment of the world order; for example, when it intervened in Iraq or chose not to intervene in Syria. Before his untimely death, President Jimmy Carter's national security advisor and noted strategist Zbigniew Brzeziński, who was the reigning realist of the Democratic Party, described the upheaval in the world order this way:

> Today, I think the world is really facing a global crisis, which is simultaneously political, economic, systemic, racial, religious. We have had major international crises histor-

---

[169] British Broadcast Channel, Trump says Putin 'a leader far more than our president', Online: https://www.bbc.com/news/election-us-2016-37303057, (London, 2016).
[170] Kevin Liptak, Trump declare himself a 'big fan' of Turkey's strongman leader Erdoğan, in: CNN, Online: https://edition.cnn.com/2019/11/13/politics/donald-trump-recep-tayyip-erdogan-turkey-impeachment/index.html, (New York City, 2019).
[171] Ben Jacobs, Donald Trump: Marine Le Pen is 'strongest candidate' in French elections, in: The Guardian, Online: https://www.theguardian.com/us-news/2017/apr/21/donald-trump-marine-le-pen-french-presidential-election, (Washington D.C., 2017).
[172] Peter Baker, Viktor Orban, Hungary's Far Right Leader, Gets Warm Welcome From Trump, in: The New York Time, Online. https://www.nytimes.com/2019/05/13/us/politics/trump-viktor-orban-oval-office.html, (New York City: 2019a).
[173] Peter Baker, Trump embraces Polish Leader and Promises Him More U.S. Troops, in: The New York Times, Online: https://www.nytimes.com/2019/06/12/us/politics/andrzej-duda-trump-poland.html, (New York City: 2019b).

ically, but the scope of these international crises gradually got larger and larger. Now the crises are practically all over the place. And the places that are not in crisis are beginning to show some evidence of probably being in crisis before too long.[174]

There is little doubt that the Trump administration is withdrawing from international leadership and from liberal values that have shaped the peace and prosperity of the last seven decades. Trump's worldview, formed in the 1980s, is best reflected in the Wall Street Journal article by H.R. McMaster and Gary Cohn:

> The president embarked on his first foreign trip with a clear-eyed outlook that the world is not a "global community" but an arena where nations, nongovernmental actors, and businesses engage and compete for advantage. We bring to this forum unmatched military, political, economic, cultural, and moral strength. Rather than deny this elemental nature of international affairs, we embrace it.[175]

However, the international liberal world order is values-based, and Chancellor Merkel set out the goals for the German relationship with the U.S. in her congratulatory message to the newly-elected president when she said:

> Germany and America are bound together by values – democracy, freedom, respecting the rule of law, people's dignity regardless of their origin, the color of their skin, religion, gender, sexual orientation, or political views. Based on these values, I am offering to work closely with the future President of the United States, Donald Trump.[176]

This values-based partnership has a firm foundation in transatlantic ties, and working with the United States remains a crucial pillar of Germany's foreign policy. Roger Cohen assessed the danger of America's loss of leadership and diplomatic power with a quote from Senator John McCain:

> To refuse the obligations of international leadership and our duty to remain 'the last best hope of earth' for the sake of some half-baked, spurious nationalism cooked up by people who would rather find scapegoats than solve problems is as unpatriotic as an attachment to any other tired dogma of the past that Americans consigned to the ash heap of history…We live in a land made of ideals, not blood and soil. We are the custodians of those ideals at home and their champion abroad. We have done great good in the world. That leadership has had its costs, but we have become incomparably powerful and wealthy as we did. We have a moral obligation to continue in our just

---

174 Zbigniew Brzezinski, On Global Crisis, Center for Strategic and International Studies, Online: https://ontheworld.csis.org/2015/09/22/on-global-crisis/, (Washington D.C., 2015).
175 H.R. McMaster and Gary D. Cohn, America First Doesn't Mean America Alone, in: Wall Street Journal, Online: https://www.wsj.com/articles/america-first-doesnt-mean-america-alone-14961874262017, (New York City, 2017).
176 Michelle Martin and Madeline Chambers, Merkel offers to work with Trump on basis of democratic values, in: Reuters, Online: https://in.reuters.com/article/usa-election-reaction-merkel-idINKBN1341ZQ?feedType=RSS&feedName=worldNews, (Berlin, 2016).

cause, and we would bring more than shame on ourselves if we don't. We will not thrive in a world where our leadership and ideals are absent. We wouldn't deserve to.[177]

Richard Haass also warned:

> America's decision to abandon the global system it helped build, and then preserve for more than seven decades, marks a turning point because others lack either the interest or the means to sustain it. The result will be a world that is less free, less prosperous, and less peaceful, for Americans and others alike.[178]

As American leadership recedes, the competition to fill this vacuum has begun. The Russian invasion of Ukraine and the annexation of Crimea violated the Charter of Paris and Budapest Memorandum agreements that agreed not to change or resolve territorial disputes using military force. The conflict remains unresolved. The Minsk Agreement has not ended the war in Eastern Ukraine and sanctions against Russia stay in effect. The EU and the U.S. have failed to broker a settlement on Ukraine. NATO members, especially the Baltic States and Poland, need reassurance that NATO can deter Russian military threats. NATO has a European Reassurance Initiative to demonstrate resolve to defend Europe. Territorial violations through the use of force led Europe and the United States to impose sanctions on Russia for violating Ukraine's border and annexing its territory.

Not only China's Belt Road Initiative but also:

> [a] series of doctrinal statements by the United States has formally declared an end to 40 years of U.S. strategic engagement with China and its replacement with a new period of strategic competition. Rather than becoming a responsible stakeholder in the global rules-based order, China is now developing an alternative international order with Chinese characteristics; and that instead of becoming more democratic in its domestic politics, Beijing has now decided to double down as a Leninist state.[179]

China's rise as a competitor to the United States has vast implications for the world order. The global power shift of rising nationalism and populism is a significant challenge for Europe. As a result, it needs leadership and has turned to Germany. In March 2017, Politico captured the global power shift with its

---

177 Roger Cohen, Donald Trump and the Erosion of American Greatness, in: Spiegel International, Online: http://www.spiegel.de/international/world/roger-cohen-on-trump-and-the-erosion-of-american-greatness-a-1176642.html, (Hamburg, 2017).
178 Richard N. Haass, Liberal World Order, R.I.P., in: Project Syndicate, Online: https://www.project-syndicate.org/commentary/end-of-liberal-world-order-by-richard-n-haass-2018-03/german?barrier=accesspaylog, (New York City, 2018).
179 Kevin Rudd, How to Avoid an Avoidable War, in: Foreign Affairs, Online: https://www.foreignaffairs.com/articles/china/2018-10-22/how-avoid-avoidable-war, (Washington D.C., 2018).

headline, "The Leader of the Free World Meets Donald Trump."[180] Whether she wanted the leadership job or not, Germany's Chancellor Angela Merkel, the article contends, is the West's last, best hope to defend the Liberal International Order. Germany's civilian power would not be sufficient enough for it to take a leading role in Europe in a time of great power politics. Can Germany make the necessary changes to accept that international responsibility?

President Donald Trump's Worldview

Diplomacy, as defined by the Vienna Convention, is how countries influence the decisions and behavior of foreign governments and peoples through dialogue, negotiation, and other measures short of war or violence. The diplomats' task is to represent his/her country to the host country, and explain the host country to his/hers. A diplomat is a person who can deal with others sensitively and tactfully.

So how well is diplomacy doing today? A fundamental conflict exists between the power of the rule of law and rule by the powerful. Walter Russell Mead argues:

> …the Trump critique of the European Union. First, some of the "new nationalists" believe multinational entities like the EU are much weaker and less effective than the governments of nation-states – so much so that the development of the EU has weakened the Western alliance as a whole. In this view, cooperation between nation-states is good, and through it, countries can achieve things they couldn't achieve on their own. But trying to overinstitutionalize that cooperation is a mistake. The resulting bureaucratic structures and Byzantine politics and decision-making processes paralyze policy, alienate public opinion, and create a whole significantly less than the sum of its parts. … the European Union is too German. As some on the president's team see it, German preferences mean the Continent is too hawkish when it comes to monetary and fiscal policy, and too dovish when it comes to defense.[181]

Chancellor Merkel sees the transatlantic relationship as based on shared values and has cautioned:

> The era in which we could fully rely on others is over to some extent…We Europeans truly have to take our fate into our own hands – naturally in friendship with the United States of America, in friendship with Great Britain, as good neighbors with whoever,

---

180 James P. Rubin, The Leader of the Free World Meets Donald Trump, in: Politico, Online: https://www.politico.com/magazine/story/2017/03/the-leader-of-the-free-world-meets-donald-trump-214924, (Arlington County, 2017).
181 Walter Russel Mead. Trump's Case Against Europe, in: Wall Street Journal, Online: https://www.wsj.com/articles/trumps-case-against-europe-11559602940, (New York City, 2019).

also with Russia and other countries. However, we have to know that we Europeans must fight for our future and destiny.[182]

The world is not a boxing ring; the West is a community of nations with shared values of democracy, freedom, the rule of law, and respect for human dignity. For U.S. President Donald Trump, it is an arena where countries compete. As Trump seeks diplomacy, he met with North Korea's leader Kim Jong-un on June 12, 2018, in Singapore. This summit meeting came at a time when international diplomacy is currently experiencing unprecedented challenges. The Kim-Trump Summit followed months of hostile exchanges between Donald Trump and Kim Jong-un. Trumpian disruption policies opened the way to the Summit.

Other actors also intervened. South Korean President Moon Jae-in seized the opportunity presented by the fiery Kim-Trump exchanges to invite the North Koreans to the Olympics in South Korea and brokered an invitation to Trump to meet Kim. The Kim-Trump joint statement opened the door to seek a possible breakthrough on the denuclearization of North Korea. Kim won a place on the world stage; Trump won a seat in reality TV diplomacy. Diplomatic results may or may not come later.

The Trump decision to withdraw from the Iran nuclear deal, or the Joint Comprehensive Plan of Action (JCPOA), was to open a path for Iran to restart its nuclear weapons program. It did little to resolve the unacceptable Iranian missile development program or Iran's support for Hezbollah terrorists and military expansion into Yemen, Lebanon, Iraq, and Syria with proxy forces. The agreement is now torn in tatters as Iran restarted its uranium enrichment program.

Trump's disruption diplomacy needs a strategy beyond threats of sanctions and bullying to be successful. Europe's challenge is to offer a plan to make Trump's disruption of the old order successful in sustaining liberal values. What should Europe do? At a dinner honoring Henry Kissinger in June 2018, President Steinmeier addressed a statesman's international responsibility. Leaders have the power that affects millions of lives, and the exercise of that power often conflicts with morality.[183] However, is all power then suspect? Indeed, those who accept leadership, accept responsibility for success as well as failure. Dr. Kissinger has written that "if the moral basis of my service were lost, public life would have no meaning for me." The dilemma of finding a balance between power and morality

---

182 Angela Merkel quoted in Guilia Paravicini: Angela Merkel: Europe must take 'our fate' into own hands, in: Politico Magazine, Online: https://www.politico.eu/article/angela-merkel-europe-cdu-must-take-its-fate-into-its-own-hands-elections-2017/, (Arlington County, 2017).

183 Frank-Walter Steinmeier, Frank-Walter Steinmeier beim Abendessen zu Ehren von Henry A. Kissinger aus Anlass seines 95. Geburtstages am 12. Juni 2018 in Schloss Bellevue, Online: https://www.bundespraesident.de/SharedDocs/Downloads/DE/Reden/2018/06/180612-AE-Kissinger.pdf;jsessionid=0438C561DB22F2BEE649C43CE07BB888.1_cid387?__blob=publicationFile, (Berlin, 2018).

is also found in Goethe's comment that the one who acts is always unjust and that nobody has justice but the one who observes me."[184]

With the Kim-Trump Summit, the Iran nuclear weapons deal in shambles, transatlantic partners increasingly unable to see eye-to-eye on almost every major geopolitical issue and tensions in Syria and Gaza escalating once more, the current era poses severe challenges for international agreements, partnerships, and peaceful solutions. Responsibility and leadership – and diplomacy – are needed.

Germany's Leadership Responsibility

Transatlantic partners need to stand up for democracy and oppose populists in Italy, France, the Netherlands, Germany, and the U.K. to preserve freedom. It's important to remember what the third American president Thomas Jefferson warned that the price of liberty is eternal vigilance.

Who will successfully manage the stress of these turbulent times in the transatlantic relationship? Germany, whether it wants the leadership job or not, is the best hope to protect the liberal international order. The Körber Foundation reported that in 2019 only 22 %[185] of Germans surveyed thought Germany should continue to rely on the United States, while 40 %[186] would like to seek nuclear protection from the UK and France. Gallup has reported Germany had a 41 %[187] approval rating as a global power tying with the U.S.[188] Germany's new international standing marks a historic shift in power relations, While the standing of the U.S. has declined even more since the study in 2013.[189]

What role will Germany accept? After the defeat of democracy in the 1848 Revolution, Chancellor Otto von Bismarck united Germany with 'Blood and Iron.' From 1871 through World Wars I and II, German militarism dominated the German security strategy. After the defeat of National Socialism in 1945, Ger-

---

184 Kissinger, Henry, in Barry Gewen, Kissinger's Moral Example, Kissinger examined whether intellectuals should get their hands dirty making policy, or preserve their integrity at the price of influence, in: The National Interest, 2017, Online: https://nationalinterest.org/feature/kissingers-moral-example-20225?nopaging=1, (Washington D.C., 2017).
185 Körber Stiftung, *The Berlin Pulse 2019/20. German Foreign Policy in Perspective*, (Körber Stiftung: Berlin, 2019), p. 37.
186 Ibid.
187 Jon Clifton, Germany Ties U.S. Again in Leadership Approval Ratings. Approval declines among most global powers, in: Gallup, Online: https://news.gallup.com/poll/161369/germany-ties-again-leadership-approval-ratings.aspx, (Washington, D.C., 2013).
188 Ibid.
189 Brett Samuels, Global image of US leadership trails China: Gallup, in: The Hill, Online: https://thehill.com/blogs/blog-briefing-room/news/431973-global-image-of-us-leadership-now-trails-china-gallup, (Washington D.C., 2019).

many for the past seven decades has risen from the horrors of the Second World War and the Holocaust to become a *Zivilmacht* and Europe's leading democracy. The question remains whether this Hegelian juxtaposition shifting from one extreme to the other will now find the synthesis balancing between peace and power.[190]

Germany's history compounds its leadership dilemma and has become an obstacle to its future. After World War II, the country set out to recover economically under the security umbrella of the United States. Lacking full sovereignty during the Cold War and struggling with its history of nationalism, militarism, and Nazism, Germany developed a strategic culture that was passive, timid, morally uncompromising, and dominated by feelings of guilt. Never again would it engage in "regular" foreign affairs that include protecting national interests and morally messy foreign policy.

Now, three decades after unification and at a time when power politics and nationalism are on the rise, Germany has to recalibrate its strategic culture to fulfill its *Staatsräson* established at unification. For several years, U.S. presidents have called for German leadership and a stronger Europe within the transatlantic partnership. Now is the time for Germany to find the right balance between its international responsibilities and its culture of remembrance. Since nothing moves forward in Europe without it, the country not only has to develop a national strategy but also to strengthen Europe's strategic role in the transatlantic partnership.

After the German Question now the German Problem

While the German Question is answered, the German Problem remains after thirty years of peace and prosperity and from an unraveling world order. The United States, the European Union, and NATO are in crisis. German international responsibility in this time of crisis requires it to help shape a security strategy for Europe. What is the German Problem, and can it be solved?

Germany seeks to balance its commitments to Europe and transatlantic security with its national interests. The German pledge of *Never Alone*, a promise to replace historical hegemony, was breached in decisions over migrants from Middle East wars, austerity in the Euro crisis, withdrawal from nuclear energy after the Fukushima tsunami, and ending the military draft. Leadership in Partnership competes with unilateral decision making in an endless series of

---

190 For further reading on the changing and shifting role of ther German Foreign Policy since 1945 please consider Wolfram Hilz, Deutsche Außenpolitik, (W. Kohlhammer GmbH: Stuttgart, 2017).

dilemmas. Can Germany keep its pledge of "Never Again," while crafting a security strategy that enables Europe to complete its global security strategy? Is Foreign Minister Heiko Maas' "Alliances of Multilateralists" able to balance the French proposal for sovereign autonomy? Does German history, from National Socialism to the Holocaust, to East German communism, form a formidable culture of remembrance that acts as a restraint on policy excess?

The Federal Republic of Germany, the Berlin Republic, remains the critical strategic actor in Europe. Even a reluctant German leader will lead either upfront or from behind. These are German dilemmas. The problem is mustering the political will for Germany to create a strategy for Europe and the transatlantic partnership, in addition to exercising its formidable skills to manage crises. America is consumed by its stress test of democracy, which will determine the resilience of transatlantic leadership. Europe is torn apart by Brexit and the strengthening of illiberal democracies, and growing populism. Can a fully sovereign Germany, exercising its sovereign obligation to the EU and NATO with leaders in partnership and restrained by history, lead in Europe to reshape the multilateral Liberal International Order?

After a long war, from 1914 to 1990, the world finally emerged from two World Wars, and the Cold War dedicated to parliamentary democracy sealed in the 1990 Charter of Paris. Unification established one nation from the two German states, and a re-invented Germany became a free and democratic sovereign nation. It has exuded a new narrative of democratic self-confidence. Germany has taken the principles of *Staatsräson* and applied them to its foreign policy, emphasizing peacebuilding and encouraging other states to build institutions premised on individual dignity and human rights.

Europe is now in a deep crisis. Dominique Moïsi described Europe's unraveling:

> ...[at] a time when America, which was always the European Union's life insurance policy against predatory threats from the East and was the world champion of democracy, begins to withdraw from the world; when Russia returns with a vengeance to global politics; when Germany turns inward and Italy rebels against EU spending limits and moves closer to autocratic Russia; when so many roads now lead to Beijing; and when the U.K. is hellbent on suicide, suddenly what happens in France goes beyond France. We are the last barrier protecting the European idea. If Macron fails, it can bring the end of Europe.[191]

Henry Kissinger warned in 2014 that the Liberal International Order was at risk. Established after the Second World War and defined explicitly by its commitment to free enterprise and representative government, it had achieved a just peace at

---

191 Thomas L. Friedman, The End of Europe?, in: The New York Times, Online: https://www.nytimes.com/2018/12/18/opinion/europe-france-economy.html, (New York City, 2018).

the end of the Cold War in 1990. The Liberal International Order has underpinned the modern era for generations, and maintaining it will require a strategy that celebrates universal principles and recognizes the reality of other regions' histories, cultures, and views of their security.[192]

Reinventing Germany

The Eurozone, and the agreed defense spending contribution of 2 percent of GDP for defense by NATO members, have caught Germany in the dilemma of having to exercise its sovereign obligation to the EU and NATO without relinquishing its national sovereignty. That choice is difficult, but John Mearsheimer argues that "people fail to realize that realism and nationalism are more powerful forces that undermine liberalism at every turn."[193] Germany needs a strategy that preserves its sovereign obligations to the EU and NATO in the face of growing nationalism, notably in the rise of both German and European populism. Two cases illustrate this problem, and a call for strategic planning offers a process to build a German strategy for its obligations to Europe and the transatlantic partnership.[194]

First, the unfinished project of the European Monetary Union will either lead to European integration or disintegration. France and Germany have worked to create the European Monetary Union but have lacked the political will for political union. German pooled sovereignty with the European Union has led to the creation of the Euro but remains in conflict with national interests. The Eurozone has failed to complete the structures needed for fiscal union and to mutualize debt. In the 2009 financial crisis, Germany unilaterally chose austerity policies over debt forgiveness for Greece, Italy, and other southern European nations. Germany prospered with low-interest rates, granting loans for German exports to Greece, Italy, and others, but chose not to accept responsibility for those countries' debt problems. As a result, Europe has seen the rise of populist, nationalist movements as Europe turns to populism to resolve the dilemma. In Germany, the populist/nationalist Alternative for Germany party began as a protest against the Euro.

Second, the current American administration questions NATO's European security architecture and asks whether it should fulfill its commitment to European security under Article 5 of the NATO Treaty. After unification, the German

---

192 Henry Kissinger, *World Order*, (Penguin Books: London, 2014).
193 John J. Mearsheimer, Bound to Fail, The Rise and Fall of the Liberal International Order, in: International Security, Vol. 43, No. 4 (Cambridge, U.S.A., 2019), pp. 7–50.
194 John J. Mearsheimer, Liberal Ideals and International Realities, Stimson Lectures, Yale University, Online: https://macmillan.yale.edu/news/john-j-mearsheimer-liberal-ideals-and-international-realities, (Providence, 2017).

Constitutional Court allowed Germany to participate in military deployments within alliances and with a parliamentary mandate. As those deployments advanced from the Balkans and then to Syria and Mali, Germany's commitment to NATO to spend 2 % of GDP on defense was largely abandoned. It abolished its mandatory military conscription, cut the size of the *Bundeswehr*, and neglected its defense capabilities. Can the unraveling of the world order, internal challenges of the EU, and a withdrawal of American leadership pressure Germany to choose to fulfill its sovereign obligations to Europe and NATO, or will it choose its national interests instead?

Germany faces dilemmas in its exercise of leadership. Europe and Germany, together, need to take on more responsibility and step up to defend and help reshape the world order to sustain Western values. However, caution, passivity, and moral intransigence dominate Germany's strategic culture, which is incompatible with new realities in international relations. This culture is difficult to reconcile with the increasingly complex facts in foreign and security policy.

French President Emmanuel Macron presented visions of reform for the European Union to prepare it for international leadership, and called on Germany, the economic powerhouse in the middle of the continent, to take a leading role. German reluctance to step out beyond crisis management lacks strategic vision. This reluctance results in halting steps toward reform of the EU, including in security issues, such as *Permanent Structured Coordination* (PESCO) and a European intervention force, as well as in Eurozone economic structures that would help to strengthen the European Union on the international stage.

German leadership is fraught with dilemmas; Germany needs a strategy for Europe. Germany's history compounds its leadership dilemma and has become an obstacle to its future. Four obstacles stand in the way of Germany, developing a new strategic culture. First, even though German political leadership set out at the Munich Security Conference in 2014 to take on more responsibility, and subsequently conducted foreign policy and defense reviews, the strategic culture and the German public's aversion to the military have not changed significantly. According to a Pew Research survey in 2017,

> two-thirds (67 percent) of Germans also hold a positive opinion of NATO but were the least supportive country when it came to defending Alliance members. Just 40 percent of Germans believe that Germany should provide military force to defend a NATO ally if Russia attacks it. More than half (53 percent) did not support such aid.[195]

---

195 Pew Research Centre, Divisions within NATO on defending an alliance ally, Online: https://www.pewresearch.org/global/2017/05/23/natos-image-improves-on-both-sides-of-atlantic/pg_2017-05-23-nato-00-06/, (Washington D.C., 2017). Also cited in: James D. Bindenagel and Philip A. Ackermann., Germany's Troubled Strategic Culture Needs to Change, in: Transatlantic Take, Online: http://www.gmfus.org/sites/default/files/Germany%E2%80%99s%20Troubled%20Strategic%20Culture%20Needs%20to%20Change.pdf, (Washington D.C., 2018).

Second, given the dominant civilian power security culture, it is politically risky to suggest a German initiative or participation in international alliances publicly unless the situation is morally and legally undisputedly clear. Dogmatic public backlash often prevents an informed debate on foreign policy issues and pre-empts policy decisions. The suggestion of a German intervention should the regime in Syria decide to use chemical weapons against its opponents was rejected. Future consideration is now blocked. Furthermore, domestic rather than international or security issues drive the political fortunes of aspiring and high-level German politicians.

Third, Germany's strategic cultural deficit leads to a lack of cooperation and coordination within the government and especially among ministries, whose independence is protected by a constitutional mandate. At the same time, foreign policy in coalition governments, which are the norm for the country, requires collaboration between ministers with often conflicting political programs adding to the lack of coherent strategic thinking and planning.

Fourth, as a civilian power, the German public supports a reluctant leadership that is based on a worldview that Europe can live in blissful isolation of world events, added now by the coronavirus pandemic.

Chapter 5: The Eurozone

The Treaty of Westphalia established world order under the principle of Sanctity of Sovereignty, the right of nations to independent existence and autonomy. The policy dilemma of the Eurozone is the unresolved question of the EU's identity. Is the EU an international organization, a state in being, a supranational structure, all of this at the same time, and evolving? The weakening of the principle of national sovereignty started with the supranational structures created in 1952 and 1957. This need for German leadership and its dilemmas in choosing between its national interest and its case for that obligation to Europe is presented here in the example of the European Monetary Union (EMU). Can Germany lead in Europe?

Franco-German Leadership in Partnership

The role of France and Germany as leaders in Europe lies in the political and economic weight of these two countries and their history. Following the Second World War, reconciliation between France and Germany meant locking them together through cooperation. As post-war European unity developed, the French embraced a new security concept with the Germans and not against them. The European Coal and Steel Community was designed to ensure that Germany would never again go to war with France, rather than any grand desire for a supranational entity. After German unification in 1990, the French understanding was that "any war between France and Germany becomes not merely unthinkable, but materially impossible," [196] remained unchanged. Franco-German initiatives advanced European integration through the European Monetary System. This initiative included closer political cooperation, the Schengen agreements, and closer partnership with other European countries. The Franco-German 'partnership' represents a subset of

---
196 William Mitchell, *Eurozone Dystopia. Groupthink and Denial on a Grand Scale*, (Edward Elgar Publishing: Cehltenham, 2015), p. 38.

the negotiations on the European scene. The partnership's most crucial function to radically reduce the number of negotiators involved, which increases the likelihood of finding a compromise solution. Summits between France and Germany are essential as the countries often represent different perspectives on issues. As happens in other types of bargaining, it is as if France and Germany are "delegated" to negotiate a settlement. Solutions were often not reached during Franco-German summits or economic consultations, but the subsequent meetings of European leaders benefited from the prior exchange of views and signals.[197] The following short vignettes seek to give impressions that illuminate the Franco-German partnership, although not exclusive to German decision making; it has shaped especially the development of the European Monetary Union.

Georges Pompidou and Willy Brandt

The French envisioned that the EMU would deepen ties with Germany. However strong the history of war has been, over time, the fear of war has eased but not the fear of German dominance. Starting with the Rome Treaties, the *European Economic Commission* (EEC) joint decision making prevailed and included the other member states and the EU Commission. In 1969 at The Hague Summit, French President Georges Pompidou and German Chancellor Willy Brandt, along with the other member states, asked Luxembourg Prime Minister Pierre Werner to create a plan for a European Monetary Union.[198] Prevention of war was the prime motivation for European unity was consequently achieved at the time for a quarter-century after the end of the Second World War. In 1969, an understanding of the relationship between money and collective identity prevailed, and the Werner Plan established the template for a fundamentally social democratic and Keynesian EMU. Monetary policy was designated to serve as an instrument of economic growth and full employment in the context of tripartite corporatist plans.[199] The path chosen meant:

---

[197] Martin Heipertz and Amy Verdun, The dog that would never bite? What we can learn from the origins of the Stability and Growth Pact, in: Journal of European Public Policy, Vol. 11, No. 5, (Milton, 2004), pp.765–780.
[198] Archives of European Integration, Meeting of the Heads of State or Government, The Hague, 1–2 December 1969, Online: http://aei.pitt.edu/1451/1/hague_1969.pdf, (The Hague, 1969).
[199] Alan W. Cafruny, European integration studies, European Monetary Union, and resilience of austerity in Europe: Post-mortem on a crisis foretold, in: Competition and Change. Vol. 19, No. 2, (Washington D.C., 2015), p. 163.

Money and identity can be both cause and effect. On the one hand, money is a purposeful political tool in the construction of identities. On the other hand, to function correctly, money requires some level of collective identity among its users.[200]

In the early 1970s, many voices echoed Werner's view that "there was a true need for European countries to start a currency union. It is simply to put an end to the periodic wars that have started in Europe".[201] Werner's monetary union committee produced a three-stage plan to create a European Economic Area and the Monetary Union that sought to balance traditional economists' demands for economic convergence and the Monetarists' requirements for monetary alignment. The French, notably the then finance minister Giscard d'Estaing, wanted the process to produce more exchange rate cooperation to reduce fluctuations against the U.S. dollar, rather than a carefully coordinated economic policy. The Germans desired to break out of the currency instability by floating the D-Mark. That came as a result of Nixon's decision in 1971 to abandon the Bretton Woods system of the gold standard for the US-Dollar. Germany decided, in 1969, to revalue the D-Mark within the Bretton Woods system. At the time, the country was facing massive capital inflows, mainly from the U.S., as a result of currency uncertainty. These capital inflows were straining their capacity to both maintain economic growth and defend the fixed parity.[202]

Against that background, Pompidou and Brandt met in January 1971 as the Bretton Woods system collapsed and postponed the compromise agreement for the European currency union meant for a European Summit. Pompidou faced significant opposition within his Gaullist party to the Werner preference for establishing supranational institutions. Pompidou had to effectively renegotiate the French position before it went to the Heads of State and government, who occasionally met after 1969 in The Hague and again in Paris in 1972. As a result, any concrete plans to transfer power to any supranational institutions disappeared.[203]

In 1972, the Europeans established the *currency snake system*. The six currencies fluctuated in a tunnel within 2.25 %, like the undulations of a snake. The French gained some traction by getting Brandt to agree to the creation of a European level reserve fund to reduce exchange rate fluctuations. While those

---

200 Matthias Kaelberer, The Euro and European identity: symbols, power and the politics of European monetary union, in: Review of International Studies, Vol. 30, No. 2, (Cambridge, 2004), p. 162.
201 Werner, Pierre, quoted in Stephen Bates, Pierre Werner. The man who dreamed the euro, in: The Guardian, Online: https://www.theguardian.com/news/2002/jun/28/guardianobituaries.euro, (London, 2002).
202 Loukas Tsoukalis, The European Agenda: Issues of Globalization, Equity and Legitimacy, in: The Robert Schuman Centre, Jean Monnet Chair, Vol. 49, Online: https://core.ac.uk/download/pdf/45681007.pdf, (San Domenico, 1998), pp. 108–10.
203 Ibid.

interests were driving the economic debate, Brandt also supported the monetary union to garner French support for *Ostpolitik*, a fundamental German foreign policy goal.[204]

In the mid-1970s, the French suggested setting the margin of fluctuation with reference to the value of the European Unit of Account (EUA). This basis line would make it easier to share the burden of adjustment more fairly as so far that burden had fallen only on weaker currencies. However, by 1977 the Werner Plan's monetary union was finally abandoned after the earlier failure of Bretton Woods. The monetary union was soon to be reborn with the help of German Chancellor Helmut Schmidt, French President Giscard d'Estaing, European Commission President Roy Jenkins, and the German business sector.

Helmut Schmidt and Valéry Giscard d'Estaing

German Chancellor Helmut Schmidt and French President Valéry Giscard d'Estaing collaborated on the Exchange Rate Mechanism (ERM) after the Snake failed. Giscard d'Estaing advocated for the European Monetary System (EMS) as a stepping stone to a European political union. Seen from the vantage point of German history, Schmidt believed that the EMU with a common currency would prevent the dominance of the D-Mark and Germany from becoming isolated.

European leaders gave a boost to the 40-year multilateral negotiation for the European Monetary Union (EMU) and a common currency, when in July 1978 in Bremen Giscard and Helmut Schmidt created the EMS. The summit leaders descended on the town to launch the ECU under the European Monetary System. By December, seeking protection from the dollar's volatility, European leaders agreed to the EMS. The next year, they launched the snake: eight states were now part of a snake-like exchange rate system that was to evolve into the more rigid ERM. The ECU, a currency unit whose value was determined by a basket of European currencies, was also created.[205] The most vigorous opposition to such a proposal came from the German government, which insisted that the key to convergence was an economic adjustment, not monetary technicalities. National sovereignty challenged the obligation to intervene on Europe's behalf. Both the German economic and finance ministries stated monetary mechanisms should

---

[204] Emmanuel Mourlon-Druol, Don't Blame the Euro : Historical Reflections on the Roots of the Eurozone Crisis, in: West European Politics, Vol. 37, No. 6., (Abingdon-on-Thames, 2014), pp. 1287–1288.

[205] Sally Bolton, A History of Currency Unions, in: The Guardian, Online: https://www.theguardian.com/world/2001/dec/10/euro.eu, (London, 2001).

not become financial transfer mechanisms for the economically weaker member states.[206]

By the end of 1979, when U.S. President Jimmy Carter launched his package of budget cuts, credit controls, and monetary tightening, the U.S. economy took a nosedive. This crisis confirmed for the Europeans the need for economic adjustments for monetary convergence via the EMS. Legal enshrinement of the exchange rate *Snake,* with inflation and fixed exchange rates in the European Exchange Rate Mechanism (ERM), dominated the technical debate. Throughout the 1980s, the struggle was whether a currency union or real economic cohesion should come first. What kind of criteria would be necessary to please the Germans, and which binding timeline would be needed to calm the French?[207] For Schmidt, the EMS was far more than a currency bloc; it was Germany's future in Europe, a defense against American financial volatility and Germany's commitment to peace and stability on the continent.

Helmut Kohl and François Mitterrand

In the early 1980s, Chancellor Helmut Kohl and French President François Mitterrand Franco-German, leaders in partnership, deepened their cooperation. Mitterrand saw an opportunity to maintain France's policy of embedding Germany in Europe by giving Germany assurances that it would collaborate on security issues. For example, he created the Franco-German Brigade and provided his full support of the deployment of American Intermediate-Range Nuclear Forces (INF) in West Germany. At the time, France demanded a promise that Germany would support the EMU in exchange for French security guarantees for West Germany.[208] In 1983, no one saw the likelihood of German unification; Mitterrand's proposal quickly became a done deal.

Mitterrand spoke in favor of U.S. nuclear missile deployments in the German Bundestag in 1983. That speech gave Chancellor Kohl the critical political support he needed to win parliamentary approval for the American Intermediate-Range Nuclear Forces (INF) deployments in Germany in November 1983. The European Council finally decided to start the three stages toward EMU in 1988. However, suddenly in 1989, Kohl and Mitterrand were surprised on November 9, 1989, when the fall of the Berlin Wall sent shockwaves throughout Europe. Kohl became

---

206 Ibid.
207 Ludger Kühnhardt, European Union – The Second Founding: The Changing Rationale of European Integration, in: Schriften des Zentrum für Europäische Integrationsforschung (ZEI), 2. Edition, (Bonn, 2010), pp. 481–574.
208 David Marsh, *The Euro – The Battle for the New Global Currency*, (Yale University Press: Providence, 2011), p. 99.

preoccupied with the revolution in East Germany. While the agreed progress toward monetary union took a back seat for many Germans, Kohl's commitment remained fixed. Mitterrand flirted with Gorbachev and Thatcher over obstructing German unification to remind Kohl of his support for the process launched in 1988. Mitterrand stated bluntly: "Without a common currency, we are all of us ... already subordinate to the Germans' will."[209]

The 1983 Kohl-Mitterrand agreement on the EMU was a power bargain that came back to the negotiation table after the fall of the Berlin Wall. EMU was part of the Delors proposals for the completion of the Single Market in 1985, and at the EU Summit in Strasbourg in December 1989, EU Member States agreed to two intergovernmental conferences, one on monetary union and another on political union. In light of the move to German unification, Mitterrand pressured Kohl calling on Germany to agree to advance the planned negotiations on the Economic Monetary Union before the end of 1990. Otherwise, in light of the push toward German unification, "Germany risked a *Triple Entente* between France, Britain, and the Soviet Union that could similarly isolate Germany on the eve of the First World War."[210] That reluctance could slow down the unification process. Shortly after the EU summit, Kohl told U.S. Secretary of State James A. Baker that he would support early moves toward EMU. Although Kohl also recognized that there would be no political union in the foreseeable future, he nevertheless supported the Monetary Union. However, it was not in the German interest without a political union.[211]

Kohl knew that European political union was needed to support a common currency. However, the search for political union faded as German unification became inevitable and died in the aftermath of the Yugoslavian breakup. Mitterrand stuck by the European Council's decision for EMU. After the East German parliamentary elections in March 1990 had given East Germany a mandate for unification, implementation of the Franco-German EMU deal struck earlier by Jacques Delors was back on track towards implementation. The European Council, chaired by the Luxembourg and Dutch presidencies, convened two inter-governmental conferences under the guidance of Karl Otto Pöhl and Jacques Delors, one on the EMU and the other on political union soon after the first all-German election on December 2, 1990.

Already in his 1989 report on the establishment of the Economic and Monetary Union (EMU), Commission President Jacques Delors pointed out the importance of an economic and monetary union. He insisted that "monetary union

---

209 Ibid., p. 135.
210 Ibid., p. 137.
211 Ibid.

without a sufficient degree of convergence of economic policies is unlikely to be durable and could be damaging to the Community."[212]

The EMU, as adopted in the 1990s, was comprised of an institutional basis of the Maastricht Treaty that included monetary union, the Euro as a common currency and the European Central Bank (ECB). It established the Single Market with the four set freedoms in the Rome Treaty in 1957 – freedoms of movement of goods, services, people, and money. European political union remains unfinished business, without which the EMU cannot constitute a whole. Political union, fiscal union, economic governance institutions, and meaningful coordination of structural economic policies are needed. Wolfgang Münchau in the Financial Times has asserted that it is easy to invent new institutions to deal with each crisis issue, and he insists this requires a fiscal union, an EU treasury secretary, a common sovereign bond, and a banking union.[213]

Gerhard Schröder and Jacques Chirac

It fell upon German Chancellor Gerhard Schröder and French President Jacques Chirac to launch a common currency, the Euro, which they implemented on January 1, 1999. The debate over the Euro included the assertion that the Euro was the price of German unification. Kohl's Finance Minister Theo Waigel had demanded and achieved the Stability and Growth Pact to balance the missing political union with a more solid EMU. He recalled that while the claim was made, mainly from France and Britain, those assertions may have had more to do with Mitterrand and Thatcher's efforts to justify to their respective publics their support for German unification. Gorbachev also heard those assertions and told Waigel that both countries wanted to delay unification. President George H.W. Bush's strong support for Germany Unification contrasted with the French[214] and British[215] support. They subsequently argued for their domestic audience that they won German support for the Euro in exchange unification. However, those

---

212 Angela Merkel citing Jaques Delors in: Angela Merkel, Chancellor Merkel European Parliament Address, Online: https://www.c-span.org/video/?309369-1/chancellor-merkel-european-parliament-address, (Brussels, 2012).
213 Wolfgang Münchau, A real banking union can save the Eurozone, in: Financial Times, Online: https://www.ft.com/content/45b36a66-abd4-11e1-a8a0-00144feabdc0, (London: 2012a).
214 Michael Sauga, Stefan Simons and Klaus Wiegrefe, The Price of Unity. Was the Deutsche Mark Sacrificed for Reunifcation, in: Spiegel International, Online: https://www.spiegel.de/international/germany/the-price-of-unity-was-the-deutsche-mark-sacrificed-for-reunification-a-719940.html, (Hamburg, 2010).
215 Timothy G. Ash, Britain fluffed the German question. Now Britain is Europe's great puzzle, in: The Guardian, Online: https://www.theguardian.com/commentisfree/2009/oct/21/britain-fluffed-german-question, (London, 2009).

views do not square with history: as seen in the Delors plan, Europeans decided on the implementation of the Euro before the unification negotiations began.

France and Germany met the Stability and Growth Pact convergence criteria to coordinate economic policies to facilitate and maintain the stability of the EMU. However, Waigel, Jürgen Stark, State Secretary in the Finance Ministry, and head of the European Section of Finance Klaus Regling argued that, before the implementing EMU and the launch of the Euro, the EU should have decided economic convergence and political union. It was not.[216]

The critical monetarist decision-makers at the time were Hans Tietmeyer, President of the Bundesbank, and Otmar Issing, his chief economist. They presented the underlying reasons for the launch of the Euro. Klaus Regling and Jürgen Stark posed the question to the Bundesbank: "What is meant when it is repeatedly argued that the European Monetary Union without political union will not work?" Does it mean a European Army to defend Europe or a shared European foreign policy? Tietmeyer answered these rhetorical questions, noting that both are valuable, but are they essential for a monetary union? Stark argued that monetary union would violate the Maastricht Treaty. Issing, who participated in that debate, stressed that the reconciliation between former arch-enemies Germany and France is the key to European integration. The result has been that nothing in Europe progresses without a Franco-German agreement. This particular example of Leadership in Partnership is crucial.[217]

The Euro's success and durability rest on trust, and the Stability and Growth Pact, with its 3 percent limit on budget deficits to GDP, offered just that. President Chirac and the Union for a Popular Movement (UMP) campaigned in 2002, calling for significant tax cuts, one of the principal presidential campaign pledges. Chirac overstretched. He and his political party, the UMP, also regularly confirmed France's commitment to meeting the medium-term Stability Pact goals. At the same time, repeated German failures to meet the 3 % deficit figure aligned the two governments on the wrong side of the Stability Pact rule. The Raffarin government formed a pro-reform alliance with the Schröder government. The French government then accepted the Schröder government's demands to suspend the application of the Excessive Deficit Procedure (EDP). The French then joined the Germans to force through the suspension at the 2003 EU's Ecofin meeting of finance ministers. Official French policy on the Stability Pact

---

216 James P. Rubin, The Leader of the Free World Meets Donald Trump, in: Politico, Online: https://www.politico.com/magazine/story/2017/03/the-leader-of-the-free-world-meets-donald-trump-214924, (Arlington County, 2017).
217 Otmar Issing, Wie die Deutsch-französische Achse neue Impulse für Europa setzen könnte, in: Wohlstand für Alle, 70 Jahre Währungsreform, Ludwig-Erhard Stiftung, (Bonn, 2018), pp. 32–33.

insisted that the non-application of the EDP did not amount to an abandonment of France's commitment to the Pact.[218]

In 1991, France was one of the few EC Member States that had consistently respected all five criteria since the Second World War, except for 1983. Throughout, France had avoided a public spending deficit higher than 3 %. The socialist French government set the 3 % deficit limit when it abandoned its Keynesian experiment of the early 1980s. With a 3.1 % deficit in 1983, President Mitterrand resolved not to exceed three percent in the future. However, the Raffarin government insisted upon a more flexible application that would – officially – take into consideration the economic situation facing a participating member state.[219]

After successfully launching the Euro, its two leading proponents, Chancellor Gerhard Schröder and President Jacques Chirac, partnered to violate the Stability Pact, which damaged it severely.[220] Theo Waigel, who negotiated the Stability Pact after criticizing Gerhard Schröder and Finance Minister Hans Eichel, was concerned that the Stability Pact placed too much reliance on fiscal policy. A biting debate followed the Franco-German undermining of the Stability Pact. Would a return to the D-Mark be an option for the Germans? What would happen to Germany if the Euro collapsed? The unasked question is where Germany would be without the Euro.[221] German industry would face a desperate struggle to export its products. The global impact of a return to the D-Mark would also be devastating.

Pieces of the EMU Puzzle

Europe could jettison its monetary union, or it could stick with the fiscal compact and adopt a complementary economic union, starting with a banking union and bank supervisor. How are the Europeans progressing with their institution-building? Five presidents of EU institutions have laid out a plan with a deadline of 2025. The negotiations to implement details remain difficult because members

---

218 Le Monde, 26.11.2004, cited in: David J. Howarth, Making and Breaking the Rules: French policy on EU 'gouvernement économique' and the Stability and Growth Pact, in: European Integration Online Papers, Vol. 9, No. 15, (Vienna, 2005), p. 9.
219 David J. Howarth, Making and Breaking the Rules: French policy on EU 'gouvernement économique' and the Stability and Growth Pact, in: European Integration Online Papers, Vol. 9, No. 15, (Vienna, 2005), pp. 11–12.
220 Petra Pinzel and Mark Schieritz, Euro-Einführung. Wir waren doch keine Idioten, in: Zeit Online, Online: https://www.zeit.de/2018/27/euro-einfuehrung-waehrungsunion-eu-refor mInterview, (Hamburg, 2018).
221 Theo Waigel quoted in Petra Pinzel and Mark Schieritz, Euro-Einführung. Wir waren doch keine Idioten, in: Zeit Online, Online: https://www.zeit.de/2018/27/euro-einfuehrung-waehr ungsunion-eu-reformInterview, (Hamburg, 2018).

are driven by contrasting national interests, although German Finance Minister Olaf Scholz in November 2019 proposed four steps toward a banking union.[222]

The unfinished business of the 40-year-long struggle to create a European Monetary Union is at the top of the agenda. The current set of negotiations is quite typical of the politics of the EMU. That is, the Europeans are crafting piece by piece the elements of the missing political union. The European Stability Mechanism (ESM), funded by national governments, stood ready to bail out countries through loans with possible debt defaults and mutualization of sovereign debt. Euro bonds remain a mere concept for a system of bank resolution and insurance but may offer a future refinancing option. Common banking regulation and supervision would help stabilize the market and maintain credibility in the banks.

European Central Bank's flooding of the market with banking liquidity resolved the sovereign debt. If the sovereign debt is collateral, it will shift debt to taxpayers. That shift is politically difficult. A fiscal compact and eventually Euro bonds or mutualization of sovereign debt through the ECB or ESM could support a monetary union.

German insistence throughout negotiations on debt management, fiscal austerity, and price stability in the Greek crisis has had a political impact. Those policies angered the public in several countries and contributed to the rise of anti-EU parties. That narrow focus on Eurozone economic and monetary governance demonstrated that the EMU was less a path to European unification than one leading to anti-Euro populist movements. European populist movements have risen along with illiberal democracy, for example in Hungary, and populist movements in several other countries. The Alternative for Germany (AfD), which began as an anti-Euro party, is also a result of these policies. Populist movements pose the risk of disintegrating European unity.

Sovereign Debt Crisis in the Eurozone: German Dominance

Chancellor Angela Merkel would later see the Eurozone crisis, without exaggeration, as "maybe Europe's most difficult hours since World War II."[223] The 2010 Greek crisis reverberated across Europe. Severe fiscal austerity and price stability managed the Greek debt problem, but the solution was that Germany

---

222 Olaf Scholz, Germany will consider EU-wide bank deposit reinsurance, in: Financial Times, Online: https://www.ft.com/content/82624c98-ff14-11e9-a530-16c6c29e70ca, (London, 2019).
223 Angela Merkel quoted in: The Guardian, European debt crisis is worst time since second world war, says Angela Merkel, in: The Guardian, Online: https://www.theguardian.com/business/2011/nov/14/eurozone-debt-crisis-angela-merkel, (London, 2011).

became the dominant leader of Europe. Merkel had characterized the threat of the global financial crises that led to the Eurozone crisis as an existential one.[224]

How did the Europeans get to this crisis in the first place? Without a political union, EMU institutions remain unfinished. Consequently, many analysts who watched the European economy dragged through the 2010-2011 financial and debt crisis have concluded that the Euro is fatally flawed and faces collapse. Has Germany, as Andrew Moravsik argued in Foreign Affairs in 2012, set the terms for nearly every agreement on monetary issues since the 1970s? Moravsik claimed that

> Germany's primary motivation for a single currency, contrary to popular belief, was neither to aid its reunification (sic) nor to realize an idealistic federalist scheme for European political union. It was instead to promote its economic welfare through open markets, a competitive exchange rate, and anti-inflationary policy. The problem is not the role of technocratic central banks or even temporary technocratic governments. The problem is rather that the European Central Bank is more independent than any comparable national bank – without any apparent technocratic or democratic justification. The reason is instead political; it was Germany's condition for creating the euro. The result is a system tilted toward German priorities: low inflation, austerity, and the repayment of creditors.[225]

Narrowly based analysis such as this shows the dilemmas Germany continues to face as the Federal Republic made and has kept the commitments from the end of the Second World War and to be welcomed back into the community of nations after the National Socialists regime. U.S. Secretary of State James F. Byrnes, in his 1946 Speech of Hope in Stuttgart, laid out the criteria for the defeated nation to turn to democracy in Europe and to respect the rule of law. Robert Schuman proposed the European Coal and Steel Community in 1950 to integrate Germany into Europe.[226] That commitment to Europe, the common good, is a reminder of Germany's obligation to the other EU Member States. During the Eurozone crisis, Chancellor Merkel called for solutions to sustain European integration. Still, German decisions were reasonably made with national interests in mind and raised questions of how much Germany is committed to acting in common European interests. The French fear of Germany's dominance in the Eurozone grew as Germans pushed to avoid the moral hazard of ECB bailouts and Eurobonds in 2010. That was stage one of the Maastricht-agreed Stability and Growth

---

[224] Angela Merkel, Chancellor Merkel European Parliament Address, Online: https://www.c-span.org/video/?309369-1/chancellor-merkel-european-parliament-address, (Brussels, 2012).
[225] Andrew Moravcsik, Europe After the Crisis, How to Sustain a Common Currency, in: Foreign Affairs, Online: https://www.foreignaffairs.com/articles/europe/2012-05-01/europe-after-crisis, (Congers, 2012).
[226] Robert Schuman, Schuman Declaration and the Birth of Europe, Speech of May 9, Online: http://www.schuman.info/9May1950.htm, (Brussels, 1950).

Pact. The fiscal compact, fixated on strict limits on deficits through austerity regimes and constitutional balanced budget amendments in each country, was a point of contention.

The European sovereign debt crisis that began in Ireland and Portugal trickled into Spain. It developed a Europeanized monetary policy and non-Europeanized, national, autonomous economic and fiscal policies. Germany feared it would pay dearly for any solution and demanded austerity. Martin Wolf wrote in the Financial Times: "Austerity is merely begetting more austerity."[227] Public debt to GDP will only rise with austerity, not fall. Fear of inflation has caused talk of stimulus and growth policies to take a back seat. Still, after the Greek and French elections, strategies for growth would hopefully rebound to become stage two of the crisis resolution.

The other side of the issue was whether increased stimulus could achieve growth without exploding inflation? These were not new debates in Germany considering its history of runaway inflation in the 1920s. A mini-stimulus was tried in 2012 when German Finance Minister Wolfgang Schäuble opined that German wage rates could rise by 6.5 % and which settled at 4.3 %, a small movement toward a stimulus in Germany. *Bundesbank* President Jens Weidmann stated in the summer of 2012 that it was not the time to raise interest rates, signaling acceptance of a rise in inflation. Finance Minister Schäuble noted that inflation could rise between 2 and 3 %, above the average of Eurozone inflation. The market has been skeptical of these proposals, which in the long-term is likely to make things worse.[228]

The crisis demanded more action to restore confidence. An initiative began with President of the European Council Herman Van Rompuy's work in the European Council after a period of blame-games from 2008 to 2012. Former European Commission President José Manuel Durão Barroso responded to the crisis by calling for a "decisive deal for Europe," starting with efforts to stabilize the Euro area and accelerate growth throughout the EU.[229] In his 2013 state of the Union address, Rompuy committed the Commission to present proposals to create a single banking supervisor and to create a banking union in line with the current Treaty provisions. The Commission gave its blueprint to build a comprehensive and genuine economic and monetary union, including political instruments. Eventually, the Council, Commission, and Central Bank presidents

---

[227] Martin Wolf, The riddle of German self-interest, in: Financial Times, Online: https://www.ft.com/content/4fe89d8c-a8df-11e1-b085-00144feabdc0, (London, 2012).
[228] Chris Byrant, Schäuble backs wage rises for German, in: Financial Times, Online: https://www.ft.com/content/54aa8246-9772-11e1-83f3-00144feabdc0, (London, 2012).
[229] José Manuel Barroso, State of the European Union 2012 Speech, European Parliament in Strasbourg, France, September 12, Online: https://ec.europa.eu/commission/presscorner/detail/en/SPEECH_12_596, (Straßbourg, 2012).

presented a joint approach, which remains the blueprint for the path toward the Five Presidents' Report 2025.[230]

German Foreign Minister Guido Westerwelle and Polish Foreign Minister Radek Sikorski recognized in 2012 that the Eurozone crisis stemmed "partly from the flawed architecture of the Economic and Monetary Union."[231] The EMU's founding father, Jacques Delors, was aware of EMU's deficiencies, but a compromise beyond a single monetary policy was not feasible at that time. They argued it was the time to remedy this mistake and made their goal known in the New York Times:

> It will take much to motivate citizens to implement these reforms. For Europe to be a genuinely solid actor and global leader, it needs a strong institutional setup, a streamlined and efficient system for the separation of powers. It also requires a directly elected European Commission president who personally appoints the members of the 'European Government,' a European Parliament with powers to initiate legislation and the second chamber for member states.[232]

The European Central Bank sought to resolve the issue with the European Stability Mechanism (an emerging European Monetary Fund). The Council, Commission, and Parliament, as well as national governments/parliaments, in consent with the ECB, agreed on a fiscal compact and a banking union that would include an EU Bank supervisor. Could these institutional steps toward economic union lead to the creation of the foreign ministers' vision of a European government and the political union Europe needs?

The EU foreign ministers' group suggestions could implement them, with the Single Market as the basis for growth and economic development along with their four building blocks for the EMU. To the public, Chancellor Merkel's determination to move toward a more political union was so cautious as to be opaque. In the first two years of the crisis, she worked tirelessly to bail out the banks by moving privately held sovereign debt to the Bundesbank and ECB, socializing private debt as needed, and saving the banking sector. The EU effort did reduce the private banks' sovereign debt exposure, and they took losses in Greece when the private banks received a "haircut." Politically, that course of action was successful in helping the bankers but did not resolve the Greek debt crisis.

Chancellor Merkel, speaking at her party's economic council (*CDU Wirtschaftsrat*) in June 2012, made clear that any near-time market solution was

---

230 Foreign Ministers of Austria, Belgium, Denmark, France, Italy, Germany, Luxembourg, the Netherlands, Poland, Portugal and Spain, *Final Report of the Future of Europe Report*, Online: https://www.cer.eu/sites/default/files/westerwelle_report_sept12.pdf, (Brussels, 2012).
231 Radek Sikorski and Guido Westerwelle, A New Vision of Europe, in: The New York Times, Online: https://www.nytimes.com/2012/09/18/opinion/a-new-vision-of-europe.html, (New York City, 2012).
232 Ibid.

unlikely to be implemented. The resolution came when European Central Bank President Mario Draghi committed the ECB to "do whatever it takes was driven to preserve the Euro as a stable currency."[233] He was signaling his willingness to finance the debt of the Eurozone 's weakest economies. Unlimited bond-buying in the primary market, EU bailout funds, ECB assistance through outright monetary transactions (OMT) and Troika (the IMF, the EU Commission, and the ECB) helped address the Spanish crisis, along with Spanish Prime Minister Rajoy's austerity budget.

Nevertheless, many obstacles will stand in the path of complete resolution of conflicts about EMU and political union. *Deutsche Bundesbank* President Jens Weidmann opposed Draghi's decision, and the issue took an ugly turn when Weidmann hinted that Draghi was the *Mephisto* (devil) in the Eurozone drama. Weidmann quoted from Goethe's Faust to suggest Draghi's solution of unlimited printing of money by the ECB would unleash uncontrolled inflation, which is the German's ultimate nightmare about fiat money and monetary union.[234]

The German Federal Constitutional Court, in defense of German national sovereignty, established another hurdle on the path to political union. It took up a court challenge to the European Stability Mechanism (ESM) to manage the debt/default. On September 12, 2012, the German Constitutional Court cleared the way for ESM for the German government to fund it but only with the approval of the *Bundestag*. Also, after the EU funded and implemented a special debt redemption fund, it could oversee and manage existing sovereign debt, along with some extraordinary measures from the ESM. Institutional steps to operate the fiscal compact and the creation of a banking supervisor will cover the existing gap in Eurozone federal structures for now. Eventually, the EU will need to create a joint deposit insurance corporation (similar to the FDIC) to stabilize bank holdings and stem capital flight.

In the continuing debate, George Soros laid out his views on the steps the Europeans needed to take. He challenged the Germans to choose between leading and leaving the Eurozone. Soros suggested the issue is one of leveling the playing field for debtors and creditors and aiming at a growth of 5 percent to get out of the debt crisis. The EU needs to build more supranational institutions, and Soros suggested a European Fiscal Authority take charge, with conditions, of the ESM and the special debt redemption fund (after sovereign debt exceeded more than 60 percent of a country's GDP). The German Federal Constitutional Court has

---

233 Ben Rooney, Draghi to the rescue, in: CNN Money Invest, Online: https://money.cnn.com/2012/07/26/investing/draghi-ecb/index.htm, (Atlanta, 2012).
234 Wolfgang Münchau, Draghi is the devil in Weidmann's Eurozone drama, in: Financial Times, Online: https://www.ft.com/content/9095a970-03dd-11e2-9322-00144feabdc0, (London, 2012a).

rejected such a transfer of German national sovereignty, which is a significant hurdle to implementing this suggestion.[235]

Soros suggested that a disorderly breakup of the Euro area would be catastrophic for the whole world. It was unlikely the Greeks would leave the Euro. The results of a 2013 poll by the Pew Research Center showed that some 69 % of Greeks approved of the Euro, even though they wished to shelve the austerity program.[236] The Germans' European commitment remained firm in 2012; they have stayed committed to the fiscal compact as it explores other options, including a transaction tax.[237] Long-term, some sort of safe assets in Europe are needed, for example, Eurobonds.[238] However, German political will to advance to complete EMU is limited. Eurobonds would require steps toward economic union, with a federal finance minister to bring the EU closer to a political union; however, such a measure needs German support. Without German support, it is likely to be made later in the political process through an intergovernmental agreement, pending a treaty change sometime in the future.

The Euro has a global impact, too. If there is another 'Lehman Brothers-like' financial collapse in Europe, it could unleash uncontrollable forces of panic. Mario Monti, a central personality in this drama, was the first to properly articulate the systemic problem behind the so-called Euro- or Greek-crisis. After 2012 he convinced Council Members to act accordingly. Monti spoke on the record at the Council on Foreign Relations in 2012 and emphasized the Euro's role as more than just a currency; it is a set of rules of governance, budgetary discipline, and a single central bank.[239] He added that since its introduction, the Euro had had a significant political impact across Europe, not only financial and economical one.[240]

While European policy-makers labor to guarantee the stability and survival of the Euro, the crisis needed all global investors and banks, country-level central banks and the European Central Bank to find the solution. Political and economic agents, stakeholders, interest groups, and exogenous forces affect the

---

235 George Soros, The Tragedy of the European Union and how to Resolve it, in: New York Review, Online: https://www.nybooks.com/articles/2012/09/27/tragedy-european-union-and-how-resolve-it/, (New York City, 2012).
236 Bruce Stokes and Sara Kehaulani Goo, 5 facts about Greece and the EU, in: Pew Research Center, Online: http://www.pewresearch.org/fact-tank/2015/07/07/5-facts-about-greece-and-the-eu/, (Washington D.C., 2015).
237 Bindenagel, James, dinner conversation with George Soros, ECFR, June 2012.
238 Marco Buti, Servaas Deroose, José Laeandro and Gabriele Giudice, Completing EMU, in: Vox. CEPR Policy Portal, Online: https://voxeu.org/article/completing-emu, (London, 2017).
239 Mario Monti, Mario Monti on Challenges for the Euro and the Future of European Integration, in: Council on Foreign Relations, Online: https://www.cfr.org/event/mario-monti-challenges-euro-and-future-european-integration, (Washington D.C., 2012).
240 Ibid.

performance and confidence in the Euro. European policy-makers degree of control over the solution is constrained. Maintaining their resolve to end the crisis is impossible without the consent of the market, the business community, the public, and civil society. These elements of the Eurozone, once only observed in Germany, are now the foundation of the European economy. European unity and stability are paramount priorities. This debate has proven the central role of Germany and its politics in such crises.

Foreign Ministers Group: Political Will and Vision

In their 2017 report on the future of Europe, the Foreign Ministers Group (Austria, Belgium, Denmark, France, Italy, Germany, Luxembourg, the Netherlands, Poland, Portugal, and Spain) described the sovereign debt crisis and the ever-accelerating process of globalization as an unprecedented dual challenge for Europe.[241] The ministers must have taken a page from Chicago's Mayor Rahm Emanuel, who has said: "Never let a good crisis go to waste."[242] The Eurozone crisis was a call to action for political leaders. They knew what the catastrophic costs of a collapse of the Euro would bring. The primary driver preventing a solution of the Euro crisis is that national fears of stepping into an abyss of financing other countries' debts. Leaders only step back from the edge temporarily, and soon Eurozone leaders will repeatedly be forced onto the precipice.

The crisis has long had a political dimension, and foreign ministers expressed concerns about the rise of nationalism and populism in many parts of Europe. Feelings of solidarity and a sense of European belonging were dwindling. Should EU disintegration lead to the resurgence of national interests, it would be at the expense of the institutions of the European Union and the world economy. Although informed observers often see this crisis as one primarily about finance, deficits, debt, and banking, it is fundamentally about the obstacles that stand in the way of coherently pooling and sharing sovereignty and a political union. Can Germany and France convince themselves and other Members of the necessity of pooling and sharing sovereignty for a common fiscal and monetary policy?

Can the Europeans find the political will to complement monetary union with a political union? Fred Bergsten commented that "the lack of confidence in the euro

---

241 Foreign Ministers of Austria, Belgium, Denmark, France, Italy, Germany, Luxembourg, the Netherlands, Poland, Portugal and Spain, *Final Report of the Future of Europe Report*, Online: https://www.cer.eu/sites/default/files/westerwelle_report_sept12.pdf, (Brussels, 2012).
242 Emmanuel Rahm quoted in : Wall Street Journal, Rahm Emmanuel on the Opportunity of Crisis, Online https://www.youtube.com/watch?v=_mzcbXi1Tkk, (Washington D.C.: 2008), min: 0:01–0:07.

is first and foremost rooted in a crisis of fundamental institutional design."[243] Other analysts have argued and will argue that the issue is one of the euro political-economy and the near absence of an institutional structure necessary to ensure, bolster, and defend a credible, sustainable common currency. Can the leaders create the needed supra-national institutions? Without a political will for solving this crisis, EU disintegration could lead to the resurgence of national interests that the foreign ministers in 2012 worried would come at the expense of European institutions and the global economy. The accelerating process of globalization accentuates the urgency.

The Foreign Ministers Group provided a remarkable analysis showing that the single market is at risk and needs sound public finances, competitiveness, growth, and employment. The ministers had proposed earlier four building blocks for the EMU: An integrated financial framework, a unified budgetary framework, an integrated economic policy framework, and measures to ensure the necessary democratic legitimacy and accountability. For twenty years, the Euro has remained a vital currency despite the ongoing crises in the Eurozone. The Euro has been stable and is a successful international currency, despite the financial and fiscal aspects of the crisis, including European sovereign debt, under-regulated banks, trade imbalances, high unemployment, and anemic growth.

At the European level, the EU Single Market is one of the EU's primary assets and the most powerful engine for growth. In resolving the crisis, the EU has opened the way for new supranational institutions in addition to the ECB, including the European Stability Mechanism and a European banking supervisor (not reporting to national governments). The ECB would finance the debt of the weakest Eurozone countries if they agreed to an EU program of budget discipline/austerity Outright Monetary Transactions (OMT). And the German Federal Constitutional Court has approved the establishment of the European Stability Mechanism.

Chancellor Helmut Kohl understood at unification the age-old German question of whether a mighty Germany at the center of Europe would be met with demands by Europeans to counter deal with rising German power. Competition between national sovereignty and the common good creates tension. In his government declaration on May 10, 1990, Chancellor Kohl reassured allies that for Germany, the common good was European unity. Kohl said West Germany was the premier beneficiary of the Western world order, and he was willing to commit to the European Monetary Union if it included a commitment to po-

---

243 C. Fred Bergsten, The Outlook for the Euro Crisis and Implications for the United States, United States Congress, Senate, Senate Budget Committee, Concurrent Resolution on the Budget Fiscal Year 2013, (Washington D.C., 2012), p. 103.

litical union with a strong European Parliament and a common foreign and defense policy.[244]

However, at a critical juncture, in the middle of the breakup of Yugoslavia in 1991, Germans moved to unilaterally recognize Croatia and Slovenia, which was opposed by most EU countries, who reluctantly followed the German lead. As a consequence, German motives were mistrusted all across the European Community. That led to stalled political union negotiations on the way toward the Maastricht Treaty. At that time, as a result, a strong proponent of Europe, Hans Dietrich Genscher, resigned as German foreign minister.

Consequently, the EU set aside goals for political union, although the Maastricht Treaty would open the single market. The treaty, however, subsequently failed to enhance the essential elements of a political union, the powers of the European Parliament, or a common European foreign and defense policy.[245] Germans, nevertheless, reached consensus on some of the elements of crisis resolution despite policy differences on Eurobonds and stimulus.

Later, Helmut Schmidt, in a 2011 speech, supported the steps taken, including rescue funds, debt limits, a common economic and fiscal policy with corresponding national tax and budget policies for spending on social and labor programs as well as labor market reforms. Some sort of Eurobond, a common debt instrument, is unavoidable on the way to a more federalized Europe. Schmidt argued that, in line with the Lisbon Treaty (Article 20), countries in the Eurozone still needed to negotiate several outstanding issues.[246]

Curbing the power of the market was needed, and Schmidt suggested the inclusion of comprehensive financial market regulation for the Eurozone, separation of commercial banks from investment, and shadow banks, including the banning of Futures short selling and trade in not officially sanctioned derivatives. He also called for restricting the unregulated rating agencies of the Eurozone.[247] Finally, he warned against an austerity policy that led to deflation and reminded us to read about the consequences of Heinrich Brünings deflation policies from 1930 to 1932 (after the hyperinflation). Schmidt called for growth policies, warning policymakers that growth policies that create jobs are required to reach budget goals.[248]

---

244 Helmut Kohl quoted in: Deutscher Bundestag, Stenographischer Bericht, 11. Wahlperiode, 210. Sitzung. Bonn, Donnerstag, den 10. Mai 1990, (Bonn, 1990). pp. 16470–16472.
245 Michael J. Baun, The Maastricht Treaty as High Politics: Germany, France and European Integration, in: Political Science Quarterly, Vol. 110, No.4, Winter (1995–1996), (New York City, 1996), pp. 605–624.
246 Helmut Schmidt, Germany in and with and for Europe. Speech at the SPD party conference, 4 December 2011, Berlin, Online: https://library.fes.de/pdf-files/id/ipa/08888.pdf, (Berlin, 2011).
247 Ibid.
248 Ibid.

Before he died, Kohl also called for politicians to remember the political foundation of the EMU and a common currency. He argued that despite comments by pundits, it is correct to say that despite the challenges and the passage of time since the end of the Second World War, the original intention behind the European Union – to unite the continent in peace – remains as relevant as ever. Kohl wrote in *Bild* in February 2012: "A look beyond one's nose into history shows: the evil spirits of the past are in no way banished, they can always return."[249]

The Nobel Peace Prize received by the EU underscores the achievements made so far for peace in Europe and, at the same time, underscores how tentative that peace could be. Kohl's comment is relevant: "Europe remains a question of war and peace, and the idea of peace the motivation behind European integration." Kohl has pleaded for political leaders not to "allow the discussion and the crisis in Greece to lose sight of a unified Europe," he believes, "The opposite is the case: we need – above all now – more and not less Europe."[250] The Nobel Committee has weighed-in to support the political will that is needed.

In the end, a vision needs the political will to implement it. Years of European summitry, multilateral consultations, and innovative proposals have not ended the protracted Eurozone crisis. Mustering political will is tough when governments all around are flirting with failure, and tens of thousands of protestors are taking to the streets against austerity. Observers have focused on the policy debate – austerity versus growth – that led to the rise of populism in Hungary, Poland, France, Italy, and Germany. Germany's economic strength so dominated that it lacked leaders, such as a weaker France, to join it in partnership. As a result, Germany dominated the resolution to the sovereign debt crisis in the Eurozone. That was until ECB President Mario Draghi announced that the ECB would do whatever it would take to resolve the crisis. Will it act in concert with its European partners in the future to achieve political union?

Even the Polish leadership has weighed in on the need to keep Europe together through the crisis. In his Berlin speech on November 28, 2011, Radek Sikorski made the political point that the EMU is condemned to succeed. He quoted German philosopher Jürgen Habermas: "If the European project fails, then there is the question of how long it will take to reach the status quo again. Remember

---

[249] Original: Der Blick über den Tellerrand und in die Geschichte macht deutlich: Die bösen Geister der Vergangenheit sind keineswegs gebannt, sie können wieder zurückkommen, in Helmut Kohl, Wie soll das Europa der Zukunft aussehen?, in: Bild Zeitung, Online: https://www.bild.de/politik/inland/helmut-kohl/wie-soll-europa-in-zukunft-aussehen-22864952.bild.html, (Hamburg, 2012).
[250] Judy Dempsey, Is European Integration Still a Question of War and Peace?, in: Carnegie Europe, Online: https://carnegieeurope.eu/strategiceurope/49651, (Brussels, 2012).

the German Revolution of 1848: When it failed, it took us 100 years to regain the same level of democracy as before."[251]

Finally, even the committed Eurosceptic Martin Feldstein writing in Foreign Affairs magazine admitted that looking ahead, the "Eurozone is likely to continue with almost all its current members."[252] European leaders can undoubtedly decide that countries as diverse in political and social culture, productivity, and taxation as the Eurozone members can come together to establish the European Monetary Union with the Euro as its currency.

Emmanuel Macron and Angela Merkel: Vision for the Eurozone

Will a renewed vision for Europe inspire sovereign obligation from the member states for European integration or political union? Ashoka Mody, in his book *Euro Tragedy*, suggests tragedy can be defined as a French vision with German rules. Macron's French ideas for Europe are still waiting in expectation of German rules.[253]

Chancellor Merkel had a vision of a future European government structure in which the European Commission would act as the executive branch of government reporting to a strong European Parliament. In her view, the Council of Europe would function as a second chamber, the European Court of Justice, as the highest authority.[254] The German Chancellor named two elements of crucial importance for the future of the Eurozone. Namely, greater financial market policy integration based on functioning and robust financial markets as well as greater fiscal policy integration by adopting the fiscal compact, which creates greater economic policy integration. In a monetary union, for instance, it's not possible to keep on demanding that governments gear national policies to strengthening competitiveness as the basis for long-term growth and employment or to enforce such policies.[255] Commission President Jean-Claude Juncker

---

251 Radoslaw Sikorski, Deutsche Macht fürchte ich wenigeeöer als Deutsche Untätigkeit, Speech at the Deutsche Gesellschaft für Auswärtige Politik, Online: https://dgap.org/de/veranstaltungen/deutsche-macht-fuerchte-ich-heute-weniger-als-deutsche-untaetigkeit, (Berlin, 2011b).
252 Martin Feldstein, The Failure of the Euro. The Little Currency That Couldn't, in: Foreign Affairs, Vol. 91, No.1, (January-February 2012), (Washington D.C., 2012), pp. 105–116.
253 Ashoka Mody, *EuroTragedy: A Drama in Nine Acts*, (Oxford University Press New York, 2018); Joseph E. Stiglitz, *The Euro: How a Common Currency Threatens the Future of Europe* (W.W. Norton: New York City, 2016).
254 Quentin Peel, Germany and Europe: A very Federal Formula, in: Financial Times, Online: https://www.ft.com/content/31519b4a-5307-11e1-950d-00144feabdc0, (London, 2012).
255 Robin Alexander, Merkels Tritte gegen den CDU Wirtschaftsrat, 12, in: Die Welt, Online: https://www.welt.de/politik/deutschland/article106533001/Merkels-Tritte-gegen-den-CDU-Wirtschaftsrat.html, (Berlin, 2012).

started informal negotiations for an agreement to make the Eurozone more resilient based on lessons learned from the crisis.

At the Sorbonne in September 2017, French President Emmanuel Macron presented a vision to complete Europe's monetary union. His initiative for the European Monetary Union was a clearly stated case for the political union:

> Europe alone can enable us to take action in the world, in the face of the significant contemporary challenges. Only Europe can, in a word, guarantee genuine sovereignty or our ability to exist in today's world to defend our values and interests. European sovereignty requires constructing, and we must do it. Confronted with each of these challenges, we now need to take tangible action. The first key, the foundation of any political community, is security. The final key to our sovereignty is industrial and monetary economic power. Making the heart of Europe an economic and industrial power naturally requires energy and digital technology policies. But long-term economic power can only be built around a single currency, which is why I am so firmly attached to the ambitions of the Eurozone. Because it is through this Economic and Monetary Union, at its heart, that we can create the heart of an integrated Europe.[256]

In the age-old debate over relinquishing sovereignty – the power to tax and spend – Macron realistically noted that no mechanism would magically solve all Eurozone problems. If there were one, the Europeans would have already created it. Pooling past debts and solving public financing problems in each other's countries are secondary. Macron has argued for a:

> long-term economic and political strategy to work out how the Eurozone economic power can compete with China and the United States. It is to create jobs and ensure that today's generation of young people is not destined for unemployment because of our failures and instability![257]

Macron's views demonstrate the real and unresolved dilemma for all in the EU: The EU founding fathers were motivated by domestic reasons and developed mechanisms to cope with internal European challenges. The Eurozone problem had a domestic and an international dimension, which has impacted the EU. Since 2008, instability has exposed the EU, which has not developed appropriate mechanisms to cope with it. Macron is the first to rethink those two dimensions – domestic (that is: EU) handling of internal challenges and international pressure and opportunities.

Chancellor Angela Merkel and President Emmanuel Macron have renewed the Franco-German partnership by exploring new ways in pursuit of a vision to complete the EMU. However, when the Bundestag election in September 2017 failed to form a government quickly, Europe drifted. Macron stepped into the

---

256 Emmanuel Macron, Initiative for Europe, Online: http://international.blogs.ouest-france.fr/archive/2017/09/29/macron-sorbonne-verbatim-europe-18583.html, (Paris, 2017).
257 Ibid.

vacuum to present a new French vision for Europe and monetary union but had to wait months for the Germans to form a government. Once again, Europe needs Germany and France as the engine of Europe to exercise Leadership in Partnership. The Franco-German tandem is a necessary, but not a sufficient precondition for success and compromise. Whether economic and monetary structures can pave the path to a political union will be tested. Can France and Germany inspire the other member states to commit to the European Commission's next steps on the road to the economic and monetary union?

With the signing of the Rome Declaration on March 25, 2017, European Union leaders reaffirmed their commitment to "working towards completing the Economic and Monetary Union; a Union where economies converge" and discovered the political will to implement it.[258] The EU has to overcome resistance found on three fronts. First, to reverse sufficiently the social and economic divergences between and within euro area members that emerged from the financial crisis. Second, to address centrifugal forces that are likely to weaken citizens' support for the Euro, creating different perceptions of the challenges, rather a vision for the future. Finally, while the EMU is more durable, to make it more shock-proof.[259]

It is in Germany's interest to take into account other Eurozone countries' interests when facing economic and financial difficulties. The Eurozone is in a continuing, severe crisis that undermines the foundation of deeper monetary integration. Solving the Eurozone crisis requires a commitment to the principles of shared sovereignty and sovereign obligation to Europe.[260] France has taken a leadership role from the beginning of the European Monetary Union. Successive German Chancellors have exercised German sovereignty to fulfill its commitments to Europe while remaining extremely risk-averse to financial transfers to other countries. For example, ruling out bailouts and seeking safe European assets – Eurobonds, Eurobills, sovereign bond-backed securities (SSBS), Blue-Red Bonds, and E-bonds that would help to create a liquid Euro area bond market.[261] The open question is whether German Chancellors are presenting a gradual trend of accepting compromises to win others in favor of German stability while enduring shared financial and decision-making understandings?

Macron and Merkel must deliver on this European promise as it:

---

[258] European Commission, *Reflection Paper on the Deepening of the Economic and Monetary Union*, European Commission COM(2017) 291, (Brussels, 2017).
[259] Ibid.
[260] Richard N. Haass, World Order 2.0, The Case for Sovereign Obligation, in: Foreign Affairs, January/February 2017, Online: https://www.foreignaffairs.com/articles/2016-12-12/world-order-20, (Congers, 2017).
[261] Marco Buti, Servaas Deroose, José Laeandro and Gabriele Giudice, Completing EMU, in: Vox. CEPR Policy Portal, Online: https://voxeu.org/article/completing-emu, (London, 2017).

requires political courage, a shared vision, and the determination to act in the common interest of Europe to work towards... a Union where...a stable and further strengthened single currency open avenues for growth, cohesion, competitiveness, innovation, and exchange, especially for small and medium-sized enterprises; a Union promoting sustained and sustainable growth, through investment, structural reforms and working towards completing the Economic and Monetary Union; a Union where economies converge.[262]

Where is the EMU Headed?

Can the Franco-German partnership take up Macron's ideas to create a Eurozone budget or cash drawing authority from the EU? Is a Eurozone finance minister that shifts of the sovereign power to tax from member states to the EU, acceptable? Only through commitments to the collective good will Europeans be able to act while their citizens still believe in the need for an integrated Europe. That belief supports the survival of the Eurozone. The success of the Euro and the long struggle for European political union demand the political will to pool sovereignty for the common good.

Solving Germany's leadership dilemma will determine whether carrying out its sovereign obligation to Europe through Leadership in Partnership can achieve political union or end in tragedy. Are German policies, such as austerity, restrained by its history? Deeply ingrained in the political culture is one of remembrance (*Errinerungskultur*) and a Germany as a civilian power (*Zivilmacht*) that indeed curb political excesses, but also allow Germany to lead Europe with partners.

Strategically, there is no doubt that the Eurozone crisis affects the U.S. and global economies. For Americans, there is a good reason to carefully follow how the Europeans seize the chance of this crisis to strengthen their global position. The political process toward political union will focus on common foreign and defense policies as well as competitiveness, trade, climate change, and energy security. Macron noted that America's role in protecting and sheltering Europe is evaporating. The global strategist George Friedman has noted:

> In the last half of the past decade, the inability to end the wars in Iraq and Afghanistan, coupled with economic problems, convinced reasonable people that the United States had entered an age of permanent decline. The sort of power the United States has does not dissipate that fast. The disintegration of European unity and the financial crisis

---

262 Ibid.

facing China have left the United States, not surprisingly, still the unchallenged global power.[263]

Europe is re-shaping itself, and the future of a more integrated Europe will demand national sovereignty that includes obligations to Brussels. Europeans have and must continue to pool their sovereignty. If national governments preserve their interests in European peace and prosperity, they can exercise national sovereignty by deciding in favor of a common fiscal and monetary policy. Can they create a European Finance Ministry with the power to tax? That would be one step on the way to political union. Chancellor Merkel had a guiding principle for resolution of the 2010 Eurozone crisis: Germany would support the periphery, but control would still come from the center.

Over the past two decades, united Germany has accepted its responsibility for EU political integration, including the European Monetary Union, by introducing the common currency through the Euro, and resolving recurring Euro crises. The role of Germany and its politics now, as it was during the Eurozone debt crisis, are causing great concern in the global economy.

The sovereign debt crisis in the Eurozone defies analysis in part because it is more than a financial issue and because Europe is not a country, a federation, nor a confederation – it is a political process among the 27 nations of the EU and the 17 states of the Eurozone. Complex crisis management requires many players and factors in the EU decision-making mechanics, not only Franco-German Leadership in Partnership. Historically, national interests and a shared commitment to Europe have helped the EU through critical decisions on European Monetary Union. The Euro is evidence of its 20 years of success and of what French-German leadership has brought to Europe. Always underlying the European Union is its founding aim: Ending the frequent and bloody wars between neighbors.[264] Securing a lasting peace through economic and political unity should remain the goal.

A vision exists. The building blocks for the EMU are:
- An integrated financial framework through the European Central Bank (ECB),
- A joint deposit insurance corporation and the European Stability Mechanism (ESM), which could evolve into a European Monetary Fund;
- A unified budgetary framework with a fiscal compact with the ECOFIN Commissioner's oversight for member state compliance;
- An integrated economic policy framework (competition, labor markets, and sustainable pension systems);

---

263 George Friedman, The Elections, Gridlock and Foreign Policy, in: Stratfor, Online: https://worldview.stratfor.com/article/elections-gridlock-and-foreign-policy, (Austin, 2012).
264 European Union, The history of the European Union, Online: https://europa.eu/european-union/about-eu/history_en, (Brussels, 2020).

- Measures to ensure democratic legitimacy and accountability (through deeper involvement of the European Parliament).[265]

However, John Mearsheimer, in his essay "Bound to Fail, The Rise and Fall of the Liberal International Order," warns that the Eurozone crisis lingers on. Not only has the crisis exposed the fragility of the Euro, but it also created intense animosity between Germany and Greece, among other political problems.[266] He argues that the euro is a crucial feature of the Liberal International Order, even though it is part of a strictly European institution.[267] When the EU established the Euro currency in 1999, it represented a giant step forward in promoting monetary union among the member states. However, there was neither a fiscal nor political union to help underpin the euro. Critics at the time predicted that without a fiscal and political union, significant problems would plague the Euro. Many advocates recognized the problem but thought that monetary union would ultimately lead to the union on all three fronts, thus eliminating the problem. But that did not happen, and the euro encountered it's a first major crisis in 2009, which produced not just economic issues, but political problems as well. The crisis and the ensuing attempts to solve it have brought hard-edged nationalist sentiment to the surface in Europe.[268]

Mearsheimer concluded that the EU had not made a significant move toward a fiscal and political union, and that means more crises are likely in the years ahead, which will further undermine not only the EU but the liberal international order more generally.[269]

Many questions remain that Germany must choose between its national interests and its commitment to Europe. Can France and Germany, as leaders in partnership, reach such an agreement with the other EU Members. Is that a deal emerging to set the path for a more integrated Europe for the next century? France and Germany, as Leaders in Partnership, can lead if they find the political will. Governments stills have many institutional issues still to resolve after the

---

265 Roel Beetsma, Niels Thygesen, Alessandro Cugnasca, Eloïse Orseau, Polyvios Eliofotou and Stefano Santacroce, Reforming the EU fiscal framework: A proposal by the European Fiscal Board, in: Vox CEPR Policy Portal, Online: https://voxeu.org/article/reforming-eu-fiscal-framework-proposal-european-fiscal-board, (Brussels, 2018).
266 John J. Mearsheimer, quoted in: Claudia Sternberg, Kira Gartzou-Katsouyanni and Kalypso Nicolaidis, *The Greco-German Affair in the Euro Crisis: Mutual Recognition Lost?* (Palgrave Macmillan: London, 2018), p. 41.
267 John J. Mearsheimer quoted in: Ashoka Mody, *EuroTragedy: A Drama in Nine Acts*, (Oxford University Press New York, 2018); Joseph E. Stiglitz, *The Euro: How a Common Currency Threatens the Future of Europe* (W.W. Norton: New York City, 2016).
268 John J. Mearsheimer, Bound to Fail, The Rise and Fall of the Liberal International Order, in: International Security, Vol. 43, No. 4 (Cambridge, U.S.A., 2019), pp. 7–50.
269 Ibid.

2008–2009 financial crisis. The vision of Europe with the Single Market as the basis for growth and economic development includes pillars proposed by the foreign ministers. Unresolved are Germany's substantial trade surpluses, austerity policies aimed at a balanced budget. More consumption within Germany and more productivity in Germany's export recipient countries are vital in ending the crisis. In the short term, the EU will seek to manage the debt crisis over the next few years, but in the long run, it must work to establish treaties that involve new European structures, and perhaps even political union.

As Olaf Scholz wrote an article in November 2019: "The need to deepen and complete European banking union is undeniable."[270] Once London's capital markets leave the EU with Brexit, and Europe should not be dependent on the United States or China for financial services. He went on to suggest collective insolvency and resolution procedure for banks, reducing the number of non-performing loans and risk from sovereign debt, banking union with a common European deposit insurance mechanism, and a common corporate tax base and a minimum effective tax and uniform taxation of banks to prevent arbitrage.[271] In response, Tony Barber commented on the 'arduous path' ahead in the plan to complete Europe's banking union. He stated: "The answers lie in Germany's unruly domestic politics, its leader's gradual reassessment of the nation's standing and the broader problems of EU integration."[272] While the Scholz plan will meet resistance over the conditions he has placed on bank regulation and a common corporate tax, it is a bold plan.

The deeper problem of this short illustrative review of Germany's decision dilemmas is its coalition governments and its *Ressortprinzip* of constitutional independence for its ministries. Overcoming those obstacles is the subject of part three of this book, a process for strategic foresight in the German Government.

---

270 Olaf Scholz, Germany will consider EU-wide bank deposit reinsurance, in: Financial Times, Online: https://www.ft.com/content/82624c98-ff14-11e9-a530-16c6c29e70ca, (London, 2019).
271 Ibid.
272 Tony Barber, Germany's Eurozone gambit could meet a swift death, in: Financial Times, Online: https://www.google.com/search?channel=trow2&client=firefox-b-d&q=Barber%2C+Tony%2C+%E2%80%9CGermany%E2%80%99s+Eurozone+gambit+could+meet+a+swift+death%2C%E2%80%9D+Financial+Times%2C+November+8%2C+2019, (London, 2019).

Chapter 6: Civilian Power or Security Guarantor, Peacekeeper or Peacemaker

> Deutschland? Aber wo liegt es? Ich weiß das Land nicht zu finden,
> wo das gelehrte beginnt, hört das politische auf.
> – Friedrich Schiller[273]

Sovereign Obligation and Security Operations

Germany's history is an obstacle to its national security debate. The process of unifying Germany 30 years ago raised the specter of Germany's history of militarism, which culminated in the disaster of two world wars and revived the German Question of its place in Europe. Through years of debate, Germany, its European neighbors, and the United States agreed that a unified Germany should find its security in NATO. Now that paradigm has come into question as the United States pushes away from its commitment to NATO Article 5. Will Germany help Europe fill the vacuum left by America's de-commitment to NATO? Can the *Bundeswehr* attain a leading role in security politics? How much of an active or influential role in Europe should the nation have? What does it mean to be a Leader in Partnership in matters of security? Can Europeans accept German leadership? Can a sovereign Germany lead, but not dominate, Europe? Will Germany lead the strategic debate for Europe's future as a pillar in the transatlantic relationship?

The German Problem of leadership in exercising national sovereignty and its sovereign-obligation to Europe appears in security issues as well. For the past three decades to ensure peace and prosperity, the country has relied on the European Union's economic policy and the NATO alliance's strategic deterrence and defense. Germany has not made all its decisions in concert with other European countries. Leadership, in its most basic form, after all, is a somewhat asymmetrical relationship between actors who influence the behavior of others. While this coercive model of singularity in leadership has been used time and time again in international relations, it is no longer a feasible or desirable approach, especially not for Germany. Consequently, Germany has relied on partners in leadership to implement its civilian power model.

---

273 "Germany? But where does it lie? I don't know where to find the nation. I know not where to find the land where the scholarly begins, and the political ends." Poem written together with Johann Wolfgang von Goethe. Poem: Das Deutsche Reich, Xenien.

The need for leaders in partnership stems, of course, partly from Germany's national history. German Marshall Fund scholar Jan Techau argues:

> [To] come to terms with itself after the Third Reich and re-establish itself as a sovereign state, Germany created a strategic posture of restraint, passivity, and multilateralism in its foreign policy. The 1950s acceptance of Germany into NATO, as well as the creation of European Coal and Steel Community and the European Economic Community, underlined the post-war tendency of Germany to think as a team player reluctant to lead.[274]

Not only was Germany reluctant to lead, and to some extent continues to be; hesitant for the same historical reasons, Germany as a unilateral leader of Europe was and remains virtually unthinkable to its allies in Europe and beyond. Domestically and internationally, due to historical responsibility and obligation, Germany is in no position to be *the* leader of Europe alone.

There are additional restraints on Germany's ability to lead. The re-emergent multipolar world order does not allow for independent leaders who freely impose their vision of the international system on others. The complex interdependence of international relations and the unprecedentedly broad dispersion of power in the global order today severely constrain even the most authoritarian of leaders' ability to influence others. The playing field level but at the same time, issue areas such as climate change or financial markets are inherently ungovernable for a single actor.

Finally, German unilateral leadership nearly impossible. The country is deeply embedded in a web of multilateral structures. The EU's principle of pooled sovereignty inherently rules out the one-sided decision-making processes required for singular leadership. In return, it also shares power and distributes responsibility among more actors.

German President Frank-Walter Steinmeier, speaking at the Munich Security Conference in 2016, warned against Germany using the refugee crisis to turn away from the world. He endorsed political negotiations with all parties – the United States, Russia, Europe, and regional players such as Turkey, Saudi Arabia, and Iran – to make a settlement possible. He also called on all parties to take responsibility not only for their own but also for regional security. Germany has engaged in the military fight against Daesh, or ISIS, by providing military equipment to the Peshmerga. Germany has also sought agreement in Libya and has continued to support the United Nations. It is necessary to recognize the unwelcome realities that come with conflicts, eroding international order, and

---

274 Dimitri Trenin and Jan Techau, Germany's Changing Role in a Changing Europe, in: Carnegie Europe, Online: https://carnegieeurope.eu/2013/03/27/germany-s-changing-role-in-changing-europe-event-4034, (Brussels, 2013).

non-state actors. Steinmeier set the course for his country to start taking responsibility to ensure that Germany does not leave the world as it has found it.[275]

Chancellor Merkel decided to increase defense spending. That decision was another essential step toward building Germany's defense posture to meet its security needs. Germany can afford it. The fight against the Islamic State and the resettlement of Syrian war refugees remain unresolved, and peace will require much more systematic cooperation between neighboring regions. The goal should be the sharing of responsibility beyond the borders of economic or political systems. Journalist Matthias Nass[276] has explained how former U.S. President Obama's cautionary strategy and reluctance to send ground troops to the Middle East demonstrated that the United States was stepping back from its role as an independent, world policeman. Now that President Trump has retreated even more from an international leadership role, Europe will have to accept more responsibility for its neighborhood, and that includes the Middle East.

In addition to more responsibility, Euro-Atlantic governments need to re-energize alliances between societies and intensify collaboration with others to develop joint strategies. Leaders in Partnership- are needed now more than ever. The role of France and Germany as leaders in Europe lies in the historical, political, and economic weight of these two countries. Following the Second World War, reconciliation between France and Germany meant locking them in cooperation. As we have seen, Franco-German initiatives advanced European integration through the European Monetary System. These initiatives have also brought about closer political cooperation, the Schengen agreements, and continued partnership with other European countries. The Franco-German *axis* represents a subset of the negotiations on the European scene. Most importantly, it has radically reduced the number of negotiators involved, which increases the likelihood of finding a compromise solution.

The benefits of letting France and Germany lead depends on the acceptance of their initiatives by others. In 2002, the rejection by France and Germany of the U.S. intervention in Iraq unleashed a debate that demonstrated that the new EU member states did not necessarily have the same geostrategic outlook as Paris and Berlin, which has led to distinct coalitions emerging as a result. Certain countries showed an aversion to what they saw as German-French hegemonic

---

[275] Frank-Walter Steinmeier, Rede des Bundesministers für Auswärtiges, Dr. Frank-Walter Steinmeier zur Eröffnung der Münchner Sicherheitskonferenz am 13. Februar 2018, Online https://www.bundesregierung.de/breg-de/service/bulletin/rede-des-bundesministers-des-a uswaertigen-dr-frank-walter-steinmeier-796670, (München, 2018).
[276] Matthias Naß, Amerikas Rückzug auf Raten. Eine Kolumne von Matthias Naß, in: Zeit Online, Online: https://www.zeit.de/politik/ausland/2016-03/barack-obama-rueckzug-usa-mittlerer-osten-verantwortung-europa, (Hamburg, 2016).

ambitions.[277] The U.S. Administration reacted to the Franco-German rejection and the subsequent dissent by suggesting there was a new Europe willing to act and an old Europe free-riding on U.S. security. At the unification of Germany, the opportunity to invite Poland into 'Leaders in Partnership' was missed. That opportunity lost has had consequences for European unity with East-Central European countries.

How can a state pursue its interests if it cannot influence the behavior of others? The answer is that it can seek instead to influence the international agenda; it can find the support of like-minded states to build sufficient international consensus for a particular decision. The Normandy format is an example of the flexible and goal-oriented strategic principle of Leaders in Partnership. Germany cannot go it alone. Germany is not the "Leader of Europe"; it must build European support if not consensus before making a decision. Otherwise, it forfeits its right to distribute obligations and must bear full responsibility. This unilateral move was evident in the 2015 migration crisis. Fears arose that Germany might overstrain its capacities by taking in so many refugees. This problem needed a long-term solution. By attacking the refugee crisis at its core, Germany showed solidarity in the fight against violent extremists.

Like in the previous chapter, the following summaries seek to illuminate the German dilemmas of choosing between national interests and commitments to the greater commons, Europe, and the transatlantic relationship.

1991: Recognition of Croatia and Slovenia in Balkan Wars

Germany took charge of the recognition of Croatia and Slovenia in the breakup of Yugoslavia. The German Problem of choosing between national sovereignty and sovereign obligation to partners arose soon after unification. In 1991, the dissolution of the Soviet Union greatly impacted Yugoslavia. Serbian President Slobodan Milošević seized power and began his consolidation of Serbian rule over the Yugoslav republics with his rally at the Kosovo Polje Battlefield with a speech about the 600th anniversary of the defeat of the Serb Kingdom by the Turks, which foreshadowed the violent breakup of Yugoslavia through nationalism.[278]

---

277 Jeremy Shapiro, Matthew Browne, Carlos Closa, Søren Dosenrode, Franciszek Draus and Philippe de Schoutheete, A View from Outside the Franco-German Couple as seen by their Partners. Our Europe, President: Jacques Delors Institute, Group E'tude et de Recherches, (Brussels, 2005).Our Europe, President: Jacques Delors Institute, Group E'tude et de Recherches, (Brussels, 2006).
278 Radio Free Europe, Timeline: The Political Career of Slobodan Milosevic, Online: https://www.rferl.org/a/1066641.html, (Prague, 2006).

The internal conflict came after the Gulf War when the American-led coalition defeated Saddam Hussein and restored Kuwait. The George H.W. Bush Administration's preoccupation with the Gulf War and Russia left Americans reluctant to intervene in Yugoslavia's internal conflict. The U.S. had focused its attention on the dissolution of the Soviet Union and thought it had no dog in the Yugoslavia fight. The U.S. chose not to have NATO intervene militarily against any party using force in Yugoslavia. The Europeans thought they could solve the crisis; it would be the first test of European power.

German Foreign Minister Hans-Dietrich Genscher, as chairman of the CSCE Council of Ministers, traveled to Belgrade in July 1991 shortly after Slovenia and Croatia announced their independence. The Yugoslav-Slovene War started on June 27 and lasted only ten days. This short conflict effectively opened the way for Slovenian independence. However, Croatian President Franjo Tuđjman had no clear borders with which to establish the country's independence. Consequently, Milošević's war against Croatia began shortly after the Slovene War to establish territory.

To internationalize and therefore end the conflict, Genscher insisted on EU recognition of the independence of Slovenia and Croatia. Most of Germany's partners, especially Britain, had grave doubts. They feared that such a move at the close of 1991 was premature and would undoubtedly trigger military conflict between Serbia and the two republics. Nevertheless, Germany pressed hard for the recognition of Croatia as an independent nation. In the end, Genscher's effort to deploy CSCE to end the violence was unsuccessful. Milošević was determined to conduct politics by other means that left little room for negotiations. A UN mission that included former UK Foreign Secretary Lord Carrington and U.S. Secretary of State Cyrus Vance sought ceasefires that did not hold.[279]

Germany presented its case in the November 1991 Franco-German Summit. French President Mitterrand sought a policy that would protect minorities and borders before recognition. On the other hand, German Chancellor Kohl argued that he was obligated to recognize Croatia citing domestic demands and the sizeable Croatian community of 500,000 in Germany at the time. However, Kohl had no answer as to whether necessary German or European military enforcement could back that diplomatic initiative. The French view was that Germany was pursuing a unilateral course. U.S. Secretary of State Cyrus Vance and U.K. Foreign Secretary Lord Carrington, seeking a negotiated settlement with Milosevic, warned that "recognizing Croatia would trigger a chain reaction culminating in a war in Bosnia."[280] Genscher ignored these counterarguments and told

---

[279] Richard Holbrooke, *To End a War: The Conflict in Yugoslavia – America's Inside Story*, (Modern Library: New York City, 1998), p. 31.
[280] Ibid.

his colleagues that if they did not support him, Germany would recognize Croatia unilaterally.[281] The Europeans followed and recognized Croatia and Slovenia.

Unity among the Europeans was at risk just as the Maastricht Treaty negotiation had reached a concluding decision point. The Maastricht Treaty, which was an essential German project for the European Union with implications for a European common foreign and security policy, was concluding days apart from the decision to recognize Croatia. European unity regarding the recognition of Croatia was the top priority for Germany. The Guardian reported later in 2016 that Genscher denied that he agreed to a secret deal involving German concessions on British opt-outs from the Maastricht treaty in return for joint EU recognition of the two former Yugoslav republics. The Guardian concluded: "Genscher will forever be associated with a move that put an end to Western hopes for a negotiated solution to the break-up of the Yugoslav federation."[282] In an interview with Deutsche Welle in 2011, Genscher argued that Bosnia's independence was not recognized at the same time because developments had not yet reached that point. He said, "I am convinced it was important to focus first on Slovenia and Croatia, where a war was raging."[283] By the beginning of 1992, the fighting in Croatia stopped with an agreement reached, but when Krajina Serbs challenged established borders a few years later, war broke out.[284]

While the war in Bosnia escalated because the West would not intervene, the decision to recognize Croatian independence was a strategic mistake that accelerated the outbreak of war in Bosnia. It also failed to prevent the Krajina War in 1995. Germany had exercised its national sovereignty and prevailed over international objections, bringing the Europeans to recognize Croatia. This success had required a careful balancing act of conflicting dilemmas. The European Community, following German leadership, recognized the independence of Croatia on December 16, 1991, and the EU agreed to implement it on January 15, 1992, allowing Germany to show it did not act unilaterally before the implementation. Genscher told the meeting of the European Foreign Ministers:

> …Of course, we [Germans] would adhere to that and would take no steps without a European Community decision. And we did adhere to the decision concerning this

---

281 Hans-Dieter Heumann, *Hans-Dieter Genscher, Die Biographie*, (Ferdindand Schönigh: Meppen/Emsland, 2011), pp. 296–297.
282 Richard Nelsson, How Milosevic stripped Kosovo's autonomy – archive, 1989, in: The Guardian, https://www.theguardian.com/world/from-the-archive-blog/2019/mar/20/how-milosevic-stripped-kosovos-autonomy-archive-1989, (London, 2019).
283 Hans-Dietrich Genscher quoted in: Deutsche Welle, Recognizing Slovenia, Croatia brought peace, Genscher says, in: Deutsche Welle, Online: https://www.dw.com/en/recognizing-slovenia-croatia-brought-peace-genscher-says/a-15182463, (Bonn, 2011).
284 Richard Holbrooke, *To End a War: The Conflict in Yugoslavia – America's Inside Story*, (Modern Library: New York City, 1998), p. 39.

issue. We made the decision to recognize the states on December 23, but it didn't go into effect until January 15, 1992. At that time, all the other European Community member states recognized the two countries, too. From the start, Germany said it would not go it alone. And, as I've said, the decision was unanimous. And it brought peace. As a result of the conflict becoming more international, in early January 1992 Milosevic declared the war to be over – the war he himself had started against the two republics. So that shows it was a decision that brought peace.[285]

However, the exclusion of Bosnia from recognition at the same time was a strategic mistake that would expose Bosnians to the nationalist wrath of the Serbs in a genocidal war. The bold act in 1991, which led the way for international diplomatic recognition of Croatia and Slovenia, tested the German culture of restraint and its lack of military capability to enforce its decisions. This recognition essentially turned the Yugoslavian civil war into a conflict in which European powers more or less took sides. The national push for internationalizing the war in Yugoslavia did not end the conflict. Instead, war and ethnic cleansing challenged the Germans to act. Still, limitations on Germany's military role, which had intensified, also dragged America into the conflict despite its lack of vital interests in the area.

When Germany and the EU were unable to prevent the escalating military conflict, a bitter experience ensued for the United States, Germany, the EU, and the UN. Only after military intervention and negotiations ended the genocide in Bosnia and the ethnic cleansing in Kosovo, was an uneasy end to hostilities achieved. This early transatlantic rift over deploying military forces continues in disputes over military capabilities in war, peacekeeping and nation-building. The German public has not yet accepted the adage of Frederick the Great: "Diplomacy without arms is like an orchestra without instruments."

1994: Bundeswehr Deployments and the Basic Law

Constitutional debates are critical to *Bundeswehr* deployments. Germany's security policy has encompassed protecting, when vitally necessary, the inviolability of human dignity under Article I of the German Basic Law. Germans follow a firmly established policy to protect human dignity through its commitments to military interventions in cases of ethnic cleansing, genocide, crimes against humanity, and war crimes under the United Nations' principle of the Responsibility to Protect. R2P is not international law.

---

[285] Hans-Dietrich Genscher quoted in: Deutsche Welle, Recognizing Slovenia, Croatia brought peace, Genscher says, in: Deutsche Welle, Online: https://www.dw.com/en/recognizing-slovenia-croatia-brought-peace-genscher-says/a-15182463, (Bonn, 2011).

The German High Court set limits on modern German military engagements through its interpretation of the German constitution in a decision handed down on July 12, 1994.[286] That decision, specifically authorizing German *Luftwaffe* crews on Airborne Warning and Control System (AWACS) missions outside of the NATO area, examined and affirmed the constitutionality of German international military deployments. The court relied on Article 24.2 of the Basic Law, which requires that Germany's deployments be part of a collective security system, and Article 59.2, which stipulates that the Bundestag must approve the mutual collective security.[287] By agreeing to the constitutionality of *Bundeswehr* deployments outside Germany, the High Court ended the strictly territorial defense role of the postwar German military. It extended it to out-of-area deployments governed by specific parliamentary mandates.

A journalist at President Clinton's news conference with European Union Leaders Helmut Kohl and Jacques Delors in Berlin, Germany, on July 12, 1994, asked both President Bill Clinton and Chancellor Helmut Kohl about the Court's decision. I attended that press conference as Ambassador Richard Holbrooke's deputy chief of mission of the U.S. Embassy in Berlin. During the press conference, the U.S. Consulate in Stuttgart, which was following the German Constitutional Court's deliberations on the AWACS case closely, called to inform me the court had decided that the *Bundeswehr* could deploy outside NATO's territory. I slipped a note about the decision to the president's valet, who handed it to President Clinton during the press conference. Although the press conference was about the European Union, the journalist engaged the president and the chancellor in this exchange on German out-of-area military deployments.

> Q. Mr. President, please permit me, a German journalist, to revisit a question that has to do with Germany taking on a greater role, taking more responsibility in the world. On that point, you are in agreement with Chancellor Kohl. Now, does the idea of German armed forces being involved in peacekeeping missions outside NATO, does that mean that you are totally comfortable with that? Aren't you the least bit uncomfortable thinking about that? And could it also mean that you could imagine German forces being involved in missions of the kind we had two years ago in the Gulf, for instance? Would that be all right?
>
> A: President Clinton. I am completely comfortable with that. And of course, I can envision German forces being involved in something like the United Nations effort in the Gulf. Why? Because of the leadership of Germany, because of the conduct of

---

286 Bundesverfassungsgericht [BVerfG] [Federal Constitutional Court] July 12, 1994, 90 Entscheidungen des Bundesverfassungsgerichts [BVerfGE] 286 (F.R.G)], Online: https://www.servat.unibe.ch/dfr/bv090286.html, (Karlsruhe, 1994).
287 Helmut P. Aust and Mindia Vashakmadze, Parliamentary Consent to the Use of German Armed Forces Abroad: The 2008 Decision of the Federal Constitutional Court in the AWACS/Turkey Case, German L.J. 2223, 2223 (2008), p. 286.

Germany, because of the role Germany has played in developing the European Union, because of the values Germany has demonstrated in taking of hundreds of thousands of refugees from Bosnia. Germany, now united is – yes, it's the largest country in Europe in terms of population and its economic strength. But Germany has been the leader in pushing for the integration of Europe, for the sharing of power among the European nations, and for setting a standard for humane conduct and support for democracy and diversity. So, the answer to that question is, yes, I am comfortable with it.

A: Kohl. One minute, I would like to add something, if I may. I feel a tendency here among you to somehow apply the constitutional court decision to the – [inaudible]. Since that is so, I would like to say that we will be deciding on the case-by-case basis with the majority in Parliament and that following the court's ruling, **we are not feeling that the Germans are now rushing to the front.** [emphasis added] I'd like to say that emphatically, because I know my fellow citizens, some of my fellow citizens and I think it's, therefore, an important statement for me to make.[288]

This court decision resolved the legal problem of deploying the German Armed Forces out of NATO's area. Germany could constitutionally deploy its military outside NATO, but the leadership still rejected sending Germans into the Front of a military conflict. Politicians needed to show the political will to fulfill international responsibility with the backing of their public. German security strategy was and is dependent on the support that the German people are willing to lend its parliament, now charged with the constitutional responsibility to mandate *Bundeswehr* deployment. As Aristotle said, "He who loses the support of public opinion is no longer king."

Later, speaking about the *Bundestag*'s decision to support NATO's 1999 bombing campaign in Kosovo, German commentator Detlef Puhl noted that governments must fight for public support for government action. Pubic support is fragile and must be handled well every day. There is no alternative to freely consented public support. Public support is especially critical in times of military action.[289] The constitutional court set the conditions for out-of-area missions operations. The court examined and affirmed, with requirements, the constitutionality of international *Bundeswehr* military deployments.[290]

Deployment debates remain a critical topic in domestic German politics. Although the *Bundestag* will decide on mandates, sometimes the court will be involved, which means that ultimately the political process will be very public and

---

288 William J. Clinton, *Public Papers of the Presidents of the United States 1994, Book I*, U.S. Government Publishing Office, Online: https://www.govinfo.gov/content/pkg/PPP-1994-book1/pdf/PPP-1994-book1.pdf, (Washington D.C.: 1994), p. 1489.
289 Detlef Puhl quoted in: James D. Bindenagel, Afghanistan. The German Factor, in: PRISM 1, No. 4, (Wahington D.C., 2010), pp. 97.
290 Bundesverfassungsgericht [BVerfG] [Federal Constitutional Court] July 12, 1994, 90 Entscheidungen des Bundesverfassungsgerichts [BVerfGE] 286 (F.R.G)], Online: https://www.servat.unibe.ch/dfr/bv090286.html, (Karlsruhe, 1994).

slow – much more complicated than the process set out in the War Powers Act of the United States. Nevertheless, the lesson of the High Court's decision is evident. German security strategy is dependent on and defined by the *Bundestag*, which represents the German public, not the executive branch of the government. Having won public support, or at least public acceptance, Germany today has had the third-largest military contingent in Afghanistan with rules of engagement governed by parliamentary mandate.

1995: Bundeswehr Deployments in Bosnia

At the time of the breakup of Yugoslavia, Germany deployed its military forces Out-of-Area NATO missions in territorial defense of the European Union during the Bosnian War. The Bundestag approves mandates for security strategy planning and execution on a case-by-case basis, since the Constitutional Court decision in 1994. This process typically means that the defense and foreign affairs ministers submit a formal proposal for a Bundestag mandate for *Bundeswehr* out-of-area NATO deployments, to be approved by Cabinet, and then sent to the Bundestag for debate and a decision on the deployments' mandates for rules of engagement. *Bundeswehr* deployments for the Implementation Force (IFOR) in Bosnia and Herzegovina and the NATO request for *Luftwaffe* Tornado aircraft missions came soon after the last Russian soldier had left Germany, and the High Court had paved the way for the Bundestag to decide on deployments.

Germany took up its responsibilities as the war in Bosnia was raging. U.S. General George Joulwan, Supreme Allied Commander Europe, approached the German government in November 1994, asking for Tornado fighter aircraft for NATO operations.[291] General Klaus Naumann sought political clearance for the request, which was delayed until a formal NATO request to protect the UN Protection Force soldiers in Bosnia was received. Immediately, the political debate began in earnest, and the seemingly straightforward request soon became mired in historical debates about German militarism and political demands to prevent any deployments of German troops to places where the *Wehrmacht* had fought in World War II. The *Bundestag* voted in June 1995, with 386 for and 268 opposed, and 11 abstentions, to approve the government recommendation that Germany contribute to the UN Rapid Reaction Force. Another vote followed on December 6th and allowed for the deployment of 4.000 *Bundeswehr* soldiers for IFOR.

---

291 Spiegel Online, Ganz verbindlich, in: Der Spiegel, Online: https://www.spiegel.de/spiegel/print/d-13686555.html, (Hamburg, 1994).

Proponents focused on solidarity with the UN Security Council, NATO, and the EU. German officials argued that national interests and Germany's role in protecting the international order were grounds for the mission. There was strong opposition in the Social Democratic Party to the use of military force, and they instead supported the position that missions should be strictly limited to non-combat roles. The *Bundestag* consequently decided in favor of requests for *Bundeswehr* logistics and support troops in Bosnia. NATO requested Tornado aircraft for combat missions, and eventually, combat infantry on the ground.

By 1997, U.S. Stabilization Force Commander General William Crouch had chosen a *Bundeswehr* general to be his SFOR chief of staff. Defense Minister Völker Rühe asked me in 1996 to request the Department of Defense to name a German general in the Bosnia-Herzegovina Stabilization Force. He argued *Bundeswehr* deployments under the command of a German general was critical for ensuring political support in the Bundestag, which decided on the mandates for such deployments. Although I explained that an American ambassador had 'chief of mission' presidential authority, it did not extend to military operations. Nevertheless, I did report the minister's request, which was immediately denied by the Pentagon, citing my lack of authority regarding military operations. A few months later, Minister Rühe again called on me to make the U.S. Government understand the political need for a German general in SFOR. This time, I conveyed the message directly to General Crouch, who decided to name *Bundeswehr* General Werner Widder to be his chief of staff in April 1997. Appointing a German general to the SFOR chain of command with *Bundeswehr* soldiers was a critical political step in the development of German security policy. It would also help to overcome the skepticism from the German public.

1999: Kosovo – "Nie Wieder Auschwitz."

Defensive operations, rather than aggressive use of military force, had been the German strategy until the *Bundeswehr* supported the NATO bombing of Serbian forces in Kosovo to end ethnic cleansing. NATO decided to protect the inviolability of human dignity and intervened militarily in Kosovo. After that aggressive use of force in Kosovo, the German slogan *Nie Wieder Auschwitz* (Never Again Auschwitz) took on a new meaning: Germany must use military force to prevent genocide.[292] The old motto that "no war could be allowed to emanate again from German soil" was not conducive to the protection of human dignity,

---

292 Joschka Fischer 'Nie Wieder Auschwitz', quoted in Nico Fried "Ich habe gelernt: Nie wieder Auschwitz", in: Süddeutsche Zeitung, Online: https://www.sueddeutsche.de/politik/fischer-ich-habe-gelernt-nie-wieder-auschwitz-1.915701, (München, 2010).

ending ethnic cleansing, or preventing war. By acting with NATO in its aggressive use of force, Germany was true to its postwar constitutional mandate to protect the inviolability of human dignity. It also led to the UN principle of the Responsibility to Protect. Following Kosovo, the aggressive use of force as an element of German security strategy was short-lived and achieved limited public support.

On February 25, 1999, the *Bundestag* debated and approved a German contribution to international troops for Kosovo under NATO command. Ultimately, 553 deputies voted in favor of a military implementation of the Rambouillet Accords (calling for a NATO force to maintain order in Kosovo); 41 voted against it (including only two Social Democrats and five Green Part members), and ten abstained. This vote laid the foundation for *Bundeswehr* participation in the Kosovo Force (KFOR).

From January to March 1999, the conflict intensified, notably in the Račak incident, where Serbian troops killed some 45 Albanians. The United Nations Security Council condemned this incident calling it a massacre. On 18 March 1999, the Albanian, American, and British delegation signed what became known as the Rambouillet Accords while the Serbian and Russian delegations refused. The accords called for NATO administration of Kosovo as an autonomous province within Yugoslavia, a force of 30,000 NATO troops to maintain order in Kosovo; an unhindered right of passage for NATO troops on Yugoslav territory, including Kosovo; and immunity for NATO and its agents to Yugoslav law.[293] Consequently, to enforce the accords, and in an all-out effort to end Serbian ethnic cleansing in Kosovo, NATO conducted a bombing campaign against Serbian forces from March 22 to June 11, 1999. This aggressive military action was the first time since World War II that the *Luftwaffe* participated in combat missions. There was no formal declaration of war by NATO; instead, NATO characterized the bombing as a military action necessary for the prevention of a humanitarian catastrophe. The Serbs withdrew, the Kosovo Force entered Kosovo on June 3, 1999, and the war ended on June 11, 1999.[294]

---

293 U.S. Department of State, *Interim Agreement for Peace and Self-Government in Kosovo*, U.S. Department of State Archives, Online: https://1997-2001.state.gov/regions/eur/ksvo_rambouillet_text.html, (Washington D.C., 2001).
294 James D. Bindenagel, Afghanistan. The German Factor, in: PRISM 1, No. 4, (Wahington D.C., 2010), pp. 95–112.

1999: Opening NATO to New Members

When the Warsaw Pact dissolved, Poland sought to join NATO in 1992. It invoked Gorbachev's decision to end the Brezhnev Doctrine and return sovereignty to former Soviet satellite States, allowing them to decide themselves which security alliance to join. Defense Minister Volker Rühe proposed the opening of NATO in an International Institute for Strategic Studies (IISS) speech in Great Britain in 1992.[295]

However, out of concern for Russia and reluctance of the NATO Defense ministers to accept former Warsaw Pact members into NATO, aspiring NATO members in 1993 were offered Partnership for Peace as an alternative to NATO membership. NATO agreed with Russians to establish the NATO-Russia Council and the 1997 NATO-Russia Founding Act. Although the Founding Act is a political agreement and not a legally binding treaty, it speaks about no "additional permanent stationing of substantial combat forces," with which NATO has complied.

When NATO accepted new members, German responsibility for its neighbors increased; however, that responsibility was again territorial defense, not a change in strategy. After the 1995 Dayton Accords, President Clinton moved to enlarge NATO and extend security guarantees to former Warsaw Pact countries. Chancellor Kohl was willing to support NATO enlargement starting in 1997 for Poland, Hungary, and the Czech Republic.[296]

Overcoming the public's residual aversion to the use of force is difficult, but necessary if Germany is to accept full NATO engagement. The public understands the importance of collective actions and the collective security purpose of the Alliance. Meanwhile, German political leadership needs to summon the will to confront its people with the reality of the need to use force to defend German interests, while continuing to provide development assistance. Likewise, the U.S. Government needs to confront its public with the need to fund civilian agencies to build American capacity for civilian projects. Re-forging common two-track, but unified combat and complex operations policies for joint missions can lead to a security strategy sustained by both publics. NATO, in its outreach early in the 1990s, assured Russia repeatedly that it was not a threat to the Soviet Union, and that it changed its strategy to make nuclear weapons indeed of last resort, minimizing the principle of "first use." The Allies changed both "forward defense" and "flexible response" concepts that had been against east European and

---

295 Volker Rühe, Opening NATO's Door, in: Daniel S. Hamilton and Kristina Spohr, Open Door: Nato and euro-atlantic security after the Cold War, (Brookings Institution Press: Washington D.C., 1992).
296 Helmut Kohl, Statement by Helmut Kohl, Chancellor of Germany at the Signing Ceremony of the NATO-Russia Founding Act, in: NATO, Online: https://www.nato.int/cps/en/SID-27AF5864-EE4A5D0C/natolive/opinions_25643.htm, (Brussels, 1997).

Soviet territory and extended a hand of friendship to establish diplomatic liaison with NATO and later signed the NATO-Russia Founding Act before accepting new members.

2001: 9/11, NATO Treaty, Art. 5 and Kunduz, Afghanistan

The terrorist attacks by al Qaeda on the United States on September 11, 2001, led to solidarity among NATO members. They decided that the attack fit the definition of Article 5 of the NATO treaty; an attack on one was an attack on all. This solidarity allowed for general backing of the U.S. decision to attack the Taliban in Afghanistan. However, the United States chose to conduct the initial invasion primarily alone. Germany, nevertheless, has participated in NATO operations in Afghanistan by assisting in civil construction, as well as police and military training. The 9/11 attacks were also a historical turning point that shook loose previous U.S. responses to security threats and set a new American course to defeat global terrorism.

When in September 2009, *Bundeswehr* Colonel Georg Klein called in a NATO airstrike against a group of Taliban who had hijacked two fuel trucks in Kunduz targeted against the German troops. That attack popped the illusionary bubble that Germany was not at war. The Kunduz attack in Afghanistan changed the German debate; Germans recognized they were at war. A significant majority of Germans at home, before that attack the description of war, rejected the explanation. After the Kunduz attack – which took place during the September 2009 German election campaign – Chancellor Angela Merkel intervened in the parliamentary debate with a statement to the *Bundestag* that defended German participation. That statement kept the Afghanistan debate out of the election campaign at a time when some 60 percent of Germans wanted an immediate withdrawal. On February 23, 2010, the Financial Times reported that 56 percent of those polled believed that the NATO mission would fail, and nearly 70 percent called for withdrawal.[297]

There is no doubt that the lack of a unified German security strategy led to ambiguity in the political decision-making process on troop deployments. German interests in NATO solidarity for collective and national defense are persuasive. Limitations on *Bundeswehr* deployments are often politically expedient, and possible if the German mandate is part of essential NATO operations. The *Bundeswehr* could potentially assume combat roles if they arose explicitly and exclusively within the context of joint NATO missions of collective defense –

---

297 Quentin Peel, Germany and Europe: A very Federal Formula, in: Financial Times, Online: https://www.ft.com/content/31519b4a-5307-11e1-950d-00144feabdc0, (London, 2012).

planned, trained, and executed together with U.S. forces. At the same time, the German government would have to slowly and deliberately seek to build domestic political support. Decision making on the conflict in Afghanistan has determined German military posture. German politicians need the political will to overcome public resistance to combat roles as well as residual, although fading, opposition from the French, British, and Russians of a remilitarized post-World War II and post-Cold War Germany.

2003: Schröder's "No" to Bush's Iraq War

Germany's dilemma of either sustaining its civilian power role or accepting more international security responsibility has set the course for future approaches to European-American security strategy. In the lead up to the Iraq War in 2002, the U.S. National Security Strategy began to decouple American security policy from its international base in Europe. One European response to the U.S. security strategy came in June 2003 from NATO Secretary General Javier Solana. He presented a draft European security strategy to extend European security, strengthen the international order under the United Nations, and counter threats from nonproliferation, failed states, and global terrorism. Germany worked multilaterally within the EU Common Security and Defense Policy process. Throughout the debates about Afghanistan, Germany's embrace of civilian solutions and rejection of the use of force – to paraphrase Defense Secretary Robert Gates' remarks at the National Defense University – was a blessing in Germany's singularly focused approach to civilian projects in complex operations.

When it came to the preparation for the Iraq War throughout the 2002 German election campaign, Chancellor Gerhard Schröder, with strong support from the electorate, objected to the U.S. plan for a preventive strike against Saddam Hussein in Iraq. After his reelection, Schröder refused to participate in the 2003 Iraq War, and French President Jacques Chirac joined him. Schröder's opposition to the Iraq War was widespread, and opponents of the Iraq War coalesced to solidify the political limits on the German use of military force. Schröder and other Europeans questioned Iraq's link to al Qaeda terrorists, despite agreement on the destructiveness of Hussein's authoritarian regime. Americans planned the war in Iraq without the support of many U.S. allies, and this caused a crack in the transatlantic alliance. The divisive issue was whether preemption or rather a preventive war by the United States and the United Kingdom in Iraq. Inspectors found no 'weapons of mass destruction' when military action was over. This lack of proof resulted in a continued unease about the "preemption doctrine" among Europeans, despite the rapid military victory against Saddam's regime.[298]

2013: Syria UNSC Res 1973 – R2P and Foreign Minister Westerwelle

On March 17, 2011, Germany abstained in the vote on UNSC Resolution 1973, authorizing the use of military force to protect civilians from Muammar Gaddafi's regime. What happened in the Libya case is not easy to understand. Germany's decision called the country's global role into question. Peace, prosperity, and security in Europe are tributes to the visionaries who have made the European Union a tremendous success. Pooling national sovereignty has enabled Europe to create a single market, enforce European law over national law, and to act in unison. Pooled sovereignty is essential for Europe. In this decision, Germany became more provincial and proved less willing to exercise its power. If the legitimacy of a UN resolution, supported by the Arab League and other Arab nations, to protect innocent civilians in Libya from the threat of annihilation was not sufficient for Germany, what is?

German scholar Hans Maull set out two critical dimensions of this decision – one, the domestic demands of coalition government management coupled with the constitutionally mandated independence of the ministries and, two, the skepticism of the decision-makers, Chancellor Merkel and Foreign Minister Westerwelle about chances of success for military intervention. The coalition government's standing in the polls had dropped following the 2010 debt crisis, and the loss to the Green Party in state elections in *Baden-Württemberg* after the tsunami in Japan resulted in nuclear fallout. A severe drop in public support would lead to a collapse of the government. A military intervention rejected by an unwilling public would likely steepen the coalition's fall in the polls.[299]

Germany, hosting the NATO Ministerial in Berlin, insisted that there could be "no military solution" in Libya. This stance contributed to the strain in NATO solidarity that the Alliance has undergone in recent years. The NATO Alliance supported the protection of human life and liberty in the developing Arab Spring. Germany was on the sidelines at a time when the challenges in the Middle East urgently needed European leadership. This shift in German policy also came at a time when the United States wished not to lead an attack against another Muslim

---

[298] Dieter Dettke, *Germany Says "No": The Iraq War and the Future of German Foreign and Security Policy*, (Johns Hopins University Press: Baltimore, 2009), p. 158.
[299] Hanns W. Maull, Außenpolitische Entscheidungsprozesse in Krisenzeiten, in: Bundeszentrale für politische Bildung, Online: http://www.bpb.de/apuz/75797/aussenpolitische-entscheidungsprozesse-in-krisenzeiten?p=all, (Bonn, 2012).

country, which could give strength to an Iranian-led "resistance block" in the next round of regional conflicts.[300]

Provincialism and isolationism have become tempting policy choices for many. Roger Cohen in the New York Times warned against prioritizing German national interests and neglecting its global responsibilities. "Here was Germany standing wobbly with Brazil, Russia, India and China – and against its closest allies, France and the United States – in the U.N. vote on Libyan military action."[301] Brookings scholar Constanze Stelzenmueller, writing in the *Süddeutsche Zeitung*, noted that opponents to the UN resolution to protect civilians through military intervention in Libya seemed to have no sympathy for the victims of Gaddafi's massacre. Constant talk of civilian action without military force was enough to sacrifice fundamental principles of German policy.[302]

Lothar Rühl in the *Frankfurt Allgemeine Zeitung* foresaw that Germany's refusal to stand with its allies would result in a loss of influence in NATO and also in the EU.[303] Germany put its desire for a permanent seat in the United Nations Security Council at risk in the Libya case. Association of German Chambers of Commerce and Industry (DIHK) President Hans Heinrich Driftmann characterized the decision with the warning that panic and party politics make bad advisers.[304]

The international principle of the Responsibility to Protect (R2P), new norms of the post-Cold War era, was invoked in the UN and calls for intervention in Libya from Arab nations. They also embody the philosophy of the German *Staatsräson* to protect human dignity. Many foreign policy experts were baffled by the German decisions taken in the case of Libya because they seemed to go against its governing philosophy. These decisions also conflict with its support for the multilateral institutions of NATO and the UN, institutions which had been pillars of German foreign policy.

---

300 Michael Scott Doran, The Heirs of Nasser. Who Will Benefir From thhe Second Arab Spring, in: Foreign Affairs, Online: https://www.foreignaffairs.com/authors/michael-scott-doran, (May/June 2011), (Congers, 2011).
301 Roger Cohen, France Flies, Germany Flops, in: The New York Times, Online: https://www.nytimes.com/2011/04/17/opinion/17cohen.html, (New York City, 2011), p. 10.
302 Constanze Stelzenmüller, Libyen, eine Deutschstunde; Vielen Gegnern des Militäreinsatzes fehlt auffälliger weise das Mitgefühl mit den Unterdrückten in Gaddafis Reich. Außenansicht, in: Süddeutsche Zeitung, (München, 2011), p. 2.
303 Lothar Rühl, Debatte über Militärintervention. Soll der Westen in Libyen eingreifen?, in: Frankfurter Allgemeiner Zeitung, Online: https://www.faz.net/aktuell/politik/ausland/naher-osten/debatte-ueber-militaerintervention-soll-der-westen-in-libyen-eingreifen-1610254.html, (Frankfurt am Main, 2011).
304 Hans Heinrich Driftmann quoted in: Main Post, Merkel hat politisch richtig agiert, in: Main Post, Online: https://www.mainpost.de/ueberregional/meinung/leitartikel/Merkel-hat-politisch-richtig-agiert;art9517,6494325, (Würzburg, 2011).

2015: EU3+3 and Iran JCPOA

Nuclear non-proliferation is a priority issue, especially for European Middle East policy. Germany banded together with Great Britain and France to address Iran's rising role within the region following Hezbollah's victory against Israel in 2006. This war led to negotiations on limiting Iran's nuclear weapons program. According to two scholars, Payam Mohseni and Hussein Kalout:

> In 2006, in the midst of a fierce war between Israel and the Lebanese militant group Hezbollah, former U.S. Secretary of State Condoleezza Rice famously stated that the world was witnessing the "birth pangs of a new Middle East." She was right – but not in the sense she had hoped. Instead of disempowering Hezbollah and its sponsor, Iran, the war only augmented the strength and prestige of what is known as the "axis of resistance," a power bloc that includes Iran, Iraq, Syria, Hezbollah, and Hamas in Palestine.[305]

Iran's Axis of Resistance is a movement which it has called on others to join Iran against "the pestilence of imperialism and America's brand of exceptionalism."[306] The Resistance has tapped the humiliation from their autocratic rulers, an "Arab Spring." Middle East scholar Nassim Taleb draws the analogy to resistance in the Middle East in his quote from Seneca, who wrote in *De clementia*. "Repeated punishment, while it crushes the hatred of a few, stirs the hatred of all ... just as trees that have been trimmed throw out again countless branches."[307]

In the context of a chaotic Middle East, Germany, France, and the United Kingdom came together to undertake a European Initiative (EU 3+3) to negotiate a deal that could keep Iran from acquiring nuclear weapons. The EU-3 – Germany, France, and Great Britain – with China, Russia, and the United States reached an agreement on the Joint Comprehensive Plan of Action (JCPOA). It set agreed limits on Iran's nuclear weapons program. A second comprehensive agreement to address the Iranian Axis of Resistance and to set a path to resolve the Iranian missiles development program as well as its military expansion into Yemen, Lebanon, Iraq, and Syria was planned but not begun. It is doubtful that Germany and its partners can again open an international negotiation on the JCPOA. There is little international will to negotiate Iran's support of terrorist groups, its expansion of political influence backed by military force, and its refusal to recognize Israel's right to exist that could sustain the deal to limit Iran's nuclear ambitions.

---

305 Payam Mohseni and Hussein Kalout, Iran's Axis of Resistance Rises. How It's Forging a New Middle East, in: Foreign Affairs, Online: https://www.foreignaffairs.com/articles/iran/2017-01-24/irans-axis-resistance-rises, (Washington D.C., 2017).
306 Ibid.
307 Catherine Shakdam, The New Thaw: Donald Trump and the Iranian Resistance Block, in: NEO. New Eastern Outlook, Online: https://journal-neo.org/2017/02/12/the-new-thaw-donald-trump-and-the-iranian-resistance-block/, (Moscow, 2017).

The U.S. withdrawal from the agreement tests European diplomacy and its ability for conflict resolution in maintaining the plan.[308] The U.S. Administration's withdrawal from JCPOA and subsequent killing of Iran's Quds Forces commander Qassem Soleimani increase conflict in the Middle East and nudge it closer to war. It opens the door for Iran to restart its nuclear weapons program and regional nuclear proliferation. Europe's neighborhood has become more dangerous. Europe's challenge is to offer a strategy to stabilize the region. That is a wake-up call for Europe to take its fate in its own hands to pursue strategic foresight, not merely crisis management.

2016: Syrian Chemical Weapons

The debate about German military involvement in Syria in late summer 2018 was a vivid example of the dilemma of intervention or non-intervention. After Syrian President Bashir al-Assad allegedly used chemical weapons on his population, the Social Democrats immediately rejected any German involvement. However, the point is not whether Germany should or should not have participated in this mission. There were several very valid reasons against military strikes that were later submitted by SPD-Vice Chairman Rolf Mützenich. However, the decision without any form of internal coordination among the governing parties precluded future judgment on an actual case. Germany did not consult international partners, nor was a thorough internal strategic debate conducted – completely disregarding the long-term strategic consequences of hastily publishing such a conclusion.[309]

Another example of the difficulties in German security policy can be seen in the ambivalence of the German response when the USA withdrew its troops from northern Syria in late 2019. Defense Minister Annegret Kramp-Karrenbauer (CDU) proposed a security zone in North Syria with contributions by the Bundeswehr with little to no coordination with the Foreign Ministry. The Foreign Minister, Heiko Maas (SPD), responded quickly with his initiative that under the independence of ministries – Ressortprinzip – to undercut the authority of the Defense Ministry. The SPD reacted accordingly by stating that the Defense

---

308 James D. Bindenagel, Kampflos aufgeben? Niemals!, in: Süddeutsche Zeitung, Online: https://www.sueddeutsche.de/politik/aussenansicht-kampflos-aufgeben-niemals-1.3997509, (München, 2018).
309 Richard Holbrooke, *To End a War: The Conflict in Yugoslavia – America's Inside Story*, (Modern Library: New York City, 1998), p. 31.

Minister's proposal was uncoordinated in the coalition.[310] As long as different political parties lead the ministries, coalition politics hinders a strategic debate. This coalition governance underlines the need for strategic foresight to assure a coordinated, independent strategic response for German security.

2002: U.S. and European Security Strategy

Germany's dilemma of either sustaining its civilian power role or accepting more international security responsibility will set the course for future approaches to European-American security strategy. In the lead up to the Iraq War in 2002, the U.S. National Security Strategy began to decouple American security policy from its international base in Europe. One European response to the U.S. security strategy came in June 2003 from NATO Secretary General Javier Solana.[311] He presented a draft European security strategy to extend European security, strengthen the international order under the United Nations, and counter threats from nonproliferation, failed states, and global terrorism. Germany worked multilaterally within the EU Common Security and Defense Policy process. Throughout the debates about Afghanistan, Germany's embrace of civilian solutions and rejection of the use of force – to paraphrase Defense Secretary Robert Gates' remarks at the National Defense University – was a blessing in Germany's singularly focused approach to civilian projects in complex operations.

Although Germany accepts its responsibility to confront threats beyond its borders, it has no comprehensive national security strategy. The Defense Ministry published in its 2016 White Paper on German Security Policy and the Future of the *Bundeswehr* a security policy that described a leading role for the *Bundeswehr* in protecting Germany's democracy from external threats. The German Christian Democratic Union, Christian Social Union, and the strategy paper itself defined Germany's national interests in terms of five issue areas: the fight against terrorism, nuclear proliferation, energy, and pipeline security, climate change, and the prevention of conflicts.[312]

German security decision making is fragmented among the chancellor's office, the defense ministry, the foreign office, and the *Bundestag*. The process is missing the vaunted German *Gesamtkonzept*, or comprehensive concept to de-

---

310 Spiegel Online, Maas greift Kramp-Karrenbauer erneut an – scharfe Kritik aus der Union, in: Der Spiegel, Online: https://www.spiegel.de/politik/deutschland/nordsyrien-vorstoss-heiko-maas-greift-annegret-kramp-karrenbauer-erneut-an-a-1294934.html, (Hamburg, 2019).
311 Javier Solana, *European Security Strategy A Secure Europe in a Better World*, (EU Institute for Security Studies: Paris, 2003).
312 The Federal Government, *White Paper, 2016 On German Security Policy and the Future of the Bundeswehr*, (Berlin, 2016).

velop policy. Instead, foreign policy is created most often in a case-by-case policy crisis management process that is confronted by a deep-seated aversion to the use of military force, which hinders a comprehensive security strategy. Despite the lack of national or European strategic planning, German soldiers have served well in UN and NATO operations. The Germans kept full membership in NATO and have deployed the *Bundeswehr* in out-of-area missions to Cambodia, Somalia, Bosnia, Kosovo, and Afghanistan.[313] In other words, Germany does have an active military, despite its lack of a national security strategy.

While Germany does not have a comprehensive national security strategy, it has defined its first principles for its national interests. Politically and through the Constitutional Court, Berlin has affirmed its willingness to act militarily in solidarity within its alliances to NATO, the EU, and the UN. However, domestic politics and coalition governments put stress on the policy process. Also, the process will remain mindful of Russian interests in light of agreements on unification. The *Bundeswehr* retains its territorial defense mission while responding to its alliance obligations. Its aversion to the use of force supports its priority to provide training, civilian reconstruction, and stabilization operations. Germany may use military force to prevent crimes against humanity, but it will not support the use of force in preemptive attacks, such as the invasion of Iraq.

What should Europe do?

First, the EU needs a strategy, and Germany can guide the debate. Europeans put a high priority on the sanctity of contracts and the rule of law, but confidence in law is low. In the Iran example, renegotiating the Iran nuclear weapons program deal, JCPOA, is not an option. Iran would lose at home with a strengthened Revolutionary Guard and Mullah Regime. China and Russia have no interest in re-negotiations. President Rouhani has rejected that option as well.

Second, diplomacy is needed. President Emmanuel Macron presented president Trump a European proposal to address the criticism of the JCPOA and a path to resolve the unacceptable Iranian ballistic missile development program as well as its military expansion into Yemen, Lebanon, Iraq, and Syria. The EU could create a similar diplomatic process to sustain nuclear non-proliferation in the Middle East and to prevent war, refugees, terrorism that threaten Europe.

Third, the EU could build confidence that they, together with China and Russia, can work together to combat terrorism, conduct peaceful space missions,

---

313 Deutsche Bundeswehr, Aktuelle Einsätze der Bundeswehr, Online: https://www.bundeswehr.de/de/einsaetze-bundeswehr, (Berlin, 2020).

develop economic ties and broaden cooperation as part of an international community of nations.

There are lessons in this overview of Germany's security policies. As stated at the outset of the book, Henry Kissinger reminds us aptly that success as a statesman rests on the study of history to understand why nations succeeded and why they failed.

Part Three: The Case for German Engagement – To Support Europe and Transatlantic Relations

Plans are worthless, but planning is everything. There is a very great distinction because when you are planning for an emergency, you must start with this one thing: the very definition of "emergency" is that it is unexpected, therefore, it is not going to happen the way you are planning... if you haven't been planning, you can't start to work, intelligently at least.
– Dwight D. Eisenhower [314]

We [Europeans] can either slow down the pace of change or speed up our ability to learn our way into the future together, by using more than one, but not too many, plausible alternative stories of the future.
– Angela Wilkinson [315]

For the past 70 years, Germany could focus on its economic prosperity, absorbing U.S. strategic leadership, and reacting to crises when necessary. As a civilian power backed by NATO's hard power, it could develop its 'Peace Project' of a Model Germany built on soft power. Germany prospered under this model. Today, the question emerges whether Germany's foreign policy process is still applicable in a world that is unraveling. As that model dissolves, does Germany have the political will to institutionalize a new one for the transatlantic partnership?

Germany and Europe urgently need to step up and meet the challenges of a rapidly changing world order, with Great Power politics, growing multipolarity, rising unilateralism, and global threats. Tension and growing nationalism within the European Union, China's Belt and Road Initiative, Russia's open challenge to the existing global order, and the unpredictability of the current U.S. administration's foreign policy make it clear that the traditional benchmarks of German and European foreign policy are shifting. Russia's breach of international law by

---

314 United States Government Printing Office, *Containing the Public Messages, Speeches, and Statements of the President, Jan. 01 to Dec. 31, 1957, Public Papers of the Presidents of the United States, Dwight D. Eisenhower*, (Washington D.C., 1958), p. 818.
315 Angela Wilkinson, *Strategic Foresight Primer*, European Political Strategy Centre, (Brussels, 2017), p. 2.

invading Ukraine and annexing Crimea with continued fighting in Eastern Ukraine. The continuous flow of refugees from Syria and Iraq to Europe is making Europeans realize that they do not live in blissful isolation of world events.

As global challenges are mounting, the United States is retreating from its role as the primary guardian of the order it created after World War II. What does it mean that the American Administration's worldview is that the world is not a community but an arena where nations, non-governmental actors, and businesses engage and compete for advantage? That worldview runs contrary to the transatlantic values-based relationship of the rule of law, democracy, and respect for human dignity that are the foundation of the seven-decades-old world order. The absence of the United leadership role in global affairs has far-reaching consequences. European foreign and security policy has relied on U.S. security guarantees and strategic planning within the framework of NATO for decades, but the structure is uncertain.

Germany and the West stand at an inflection point in history, not knowing when the tipping point will arrive. The "Long War" in the 20th century defeated imperial powers, fascism, National Socialism, and communism, and parliamentary democracy won. Today, democracy may not prevail as nationalism, illiberal democracies, and authoritarianism rise yet again. This unraveling of world order makes leadership from transatlantic allies who shaped it all the more necessary. In the face of geopolitical upheavals that are shaking the current global order to its core, Germany and Europe's "new responsibility" is uncertain. For the European Union, protecting its values and principles in a changing global environment will only be possible by following an integrative group leadership approach with Germany and France leading with the other EU Member States as partners in leadership. And since nothing moves forward in Europe without Germany, the country not only has to develop foreign policy and security strategies, it also must be able to strengthen Europe's strategic role in the transatlantic partnership.

Thus, as the external circumstances are changing, so are the demands on German and European foreign policy. Germany has begun to accept more international responsibility since President Joachim Gauck and Ministers Frank-Walter Steinmeier and Ursula von der Leyen called on Germany to accept more international responsibility at the 2014 Munich Security Conference. Since then, Germany published in 2016 a new Defense White Book, stating the country's intention to act more proactively. At least, in theory, Germany has tentatively agreed to accept responsibility, and it is poised to take a leadership role in Europe. Politico even called Chancellor Angela Merkel, the "Leader of the Free World." In practice, however, Germany has still often shied away from leading in Europe. Without Germany leading, the future of a strengthened European Transatlantic Pillar is an open one. Thirty years after unification, balancing national interests within its parliamentary democracy with Germany's sovereign obligation to Europe and NATO institutions still presents dilemmas. Navigating the tightrope between Germany's culture of self-restraint not only in military mission, and the need for increased engagement (cum leadership) in times of growing global problems remains a source of constant conflict.

Chapter 7: Germany's Inflection Point: From Crises Management to Strategic Planning?

Germany's foreign policy is at a critical turning point. Its traditional benchmarks – Europe and the United States – are affected by a fundamental change, making reorientation of German foreign policy and the development of strategy a necessity. Is it time for Germany to enter and lead the strategic debate? Even though German leadership set out at the Munich Security Conference in 2014 to take on more responsibility, a strategic cultural deficit hinders debate. Despite Angela Merkel's surprisingly energetic speech at the 2019 Munich Security Conference, Germany, for five years now, has only begun to operationalize its 2014 Munich Consensus pledge for "more responsibility."

Meanwhile, Germans are also still at odds with the role Germany should play in international politics. Given the dominant culture of civilian power, reinforced by the peaceful resolution of the Cold War and German unification, it is politically risky for politicians to suggest Germany can contribute militarily to foreign policy goals. The German public is skeptical about participation in international alliances that are morally or legally unclear. This civilian power dominance remains an obstacle also to a robust foreign policy. The inevitable public backlash against military means often prevents an informed debate on foreign policy issues.

Nevertheless, today, we are floating in systemic fluidity, a point in history, not knowing when firm ground will arrive. We are witnessing growing multi-polarity, rising unilateralism, and global threats that are changing the world order rapidly. Numerous crises, rifts, and the disintegration of long-standing international structures are increasingly affecting traditional cornerstones of German foreign policy. Meanwhile, the United States is stepping down from its decades-long leadership role in global affairs.

What has changed? The short answer: America seems to be phasing out its grand strategy in the values-based liberal world order. External conditions are changing, and a fundamental challenge confronts Germany's foreign policy foundations. What responsibilities should Germany assume in this changing global environment? On what principles, goals, and guidelines should this new role follow? As one of Europe's biggest and most powerful states, Germany's stance on foreign policy is of vital importance to the EU's shared foreign policy. When discussing Germany's evolving role in international politics, however, there is one factor of particular importance that urgently needs attention: Germany's strategic thinking capabilities, its general strategic culture, and its ability to engage in strategic foresight.

The German constitution, the Basic Law principles, are anchored in the lessons from Germany's past and in its commitment to seeking a better future and have shaped Germany's role on the global stage. Since the end of World War II, Germany has had two significant priorities: pronounced restraint, captured in its pledge that never again will war emanate from German soil, and a firm commitment to multilateral cooperation, treaties, and international institutions. Germany is committed to lead in partnership, not unilaterally.

The 1990 Treaty on the Final Settlement with Respect to Germany (known as the 2+4 Agreement) restored full sovereignty for united Germany. The victorious four powers of the Second World War relinquished their rights and responsibilities for Berlin and Germany as a whole in 1990. The country has balanced its growing economic and political weight against its reluctance to claim power. Still, as one of Europe's economic heavyweights, it is becoming increasingly difficult to stay out of international conflicts and challenges. However, the country firmly rejected renewed power projections and has continued to pursue its assumed a role as a *Zivilmacht*, or civilian power, as coined by Hanns W. Maull.[316] Resting on the premise of an increasingly interdependent global system that prompts states to establish reliable institutions and internationally recognized norms, the country is committed to contributing to a stable and rule-based international order. Relying on NATO for its security, Germany could develop economically and conduct diplomacy in protecting and promoting human dignity. It does so by strengthening internationally recognized standards, cooperation, and multilateral institutions, instead of engaging in power politics and military intervention. Germany strives to replace the concept of *politics by force* with *politics by legitimacy*.

These are the core elements that determine Germany's political identity and its foreign policy, which have strongly emphasized peacemaking, democracy, and human rights over the last few decades. More recently, these same pillars of German political identity have adapted to global engagement. The principles of German foreign policy engagement explain Germany's current efforts to recalibrate its role in foreign policy. It faces challenges in doing so. Russia's breach of international law by invading Ukraine and annexing Crimea and the continued fighting in Eastern Ukraine are unsolved conflicts. The ongoing flow of

---

316 Knut Kirste and Hanns Maull, Zivilmacht und Rollentheorie, in: Zeitschrift für Internationale Beziehungen, 3. Jhrg. (Nomos Verlagsgesellschaft: Wuppertal, 1996), pp. 283–312.

refugees from Syria and Iraq to Europe make it increasingly clear that Germany and Europe no longer live in the banality of good times. Meanwhile, the United States is retreating from its role as the primary guardian of the order it created after World War II. China's Belt and Road Initiative, Russia's open challenge to the existing global order, and the unpredictability of the current U.S. Administration's foreign policy make it clear that the traditional foundations of German and European foreign policy are shifting.

Recognizing these changing realities, leading officials in Germany have begun to accept more international responsibility. Germany is coming to terms with its historically-determined limitations and the growing requirements of today's foreign policy demands. Germany is slowly starting to assume more responsibility on the global stage. For one, such analysis misjudges Germany's geopolitical leverage and the restrictions that arise from the country's strategic culture. Secondly, Germany's relevance as a foreign policy actor is dependent on Europe, specifically on the European Union. Even if the country manages to overcome its strategic culture deficits, it can only take part in shaping the emerging world order as a part of Europe.

For some time, analysts have increasingly criticized the lack of strategic thinking in German foreign and security policy, arguing that Germany lacks coherence, vision, guidelines, and departmental coordination. Germany also falls short in setting clear policy goals and in developing alternative options for political action. Decision-makers focus on crisis management or choosing a crisis when it fits with Germany's self-image of a leading diplomatic actor, especially in humanitarian issues or accepting NATO tasks reacting to pressures due to its membership. As a result, Germany does not act strategically, but instead reacts and repeatedly finds itself confronted with unfavorable courses of action.

This strategic deficit and the pressure to overcome it became acute with the financial crisis, the Arab Spring, the annexation of Crimea, the Syrian civil war, and the resulting migration crisis. These events took the German government by surprise and thus forcing it to make crisis management decisions that would have long-term consequences. For example, there were little to no feasible options for alternative courses of action in the Arab Spring. There were no underpinned strategic plans or anticipatory scenarios to draw from that could have assisted in increasing the government's resilience.

Today, challenges arise from the coronavirus pandemic, Brexit, the election of Donald Trump, the Middle East, and North African conflicts and the continuing repercussions of the financial crisis. In dealing with compounding crises, then Foreign Minister Frank-Walter Steinmeier said in 2016: "The world has gone completely off the rails."[317] While Brexit undermines faith in the inevitably of

---

317 Frank-Walter Steinmeier, Interview mit dem Magazin Stern, Online: http://www.bunde

European integration, populism has catapulted to the top of the agenda in Europe. President Trump is questioning the pillars of transatlantic cooperation by unilaterally retreating from the Iran nuclear agreement (Joint Comprehensive Plan of Action – JCPOA), introducing tariffs on steel and aluminum and other decisions to withdraw America from international leadership. He is establishing a foreign policy based on his views of national interests. Additionally, the pressure on German policymaking can no longer ignore long-term issues that require reforms in the Eurozone, which continue to arise from the consequences of the financial crisis.

Germany's role in the international order is undergoing a significant shift in response to such fundamental changes in global political relations. Germany's watershed moment is now. It must begin to make precedent-setting decisions regarding its policy in the Middle East and Russia, on the future of the European Union and the transatlantic partnership as well as the future of the global order.

It is crucial to increase Germany's strategic planning capabilities significantly and to conduct a broad strategic debate if reorientation and shifts towards a new leadership role in foreign policy are to be successful. Mastering the complexities connected to the current transformation of world order is only possible by identifying trends, defining long-term goals, indicating clear guidelines, developing conceivable courses of action, and identifying appropriate tools to reach said goals.

Germany's Strategic Deficit: Lack of Foresight and Scenario Building

One crucial element in developing a strategy is foresight, and thus the formulation of possible scenarios for future development. Strategic foresight as a method tries to include key driving factors, which might affect future events to formulate strategic goals, based on firm analysis, to help policymakers to be aware of different courses of action. It is a tool to try to understand the nation's possibilities of action, those of opponents and partners, as well as implications of the terrain and time. The goals of foresight are highly applicable to coherent policymaking. They vary from trying to strengthen the reaction and strategic abilities of a country to preventing conflict, hunger, and poverty, making democracy more resilient, and foster human rights and environmental sustainability.

Without taking into account possible trends, threats, and risks, it becomes more likely that strategies will fail due to unexpected events. While a strategy will

---

spraesident.de/SharedDocs/Reden/DE/Frank-Walter-Steinmeier/Interviews/2017/170720-stern-Interview.html, (Berlin, 2017).

never fully anticipate future developments, scenarios assist in the development of strategic plans and possible courses of action. This process can serve as a guideline, should an anticipated trend or situation occur, but also if they do not happen. For planning to be successful, governments need to be willing to act early based on insights gained from strategic foresight. President Dwight D. Eisenhower described the wisdom of strategic foresight when he argued that "Plans are worthless, but planning is everything."[318] Emergencies are unpredictable, but strategic foresight offers a way to inform the political debate without pre-empting policymaking. Such strategic foresight is underutilized in Germany. Various developments over the last ten to fifteen years did provide grounds for and the opportunity to draw up scenarios strategic planning at an early stage.

For instance, at the 43rd Munich Security Conference in 2007 and in subsequent speeches, Russian President Vladimir Putin openly communicated that Russia considered NATO's eastward enlargement an intrusion into the Russian spheres of influence and paints the so-called "color revolutions" as attempts by the West to overthrow regimes with close ties to Moscow.[319] In response, Russia stopped implementing parts of the Treaty on Conventional Armed Forces in Europe (CFE), conducted war in Georgia in 2008, announced an aggressive new military doctrine, and finally, in 2014, engaged in hybrid warfare in Ukraine, occupying and subsequently annexing Crimea. Meanwhile, the United States and the European Union continuously emphasized the peaceful intentions of the European Union and the fundamentally defensive character of NATO as well as their commitment to democracy and human rights. They expected Russia to become like the rest of the West.

Russia's actions and conflicting viewpoints should have prompted Germany and the European Union to draw up scenarios that could foresee possible Russian reactions to the West's policies. Such plans could have prepared them for Moscow's interpretation of events that would remain intact, despite all explanation attempts and peaceful intentions. However, NATO did not seriously consider the scenario of Russia turning towards a more aggressive foreign policy that wholly rejects Western values to protect the Russian spheres of influence. Scenarios should have included possible Russian actions based on its modernized military, active involvement in its neighboring countries' foreign policy, and military interventions to protect national interests. Even now, Germany lacks a strategy and guidelines for how to deal with Russia's new approach to foreign policy.

---

318 United States Government Printing Office, *Containing the Public Messages, Speeches, and Statements of the President, Jan. 01 to Dec. 31, 1957, Public Papers of the Presidents of the United States, Dwight D. Eisenhower*, (Washington D.C., 1958), p. 818.
319 Vladimir Putin, Speech and the Following Discussion at the Munich Conference on Security Policy, Online: http://en.kremlin.ru/events/president/transcripts/24034, (Munich, 2017).

One can make a similar case for the current crisis in the transatlantic relationship. During Obama's presidency, the United States was slowly stepping back from its role as the world policeman that it had carried out in previous decades. Instead, Washington started focusing on vital interests that shifted its focus towards Asia and left the job of overlooking its peripheries to its allies. The "pivot to Asia" policy and "strategic patience" as well as Washington's restraint in the Ukraine crisis deferred responsibilities to the Europeans. President Barack Obama's pivot to Asia worried Europeans and led to accusations that the U.S. was leaving Europe. The allegation that America was "leading from behind" came from its approach to conflict in Libya. Nevertheless, the Obama Administration held to the values-based liberal international order. This American shift was a signal that responsibility for the international liberal order increasingly fell more on Europe, but the Europeans were unable to take the reins.

Even though political leaders could have anticipated the consequences of the 2016 presidential election outcome resulting in an even more pronounced U.S. retreat from Europe, Germany, and Europe hoped otherwise. In the initial analysis, it was significantly harder to foresee that the U.S. would end up abandoning international agreements, questioning NATO's Article 5 security guarantee, disregarding WTO rules, and massively hampering long-standing peace processes. However, this should have become a more poignant scenario once Donald Trump became the Republican Party's nominee for president. At this point, it would have been advisable to develop a scenario in which Donald Trump, as the 45th U.S. president, would seek to implement his campaign promises toward national interests and away from the values-based transatlantic partnership. That did not happen. Instead, in the aftermath of Trump's election to the presidency, there was a general hope among allies that U.S. foreign policy would remain consistent and that the presidential office would have a moderating influence on the newly elected president. Whatever the likely root causes – wishful thinking, group-think analysis, absence of a crisis, the habit of free-riding, unwillingness to prepare the public, or short-term planning – the lack of foresight, as a result, has caught Germany and Europe in reacting with crisis-management solutions since January 2017.

Although the Arab Spring would have been hard to predict ahead of time, it could have been included in strategic scenarios in the examination of the possible consequences of state collapse in various Northern African and Middle Eastern countries. The operation in Libya was an early indicator that reconstructing and stabilizing countries with similar cultural, religious, and political diversity would be an enormous challenge. Furthermore, European countries had been engaged in a deal on illegal immigration with Muammar al-Gaddafi before the operations in Libya. Against this background, it is particularly surprising that the German government did recognize possible consequences of collapse, also on domestic political fortunes, and withheld their vote in the UN Security Council due to impart the uncertainty of what an operation there would bring. Nevertheless, Europeans failed to prepare with foresight the repercussions of the military operation.

Although foresight has many benefits, one cannot underestimate the inhibitions strategic foresight faces. From mirror imaging to the influence of elections cycles, intuitive thinking, hubris and paradigm shifts, group thinking, many forces can hinder strategic foresight, which is why it is so important to apply the method with as much precision and academic durability as possible. It is not a method that tries to predict the future, but a scientific tool to estimate the effects of implications, consequences of current actions, decisions, and trends – trying to foresee problems and avoid them, if possible. Try to predict developments, based on rational analysis, and paint a vision or grand strategy for what one would like to achieve in the future. Strategic foresight is a method that tries to incorporate an interdisciplinary approach to understanding all implications, drivers, and actors. Strategic foresight methods are quite appropriately based in theory, including theories of political science such as realism, constructivism, and game theory.

The German Problem: Germany Shies Away From Strategic Foresight

While German security policy has already started to change substantially over the last years, four obstacles still stand in the way of Germany developing an acceptable leadership role and effectively addressing critical challenges. The first is the missing culture of strategic planning in Germany. The country's dominant strategic culture has revolved around its civilian power since the end of World War II: One main reason why neither foresight nor early action plays a central role in German foreign policy. According to Jan Techau[320], two critical factors characterize Germany's current strategic culture: One, coming to terms with the crimes committed by the National Socialists, and two, working through the more general lessons learned from the war. As a result, Germany has adopted a feeling of shame, guilt, and national responsibility regarding foreign policy engagement that views "regular" foreign policy with a suspicious eye, including articulation of national interests. Instead, the German self-image is significantly grounded in pacifism, anti-militarism, a strong sense of morality, and the desire to disconnect from international interest-based and power politics. Historical shame is no longer the most prominent feature of policy restraint. Germans have mastered ways to deal with the past. Guilt from the Second World War focusses on Israel

---

[320] Jan Techau, Greater Ambition, Please!, in: Berlin Policy Journal, Online: https://berlinpolicyjourn-a-l.com/greater-ambition-please/, (Berlin, 2017).

and Poland. A positive approach to its pro-active policies for European integration and in improving relations to Russia dominate the historical foreign policy debate, but Germany less active outside these neighboring countries. As a result of restrained foreign policy, the German Armed Forces have a reputation that is not militaristic.

In comparison to other Europeans, Germany's lack of significant colonial legacies is an asset. It is better to take pride in the country's positive soft power image in a world-class exporting nation and a leading manufacturing country. At the same time, restrictions on German sovereignty after the war led Germany to have minimal influence on security policy, while its Western allies dealt with international security issues. Thus, the lack of broad public debate about strategic and geopolitical questions hindered strategic planning.

Second, the country's history weighs heavily against a German national strategic debate that meets stiff resistance from its neighbors and friends. Germany's history compounds its reluctant leadership dilemma. Despite Chancellor Angela Merkel's surprisingly energetic speech at the Munich Security Conference in 2019, Germany has begun to operationalize its 2014 Munich Security Conference pledge for "more responsibility" only reluctantly.[321] Meanwhile, Germans are also still at odds with the role Germany should play in international politics. In a 2019 poll by the Friedrich-Ebert-Foundation, 59 % said Germany should be internationally neutral. In the very same survey, 70 % also said Germany should pursue an active foreign policy and have a significant role in solving international confrontations, crises, and conflicts.[322]

Germany's culture of remembrance and neighbors' concerns about a dominating Germany still seriously hamper its ability to assume a more active role within Europe. Overcoming historical obstacles to its future still eludes German policymakers. The country remains determined to avoid returning to its history of a special German Way (*Sonderweg*). By sharing leadership with France and the other EU Member States, Germany finds leadership. Such a style of '*Leaders in Partnership*' in Europe is consistent with Germany's commitment to avoid hegemony and to embed its security in the EU and the transatlantic relationship. Since its European neighbors, just as much as the Germans themselves continue to view the idea of German leadership skeptically, the country had defaulted to a form of "reluctant leadership." That is particularly true in those cases when a

---

321 Angela Merkel, Speech by Federal Chancellor Dr Angela Merkel on 16 February 2019 at the 55th Munich Security Conference, Online: https://www.bundeskanzlerin.de/bkin-en/news/speech-by-federal-chancellor-dr-angela-merkel-on-16-february-2019-at-the-55th-munich-security-conference-1582318, (Munich, 2019).
322 Christian Trippe and Ben Knight, Munich Security Report: The world is in crisis, in: Deutsche Welle, German News Service, Online: https://www.deutschland.de/en/topic/politics/munich-security-report-the-world-is-in-crisis, (Frankfurt am Main: 2019).

more proactive German foreign policy was deemed unavoidable, as in the welcoming culture for war refugees in 2015.

Constitutional *Staatsräson*, commitments to democracy, human rights, and for Europe guides and binds Germany's leadership in a culture of self-restraint. Its remembrance culture also acts as a restraint on policy excesses. However, since unification, Germany's size, growing economic weight, and geographic position have pushed the country towards a more active role in European affairs.

Third, the transatlantic partnership grew out of the Cold War when NATO provided security and strategy that allowed Germany and Europe primarily to pursue diplomacy and economic prosperity. Two essential principles have characterized Germany's role. One, pronounced restraint, is captured in its pledge that never again war will emanate from German soil. The other is a firm commitment to multilateral cooperation, treaties, and international institutions, combined with a commitment to lead in partnership, not unilaterally. The German foreign policy problem is how to seek and build an overall stable, reliable, and predictable global multilateralism in the unraveling world order. The political leadership hesitates to engage in a more strategic approach to future challenges and explore the full range of possible scenarios that might unfold. Particularly as Washington, in the global power shift, is reducing its role as Europe's primary security guarantee and closest ally, the vision of stability reveals itself as hope or wishful thinking.

Although hope dies last, to live up to its objectives, Germany will have to implement change. Europe's most powerful country will have to rethink its approach to foreign policy: Germany needs to overcome its strategic deficit and establish a broad public debate about the security, foreign policy, goals, and guidelines. While remaining rooted in the principles laid out in the Basic Law, Germany can initiate a broad, informed strategic debate about current and future challenges to Europe in foreign and security policy through strategic thinking and foresight. Thus, Germany could spare the costs – not just financially – of maintaining a geostrategic balance, constructing and defending a rule-based order, and engaging on a global level. In sum, this led to a culture of restraint, passivity, and reactive engagement, which continues to this day. Until now, the convenience of exercising restraint in a transatlantic, geopolitically stable environment made it obsolete to engage in strategic foresight.[323]

German unification, the wars in the Balkans, the attacks of 9/11, the operation in Libya, and the crises in Ukraine and Syria made it clear that this strategic culture stands in contrast to new foreign policy realities. The country faced a situation that required it to actively participate in international operations – operations that were ambiguous regarding the moral assessment and legal case,

---

323 Ibid.

but that also made passivity impossible. As a result, observers accuse Germany of lacking an overall concept (Gesamtkonzept) in these types of situations.

Fourth, coalition governments are the norm in Germany, and the constitutionally-based independence of the ministries (*Ressortprinzip*) often result in ministries pursuing diverging and sometimes even conflicting goals or implementing strategies that are not coordinated with each other.

German policymaking is organized around legislative periods, election campaigning, and coalition governments, which are the norms in Germany. The country's culture of restraint has a clear sense of shame and guilt as well as an intense striving for moral correctness. German initiative or participation in morally and legally unclear policies, such as the Libya UNSC debates, Russia policy with a divided public, or conflicts in former French or British colonies, can amount to domestic political suicide. As long as an early engagement might also have negative consequences, evoke backlash, or even fail, German politicians typically refrain from starting initiatives. Germany shies away from the tough job of making moral compromises, which are entirely unavoidable in foreign policy. However, it doesn't do so because risky interventions might hurt others, but somewhat because, whenever complications arise, the country itself is afflicted the most. Foreign policy decisions are often choices of choosing the lesser of two evils. In Germany, political difficulties public criticism and calls for restraint and passivity prevail.

This reluctant leadership is also one of the reasons why foreign affairs issues are seldom the focus of federal election campaigns. This absence was particularly evident in 2017 when neither the migration crisis, the conflicts in Europe nor the crises in Ukraine and Syria received much attention by the established parties. Attempt to depoliticize foreign affairs might have contributed to the ascendancy of Germany's right-wing populists', the Alternative for Deutschland (AfD). The importance of the debate about Germany's future role on the international stage in the face of various crises, conflicts, and shifts was all but non-existent. A foreign policy debate would have meant entering the problem area of German strategic culture – resistance to the expression of precise foreign policy positions and visions – which would have resulted in a loss in electoral support. The foreign minister position is often passed around like a hot potato when allocating minister portfolios of a new coalition government. Without a broad public and political debate about strategic questions of foreign and security policy – which could balance out geopolitical realities and the strategic culture – Germany lacks the political will to engage in strategic foresight and address threats and risks at an early stage.

Especially concerning power politics and party politics, this can lead to a strategic downfall. As long as the constitution protects the ministries' independence, the *Ressortprinzip* will hamper Germany's ability to develop an overarching strategic concept for foreign and security policy. The "Independent Ministries Principle" (*Ressortprinzip*)[324] that the German Basic Law (Article 65, para 2, Grundgesetz) prescribes, empowers cabinet departments with independent responsibility that significantly hinders the effective coordination of the various branches of government regarding foreign and security policy. That principle grants ministries independence in pursuing diverging and sometimes even conflicting goals or implementing strategies uncoordinated policies, but this lack of coordination hampers Germany's ability to develop an overarching, coherent strategic concept for foreign and security policy. This constitutional provision against the coordination of departments makes strategic foresight close to impossible. Without establishing an overriding foreign policy concept that integrates all departments and ministries, a coherent strategy is elusive. There is no reference point for future scenarios without clearly creating goals and interests as well as guidelines.

The analysis of German foreign policy since 1989, the changing external circumstances that are altering the country's foreign policy benchmarks today, and the identified challenges and strategic deficits lead me to this conclusion: Germany has to "reinvent itself." I offer a perspective on the German Problem to overcome the hindrances to a path forward under today's changing circumstances. Typically, departments exercise their constitutional mandate in their areas of responsibility and only engage in cooperation if forced to do so in the face of the realities of the situation on-site, and most cases, out of pure pragmatism on the level of execution. Meanwhile, ministries insist on a policy of independent responsibility, although the situation has improved since 2016 when the Whitebook and the guiding principles (*Leitlinien*) made a difference. The desire to distinguish oneself and the unwillingness to cooperate with ministers of a different party affiliation inhibit shared approaches as it is nearly impossible to overcome the wish for preeminence among ministries. As a result, foreign policy often assumes an ambiguous character with the goals of different ministries sometimes downright contradicting each other. For instance, one ministry may make its mark in building schools, another in securing sea routes, and the third one in deescalating conflicts, all the while a fourth ministry undoes all of these efforts by entering into a trade agreement and engaging in an arms deal on top.

Efforts to create a national security council to coordinate policy among ministries have difficult hurdles to overcome. The exercise of the constitutional mandate for independent ministries headed by coalition partners of different parties is an obstacle to a coherent set of policies. In October 2019, Defense Minister Annegret Kramp-Karrenbauer advocated for the establishment of an

---

324 The Basic Law of the Federal Republic of Germany, Article 65, para 2, Online: https://www.cvce.eu/content/publication/1999/1/1/7fa618bb-604e-4980-b667-76bf0cd0dd9b/publishable_en.pdf.

internationally controlled security zone in Syria, with the possibility of German and European military deployments to the region in cooperation with Turkey and Russia. She stressed that Europe and Germany have a strong imperative to take action in Syria.[325] Foreign Minister Heiko Maas (SPD), received news of the proposal via text message shortly before the announcement.[326] Katarina Barley, also SPD, commented that "this proposition came as a complete surprise not only to us as parliamentarians but also to the foreign minister… this is not the way to introduce any diplomatic or military mission."[327]

This uncoordinated policy process is not unique. Coalition government policy incoherence was especially apparent during the confrontations during September 2019 with Iran in attacks on ships in the Strait of Hormuz. A military conflict with Iran was increasingly likely, and Europeans brought up three options to counter Iranian military threats. First, they could choose to do nothing to keep the Strait open, thereby capitulating to the Iranians seizure of ships. Second, Europe could organize its military mission that would risk armed conflict with Iran. Or, third, the Europeans could watch the situation and conduct surveillance of the strait with aircraft. In response to a request to send the German Navy to participate in protecting the freedom of navigation through the Strait, Defense Minister Annegret Kramp-Karrenbauer suggested joining a European mission. At the same time, Foreign Minister Heiko Maas was reluctant and opted for surveillance. Other German political parties outright rejected the idea of a *Bundesmarine* operation.

As discussed in the chapter on the European Monetary Union, Finance Minister Olaf Scholz proposed deepening and completing the European banking union to avoid dependence on the United States or China for financial services. In November 2019, Scholz suggested collective insolvency and resolution procedure for banks. He made four points; reducing the number of non-performing loans and risk from sovereign debt, creating a banking union with a common European deposit insurance mechanism, and establishing a common corporate

---

325 Annegret Kramp-Karrenbauer quoted in: Deutsche Welle, Krampkarrenbauer im Interview mit der Deutschen Welle: Eine internationale Sicherheitszone in Syrien, Annegret Kramp-Karrenbauer im Interview, Online: https://www.youtube.com/watch?v=VK8t0Ti9WfQ, (Bonn, 2019a).
326 Frankfurter Allgemeine Zeitung, Maas kritisiert Kramp-Karrenbauers "SMS-Diplomatie", in: Frankfurter Allgemeinen Zeitung,Online: https://www.faz.net/aktuell/politik/ausland/syrien-maas-beschwert-sich-ueber-kramp-karrenbauers-sms-diplomatie-16445725.html, (Frankfurt am Main, 2019).
327 Deutsche Welle, Germany calls for international safe zone Syria, in: Deutsche Welle, Online: https://www.dw.com/en/german-defense-chief-recommends-international-security-zone-in-syria/a-50924304, (Bonn, 2019b).

tax base and a minimum effective tax, and uniformly taxing banks to prevent arbitrage.[328] He did not consult other ministries.

The German Problem, as Financial Times' editor Tony Barber commented, lies in "Germany's unruly domestic politics, its leader's gradual reassessment of the nation's standing and the broader problems of EU integration."[329] While the Scholz plan will meet resistance over the conditions he has placed on bank regulation and a common corporate tax, it is a bold plan.[330] The deeper problem is Germany's coalition government and its *Ressortprinzip* of constitutional independence for its ministries.

Finally, constitutions govern our democracies, and in times of significant change, like those we are facing today, we need to consider and test changes under the law before public opinion. However, given the dominant civilian power culture, it is politically risky for politicians to suggest a German initiative or participation in international alliances publicly when the conflict is morally or legally unclear. Dogmatic public backlash often prevents an informed debate on foreign policy issues. Of course, we all understand that domestic rather than international or security issues drive the political fortunes of aspiring and high-level German politicians. Although politicians know what needs to be done, they do not know how to be re-elected once they have done it. Nevertheless, democracies that fail to deal effectively with the concerns of the public make themselves vulnerable to appeals from fear-based populists. The Bundestag is the best home to debate the risks democracies face.

In Uncertain Times: Recalibrating Germany's Foreign Policy Role

In this conundrum of uncertain times, the transatlantic partnership has constituted a vast zone of peace, prosperity, and democracy for most of the last 70 years but has now has moved into uncertain times. Looking back at the formation of the transatlantic partnership, President Harry Truman's decision to share the power of the United States with Europe was the foundation of peace in Europe. He turned America away from the earlier policy of isolation following the First World War. Along with his European partners and others, he created a multilateral institutional structure that included the United Nations, the World Bank, the International Monetary Fund, NATO, and the Organization for European

---

328 Tony Barber, Germany's Eurozone gambit could meet a swift death, in: Financial Times, Online: https://www.google.com/search?channel=trow2&client=firefox-b-d&q=Barber%2C+Tony%2C+%E2%80%9CGermany%E2%80%99s+Eurozone+gambit+could+meet+a+swift+death%2C%E2%80%9D+Financial+Times%2C+November+8%2C+2019, (London, 2019).
329 Ibid.
330 Ibid.

Economic Cooperation (OEEC). Meanwhile, (Western) Europeans worked to overcome their own, centuries-old differences and built the predecessors to the European Union.

Together Americans and Europeans united Germany and Europe through combined military and economic strength and, with a Peaceful Revolution thirty years ago, contributed to stability not only in Europe but in the world as well. The community has grown to over 900 million inhabitants of more than 30 countries and has set an example for regional cooperation in Africa, Latin America, and Southeast Asia. It serves as a mainstay of the liberal world order.

Germany is in the process of recalibrating its foreign policy and aspires to its role as a leader in partnership with other countries. The country remains firmly opposed to any form of renewed unilateralism of dominance. It exercises its full national sovereignty but in a sovereign obligation to the EU. It deploys *Bundeswehr* soldiers only in alliance with NATO or the United Nations and with a parliamentary mandate. Its commitment to Europe in the Basic Law's preamble is deeply ingrained. As Minister for Foreign Affairs, Heiko Maas, emphasized in a speech in Tokyo in July 2018, Germany's current foreign policy constitutes a model of multilateral leadership under the guiding principles of rules-based cooperation, integration, and multilateral institutions.[331] In this sense, Berlin's current approach to foreign policy directly opposes Donald Trump's nationalist, antagonistic understanding of foreign policy that has resulted from the "Make America Great Again" policy.

For Germany, the European Union plays a central role: German and European foreign and security policy are deeply intertwined. Former Minister for Foreign Affairs, Frank-Walter Steinmeier, concluded in his 2014 foreign policy review, the Federal Republic's international role can only emerge through a global Europe. It is through the broader framework of the European Union, which turns Germany's economic power into either a strategic and political asset or a strategic and political liability.[332] Regardless of the change in global realities, the German Basic Law commits Germany to peaceful cooperation, which remains at the heart of German foreign policy.

---

[331] Heiko Maas, Rede von Außenminister Heiko Maas am National Graduate Institute for Policy Studies in Tokyo, Japan, 25.07. 2018, Online: https://www.auswaertiges-amt.de/de/newsroom/maas-japan/2121670, (Tokyo, 2018).

[332] Frank-Walter Steinmeier Foreign Policy Review.

Reluctance, Strategy, and Foresight

In practice, however, Germany's foreign policy avoids any declaration of assumption of leadership or providing impulses, as the Defense White Paper on German Security Policy and the Future of the *Bundeswehr* from 2016 states.

> Germany is prepared to provide a substantial, decisive, and early stimulus to the international debate, to accept responsibility, and to assume leadership. This includes a willingness to contribute to the management of current and future security and humanitarian challenges. We are, however, aware of the limits of our capabilities.[333]

Germany remains, for the most part, firmly settled in a strategic culture that lacks the kind of clear goals and strategic thinking that are needed to fulfill these demands. The prevailing strategic culture is still reluctant, shies away from leadership, and avoids compromises in morally ambiguous situations where there is no easy way out – the kind of moral ambivalence that is characteristic of foreign policy. Instead, Germany often tends to opt for non-action.

The 2016 White Paper a step in acknowledging the changing global realities and addresses answers to them. The paper's first section may a rough draft for a national security strategy. In a bold move in the Federal Republic's history of avoiding national interest debates, it outlines vital national interests and foreign policy goals. These include the protection of Germany's citizens, maintaining the country's sovereignty and territorial integrity as well as that of its partners and allies, upholding the rules-based international order by international law, promoting responsible handling of natural resources and deepening European integration.[334] In practice, however, the White Paper is more of a plan for crisis management. It has one critical flaw: It fails to explore possible foreign and security policy scenarios and engage in strategic foresight that fully recognizes current trends and potential shifts in the framework within which German foreign policy operates. While acknowledging the upheavals shaking the international system, it nevertheless still assumes a vision of overall geopolitical stability and predictability that is becoming increasingly elusive, especially given Washington's current alignment.

As a result, the 2016 Defense White Paper does mark a milestone in the development of Germany's strategic culture. However, it still isn't enough to reach the goal of establishing a broad debate about foreign and security policy that can engage the public. The Paper already outlines some fundamental interests and goals in a relatively precise manner. Still, Germany will also have to develop a coherent security strategy based on a clear vision that integrates goals,

---

333 The Federal Government, White Paper, 2016 On German Security Policy and the Future of the Bundeswehr, (Berlin, 2016), p. 23.
334 Ibid. p.24f.

values, instruments, and priorities. The list of Germany's foreign policy goals is long. It includes supporting France as an equal partner within the EU, deepening cooperation with China, managing Brexit and the resulting fallout, dealing with the consequences of the Trump presidency for the international order, and effectively managing the refugee crisis starting by addressing the causes of global refugee flows. Instead of trying to resolve these issues on a case-by-case basis, however, Germany's foreign policy efforts need to be guided by an overarching strategy. If the country establishes a broad and informed strategic approach in public debate about challenges, goals, and possible instruments of German foreign and security policy, it will find political answers to these challenges, underpinned by broad democratic legitimization.

Given the long history of a similarly reluctant positioning, it is precisely this lack of coordination and strategic thinking that is leaving Germany's allies disillusioned with Germany's strategic policies. Its partners seem to be taking Chancellor Angela Merkel's expression of the necessity that Europeans take their fate into their own hands as not much more than lip service without tangible consequences. In Paris, for instance, Germany is seen as "hiding" behind France. Four years after high-ranking German politicians first announced their intention to shift gears at the Munich Security Conference in 2014, the German government's crisis management appears stuck in old patterns. When push comes to shove, Germany often remains on the sidelines, leaving the heavy lifting to others.

This reluctant leadership is partly due to constitutional restrictions; however, decision-makers often cite the German *Bundeswehr*'s insufficient capacities as the reason for staying out of armed conflicts. But the German Problem goes way beyond this reluctance. Europe's most significant and most economically robust country doesn't have a strategic approach to foreign and security policy. In Germany, the lack of strategic thinking, the missing public debate about security issues, and the country's historical resistance against an excess of foreign policy engagement are all closely interlinked. The Körber Foundation has called for greater German engagement with the German public's opinion: 49 % prefer international restraint over increased participation, a value similar to past years,[335] and more than half of Germans believe defense spending should stay at current levels.[336] For the most part, Germans remain deeply skeptical of all issues related to international engagement, security, and the identification of national interests. Assessing Germany's current role in the world, Timothy Garton Ash

---

335 Körber Stiftung, *The Berlin Pulse 2019/20. German Foreign Policy in Perspective*, (Körber Stiftung: Berlin, 2019), p. 33.
336 Ibid., p. 37.

concluded that "there has been no historical caesura since October 3, 1990, large enough to justify talking about a 'new Germany'." [337] Until now, that is.

The German culture of remembrance acts as a restraint on German foreign policy excess. It is neither possible nor advisable to draw a line under Germany's history and move forward without looking back. Still, after Germany's Hegelian transition, from one extreme to the other, the current global upheavals raise the question of whether it will be possible to find a balance between military power projections and apprehensive inaction. Using its devastating historical experience as a justification not to act in the present is becoming increasingly untenable and is starting to wear on Germany's allies. The assumption of German foreign policy is the idea that there is an overall stable, reliable, and predictable global framework for Germany to act within is withering. The country refuses to engage in a more strategic approach to future challenges and explore the full range of possible scenarios that might unfold in the future. Germany has indeed started talking of responsibility and is showing significantly more presence in international conflicts – but it is still shying away from making tough calls. To live up to its objectives, Germany will have to implement some changes. Particularly, Europe's reputedly most powerful country will have to rethink its approach to foreign policy. Germany needs to overcome its strategic deficit, particularly in the sense that it must establish a broad public debate about security, foreign policy, goals, and guidelines. While Germany remains firmly rooted in the principles laid out in the Basic Law, it needs a broad, informed strategic debate about current and future challenges in foreign and security policy and deeper engagement in strategic thinking.

Strategic Foresight is not a Predictions' Plan

First and foremost, it is necessary to distinguish between predictions of the future on the one hand and strategic foresight on the other. The point of strategic foresight is not to forecast the future or even assess which scenarios are most likely to occur. Instead, strategic foresight aims to outline various possible scenarios that might come to pass under certain circumstances based on current trends and developments. By carefully evaluating interests, values, and goals, and subsequently developing clear guidelines for political action, strategic thinking allows for the development of various courses of action for these possible scenarios.

---

337 Timothy G. Ash, Think Global Act Regional, in Berlin Pulse, Online: https://www.koerber-stiftung.de/en/the-berlin-pulse/2017/garton-ash, (Berlin, 2017).

The crucial characteristic of strategic thinking is the element of preparation. It opens space to proactively and considerately shape foreign policy issues instead of having to resort to purely reactive crisis management. To engage in strategic thinking means to evaluate current trends and developments as objectively as possible to map out a wide range of possible scenarios. Strategic foresight has two pillars: a strategic vision that includes a clear understanding of the vital interests, goals, and guidelines for foreign and security policy, and the development of the essential components required to realize this vision. These two pillars determine the resources needed to implement the strategy.

German and European Security Strategy

The numerous disruptions of the international system and Washington's retreat from leadership raise the urgent question of what order will emerge next and who will lead it. A civilian power relies on a stable global framework within which it can act. But the world has been changing since Germany developed its post-war foreign policy profile. The United States no longer serves as Europe's security guarantee, and the international order that allowed Germany to focus on its economic growth while keeping a low profile in foreign and security policy is no longer uncontested. The British and American leaders are passing the torch of the vales-based order.

Will Germany, which depends vitally on the liberal order as it is located right in the heart of Europe, reach out to accept the torch? Its export-dominated economy is deeply reliant on international trade and has a preference for a foreign policy based on diplomacy and multilateralism. Keeping up a rule-based global order is a matter of quintessential national interest. For Germany, defending the values laid out in the Basic Law will only be achievable by stepping up, and by extensively cooperating with its allies and partners. Germany and most of its partners – particularly the other European powers, but also others such as Japan – are far too small to make the rules for a new international order by themselves. Still, over the last seven decades, the EU has grown into a political union that, as the world's second-largest economy, holds 22.8 percent of global economic output and has steadily developed its foreign policy footprint with a common foreign and security policy. What this suggests is that Europe might be able to do more than watch the global upheavals from the sidelines. By pooling their strengths to a greater extent than they have in the past, Germany, the EU, and its partners could become what Heiko Maas recently called "rule shapers." That is a coalition of states committed to cooperation and democratic principles that jointly contribute to shaping the framework of global politics and stabilizing the international system.[338]

Security concerns and demands differ substantially across Europe. For instance, the Baltic countries, with proximity to Russia, struggle with entirely different security concerns than Southern European countries bordering the Mediterranean. Nevertheless, Germany and its partners are united in various overarching goals and values. These range from maintaining territorial integrity and peace on the European continent to strengthening multilateral institutions and promoting shared European values such as civil rights and liberties, democracy, free trade, and the rule of law as guiding principles of international politics. The European Security and Defense package, built on the 2016 EU Global Strategy and approved by the European Council in December 2016, already aims to demonstrate heightened European cohesion on the international stage. It also created some urgently needed tools and measures for cooperation in the area of security and defense, such as supporting the European Defense Action Plan (EDAP) with new financial instruments for capability development and defense cooperation.

However, the EU's underlying strategic vision still needs to be further developed and put on a much broader footing. It does appear that most of Europe agrees on the fact that the European approach to foreign policy and security needs to be revised and requires intensified cooperation. Emmanuel Macron has presented his vision for a reformed European Union to step up to global leadership, suggesting that change might be on the way. However, Europeans will need to become more confident and more concrete. A vague consensus is not the same as a strategy. This lack of strategy is becoming an especially urgent issue now that the strain on the transatlantic relationship is weakening one of the main pillars of European foreign and security policy. Trump has reinterpreted the EU as a foe of the United States in issues of trade, and he may become a catalyst for the EU to advance further this endeavor of crafting a common strategy, particularly if he wins a second term of office in 2020. If it doesn't want to get overrun by the upheavals shaking international politics, Europe will need a fully coherent joint approach to foreign and security policy. Such policies need public support, which is democratically sustained and underpinned by a clear strategic vision for concrete problems of managing relations with Russia, the Middle East, China, the US, and issues of migration, defense, security.

The EU faces collective action problems due to its size and its incomplete supranational structure. Europe is an imagined community, not a unified actor,

---

338 Heiko Maas, Rede von Außenminister Heiko Maas am National Graduate Institute for Policy Studies in Tokyo, Japan, 25.07. 2018, Online: https://www.auswaertiges-amt.de/de/newsroom/maas-japan/2121670, (Tokyo, 2018).

with competing interests, powers, norms, priorities, preferences, geographic locations, and legacies. Although the questions of whether it should pool sovereignty (supranationalism instead of mere intergovernmentalism) were never decisively resolved, areas of supranationalism are limited. More influential members are keen to constrain the move of sovereignty to the transnational level. All these issues complicate strategic planning, but German and European security are inextricably linked. Germany can only emerge as a credible foreign policy actor through its role in the European Union. On the other hand, due to its size, location, and economic weight, Germany is also a critical strategic actor for Europe. For the EU to come up with a coherent strategy, it is paramount that Germany takes a clear stand on foreign policy and security issues.

Against this background, the crucial question is: Will Germany develop a coherent security strategy together with its partners given rapidly changing global conditions? Even though Germany holds a key position in Europe, it cannot and may not impose its will on its European partners. Germany cannot strive to unilaterally dominate the European Union on foreign policy and security issues. A common European security strategy differs substantially from a German one in that regard in that it must take other national interests and approaches into consideration as well. Due to Germany's size and weight, it is also nearly impossible to remove Germany from the equation when it comes to establishing a practical joint EU approach to foreign policy. The way out of this dilemma is to create a broad, open strategic debate about European foreign policy and security with all European partners. Germany, thoroughly evaluating and openly communicating its strategic positions to its partners, can and should lay the foundation for this process. For Europe to develop a broad, joint debate on its strategic goals, interests, and guidelines, Germany must develop one too.

Chapter 8: An Independent Council of Experts to Support Strategic Thinking

Without falling in the trap of returning to German dominance in Europe, the last part of this book suggests a council of experts to help resolve the German Problem. It is two-fold: to create an updated strategic culture in Germany and to establish a "leaders in partnership" approach in Europe based on cooperation and the concept of "sovereign obligation."

The proposal to help overcome Germany's strategic deficit and help Germany rise to meet its international responsibilities is to introduce a Council of Experts for Strategic Foresight hosted by the German *Bundestag*. Such a Council could lay the foundation for a continuing, informed public debate on strategy and foreign and security policy, based on annual and intermittent experts' reports that include scenarios to inform the policy debate on current as well as likely future challenges. *Bundestag* committee hearings allow discussions that should consist of other Europeans, the British, and Americans. The *Bundestag* could hold regular hearings soliciting views from domestic and international think tanks, allies, and neighbors in a transparent, open debate. Strategic foresight provided by a Council of Experts would contribute to an informed public discussion to sound policymaking. A Council could add significantly to more strategic consideration of German foreign policy for Europe. Transparent and inclusive debates could help fulfill the country's constitutional obligation to Europe and its international responsibility for the global commons.

Looking ahead, identifying risks and opportunities could add significantly to more strategic consideration of German foreign policy for Europe. In the short run, it could inform the policy process and reassure *Bundestag* Members' constituents that their Members are managing the issues that determine Germany's future. In the long term, this could lead to a change in the strategic culture, enabling elites and politicians to develop a strategy for Germany and Europe.

Overcoming Obstacles to a strategic future

Obstacles to coherent and consistent policymaking are blocking Germany's and Europe's future. The clarion call is for a new strategic policy process. Germany began in earnest to accept more international responsibility since the 2014 Munich Security Conference. The Government wrote the 2016 Whitepaper for Security Policy and the Future of the *Bundeswehr* that Germany has to start acting more proactively.[339] Germany has agreed, in theory, to accept responsibility and is poised to take a leadership role in Europe. Steinmeier also made this clear during his tenure as Minister for Foreign Affairs. In 2017, then-Minister for Foreign Affairs, Sigmar Gabriel, said in a speech at the Körber Foundation: "We have to accept the fact that either the rest of the world will shape the future unless we try to contribute to shaping this world."[340] For Germany, he said, there isn't a spot on the sidelines of international politics anymore.

However, Germany has achieved little strategic foresight in the past five years. A strategic approach to foreign and security policy based on foresight indicated goals and interests, overarching guidelines, and broad strategic debate that extends into the public sphere is needed more than ever. In the future, strategic planning can translate the 2014 commitment for more international responsibility, a new-found expression of the political action Germany and Europe must take to help overcome past shortcomings, lack of preparation for possible foreign policy crises, and unexpected security issues.

These shortcomings are recognized by the political establishment already. The Federal Government's efforts for a strategic approach fell within the framework of the PeaceLab process, the Defense White Paper. The current coalition agreement did seek strategic approaches and comprehensive cooperation between ministries.[341] The Government has the intention to strengthen strategic analysis in government-supported think tanks, to better coordinate among departments, and to develop a National Security Council.

While this is a positive development, it nevertheless will not overcome the structural problems concerning a strategic approach and foresight. Expanding existing policy institutes such as the Stiftung Wissenschaft und Politik (SWP), the

---

339 The Federal Government, White Paper, 2016 On German Security Policy and the Future of the Bundeswehr, (Berlin, 2016).
340 Sigmar Gabriel, Rede zur Eröffnung des Berlin Foreign Policy Forum 2017 von Sigmar Gabriel, Online: https://www.youtube.com/watch?v=kcljjSBLBg4, (Berlin, 2017).
341 James D. Bindenagel and Simone Becker, Strategic Thinking, Planning, and Culture in Germany as an Integral Part of European Security Policy, in: Gunther Hellmann and Daniel Jacobi, Germany, The German White Paper 2016 and the Challenge of Crafting Security Strategies, Online: https://www.fb03.uni-frankfurt.de/76345851/Band_Crafting_Security_Strategies_Aspen_englisch.pdf, (Berlin/Frankfurt am Main, 2019), pp. 115–122.

German Society for International Cooperation (GIZ) and the German Institute for Development Policy (DIE), Deutsche *Gesellschaft für Auswärtige Politik* (German Council on Foreign Relations (DGAP), the Koerber Foundation, and others behind the scenes will not be enough to promote public strategic debate, and neither will the boost of expert discourse by financially supporting think tanks. Disruption of the current dynamics of political processes in foreign and security policy may help create coordination between departments. Otherwise, the planning process will remain marginal, and German politics will keep its reactive character.

Due in part to these concerns, suggestions for the introduction of new structural features – including a National Security Advisor or the idea of a National Security Council[342], were also made during the PeaceLab process. However, these institutions should be embedded, for example, within the Chancellery, a ministry, or the Federal Security Council. These suggestions could automatically result in a debate about competencies and powers that need to be avoided, particularly in a coalition government. Discussions about the introduction of a National Security Council held between 2008 and 2010, at the suggestion of the CDU-CSU parliamentary group, demonstrated the conflict between policymaking and foresight.

Germany can resolve this dilemma by implementing a more strategic process in its political structure to overcome its reactive, crisis-management culture. Discussions on a National Security Council have not led to a national coordinating council. The Bundestag offers a way to resolve *Ressortprinzip* dilemmas and the dependence of think tanks on a specific ministry. A strategic foresight approach does not replace policymaking; it builds an informed public debate that is the foundation for effective policymaking. Germany needs to create an independent expert council for strategic foresight, one that is not identical to a German National Security Council. A Council for strategic foresight is one that supports an informed public discussion and is separate from inter-ministerial or intra-coalition rivalry. To create a balance, a comprehensive public debate on foreign and security policy based on undogmatic analyses and prognoses is crucial. An open discussion is an essential requirement to balance Germany's interests and obligations to overcome a strategic culture deficit in foreign and security policy.

Strategic planning, projecting possible scenarios, and gauging risks and threats allow for a chance to create such a balance. In its 2016 White Book, its

---

342 Sarah Brockmeier, A German National Security Council: If Kramp-Karrenbauer is Serious, Her Work Starts Now, in: Global Public Policy Institute, Online: https://www.gppi.net/2019/12/05/a-german-national-security-council-if-kramp-karrenbauer-is-serious-her-work-starts-now, (Berlin, 2019).

Review 2014 for foreign policy, and its most recent coalition agreement, the German government has recognized the need to strengthen existing structures within the ministries and think tanks linked to the government's strategic analysis. A *Council of Experts for Strategic Foresight* could increase Germany's strategic planning capabilities and contribute significantly to a more strategic consideration of German foreign policy.[343]

A Council on Strategic Foresight as an instrument of the Bundestag could foster the basis for such a strategic debate in Germany. Through discussion scenarios of the future and their implications as well as alternatives for actions before events happened, one could avoid crisis management and open up new possibilities, by creating an atmosphere of acting rather than reacting. Simultaneously, debates such a Council will bring will inform the public debate and would, therefore, inform politics but without infringing on the policymaking process. To look ahead, anticipating concrete risks and opportunities as well as evaluating alternatives and can focus on trends and their impact on international politics. However, that calls for a new German strategic culture.

By holding regular strategic foresight parliamentary committee hearings on global trends, scenarios, and action plans, the Bundestag would ensure a transparent and informed discussion of the challenges and policies to meet them. Inviting Germany's allies, think tanks, government experts, and others to such committee hearings would create cross-cutting European ideas and build confidence in European consideration of Germany's political debate. In the short-term, this would lead to more informed politics and the public, which assures voters that politicians are managing vital topics in the parliament. An independent Council of Experts for Strategic Foresight could foster strategic discussions, which could lay the foundation for a continuing, informed public debate of strategy and foreign and security policy. Annual and irregular experts' reports that include scenarios and policy options for current, as well as likely future challenges, would, in the long run, lead to a change in the strategic culture. And such continuing debates can enable elites and politicians to more easily develop a strategy for Germany and Europe that could help to strengthen or reshape world order with a robust transatlantic pillar.[344]

While taking into account the need for debate on policy, one fact becomes increasingly evident. The Federal Republic of Germany is a crucial EU member state, but only by developing with its partners clear, concise, and coherent positions will Germany be able to effectively contribute to establishing a firm, united EU

---

343 James D. Bindenagel and Philip A. Ackermann, Deutschland strategiefähiger Machen. Ein Sachverständigenrat für strategische Vorausschau ist nötig, in: Sirius 2018, Vol. 2, Nr. 3, (Bonn, 2018), pp. 253-260.
344 Ibid.

foreign and security policy. A viable option to overcome the deficits that hinder strategic thinking in German foreign policy would be the introduction of a new element into Germany's strategic culture: an expert advisory board as an independent body on Germany's foreign policy, reporting to the Bundestag. An independent council of experts could complement the White Paper, the responsible ministries, and the other actors who are involved in the realization of German foreign policy processes. As a complement to the work of the German Institute for International and Security Affairs (SWP), the German Society for International Cooperation (GIZ) and the German Institute for Development Policy (DIE), Deutsche *Gesellschaft für Auswärtige Politik* (DGAP), among others. Such an independent board of experts could contribute to a sound, coherent, coordinated foreign policy and defense strategy. The German Council of Economic Experts, which publishes an annual report outlining possible scenarios of economic development and reports directly to the government, provides a model for strategic foresight. Accompanied by extensive media coverage, the Council's economic report regularly serves as the basis for broad public debate about the priorities, goals, and instruments of German economic policy.

Similarly, a Council for Strategic Foresight composed of experts on foreign policy and security issues could provide a scientifically substantiated report of global trends and scenarios to serve as a starting point for strategic debates. Instead of economic prognoses and scenarios, the new council's analysis would focus on strategic challenges to Germany's current global and security environment. It might thus help resolve the dilemma of Germany's strategic culture. By mapping out trends through scanning and possible developments connected to foreign policy and security issues, a comprehensive security report would provide impulses for a broad, fact-based, and informed debate about threats, goals, and guidelines of German foreign policy engagement. As a politically impartial body, such a Council of Experts would be neither caught up in interministerial or intra-coalition rivalry nor influenced by political bias, interests, and election campaign trade-offs. The point of such a new body would not be to make forecasts or give governmental political assessments of possible security threats and foreign policy trends, nor would it compete with democratically elected politicians in their task to find solutions, determine priorities and make political calls on the issues at hand. Instead, it would promote open debate and strategy development at a point where it is still early enough to prepare for various scenarios. This policy process would make it possible to debate and gauge priorities, goals, and possible courses of action as well as their long-term strategic implications based on politically neutral analyses and are not day-to-day operations. It could also help overcome barriers to a strategic approach that arise from Germany's strict separation of departments and ministries, and the resulting lack of coordination between them, by providing an overarching, long-term perspective.

An informed public strategic debate is a building block in the foundation of policymaking. An informed public does not infringe on policymaking itself, which is a prerogative of the executive. Introducing a Council for Strategic Foresight that reports to the Bundestag might help Germany to overcome its reactive, crisis-management style and implement a more strategic approach to dealing with the complexity of today's foreign policy realities by providing an impartial, fact-based basis for discussion. The lessons from Germany's horrific historical experiences need to guide its foreign policy engagement. Instead, they should avoid becoming a hindrance to the country's future that could ultimately do more harm than good. Recognizing and tackling security issues at an early stage make it possible to engage in clear thinking, reach goals can at acceptable costs, and make informed decisions about possible courses of action. In this way, strategic thinking increases the likelihood of upholding values, such as the principles laid out in the German Basic Law.

This Council could engage in foresight and in the identification of global trends based on a widened definition of security that includes both traditional and non-traditional security threats. On that basis, the Council would present a catalog of future scenarios for foreign and security policy in parliament that could then serve as an impetus for a broad parliamentary and public debate. In the long run, this might help defuse the tension between Germany's strategic culture and current geopolitical realities. The Council's reports would mainly contribute to German strategic planning capacities by serving as a comprehensive basis for parliamentary discussion. They could contain a wide array of scenarios ranging from optimistic to threatening and could subsequently provoke a broad, open, and fact-based debate on questions of foreign and security policy. Ultimately, this would also tightly tie in with the Foreign Office's project Review 2014, as well as the White Paper process.

Furthermore, creating such a Council would help persuade the government to develop an overarching strategic concept that integrates all departments' policies and defines security indicators that could serve as the basis for the council's analyses and foresight. This process would support the government's strategic planning process and serve as an independent complement to the initiatives laid out in the German Government's 2017 coalition agreement.

The Council's composition could also extend its definition of security to include interdisciplinary membership of no more than seven experienced scholars and experts. The experts could come from the areas of security policy, defense, development, climate, law, and economy. They would, therefore, be capable of analyzing a diverse range of strategic challenges, developing scenarios, and simultaneously following an overarching strategic concept.

Overall, this might alleviate Germany's structural problems regarding the development of its strategic planning capabilities. The Council would not impinge on ministers' and their departments' responsibilities and powers guaranteed by the Basic Law, nor would the Council intervene in or comment on day-to-day policymaking, but instead would focus on long-term developments. Particularly in the face of numerous crises and conflicts, ministries often lack the time and resources to engage in this type of long-term strategic thinking. The Council should thus be an independent complement rather than a rival of the ministries.

Developing scenarios based on strategic concepts would generate conceptual coherence that would offer guidelines for all departments. Several Countries have vast experience with strategic foresight to tap, including RAND in the U.S., Clingendael in the Netherlands, Foresight Canada, Strategic Foresight in the Finnish Prime Minister's office, and others. The establishment of a Council of Experts for Strategic Foresight is also a viable political option under current conditions and a coalition agreement. The 2018 coalition government agreement states a clear political need for such a council.[345] Similar councils, such as the Advisory Council on the Environment, show the potential success and problems of such a project.

As noted above, there is no shortage of possible topics for the Council. While the last 15 years contained a large number of developments that would have required strategic foresight, the geopolitical conditions are even more challenging today. Examples include the deteriorating transatlantic relationship with repercussions of a possible full-blown trade war between Europe and the United States, Washington's consideration to repatriate U.S. soldiers from the NATO eastern flank, and even more pronounced support of anti-European parties and movements on the continent. Heightened tensions in the South China Sea and its possible military, but also economic consequences of trade disputes with Germany's second-largest trading partner, make strategic planning vital. In the Middle East and North Africa, the Iran nuclear weapons agreement's ultimate failure and resulting in violent conflict or the beginning of a nuclear arms race in the region would affect Germany as one of Israel's closest allies. Other topics could include the on-going COVID-19 pandemic, hybrid warfare threats, technological developments (Artificial Intelligence, Big Data, Digitalization), demography, refugees, migration, Climate Change, Futures of the EU and transatlantic relations and more.

---

345 Coalition Contract for the Federal Government of Germany, Ein neuer Aufbruch für Europa. Eine neue Dynamik für Deutschland. Ein neuer Zusammenhalt für unser Land. Koalitionsvertrag zwischen CDU, CSU und SPD, Online: https://www.bundesregierung.de/resource/blob/656734/847984/5b8bc23590d4cb2892b31c987ad672b7/2018-03-14-koalitionsvertrag-data.pdf?dow-n-load=1, (Berlin, 2018).

In addition to these somewhat realistic scenarios, it would also be advisable to analyze long-term trends. For instance, further digitalizing the social, political, and military spheres will have a significant impact on German security and its functional capabilities. If the development of drones, cyber warfare, pandemics, and artificial intelligence technologies continue at its current speed, Germany will have to investigate possible implications of these technological advancements at an early stage. The same goes for crises and conflicts related to climate change, financial stability, and energy security. Politicians decide the areas focus underscoring the need for an overall national concept and the formulation of priorities.

The *Bundestag* could establish such a Council of Experts for Strategic Foresight, and that indisputably requires corresponding political will to address strategic issues. It should be in the interest of German policymaking to create a steady point of reference independent from day-to-day and crisis management operations. Such a Council without getting lost in theoretical debates could focus on long-term developments in an ever-accelerating great powers shift among the United States, China, and Russia. The political debate in Germany supports a vision to build Europe. European security and prosperity rest on this order. Germany has national legitimacy and exercises its sovereignty with a sovereign obligation to Europe and the international order. Germany is called on to lead in Europe, and to succeed needs a bold, strategic vision to sustain democracy, peace, and prosperity in Europe.

Through annual expert analyses in reports on global trends, scenarios, and action plans, the Bundestag could contribute to an ongoing, informed public debate on strategy, foreign- and security policy. Perhaps a new Bundestag Committee for Germany's Future could hold regular strategic committee foresight hearings in the Bundestag that would ensure transparent and informed discussions of the challenges and strategies to meet them. Inviting Germany's allies to such committee hearings would create cross-cutting European ideas and build confidence in European consideration of Germany's political debate. In the short-term, this would lead to a more informed process, which ensures voters that the Bundestag is discussing essential topics.

The political debate in Germany supports a vision to build Europe. Europe can rise as a more stalwart transatlantic pillar will not let America's uncertain path question the ideas and institutions of the international liberal order. European security and prosperity rest on this order. Germany has national legitimacy and exercises its sovereignty with a sovereign obligation to Europe and the international order. Germany is called on to lead in Europe, and to succeed needs a bold, strategic vision to sustain democracy, peace, and prosperity in Europe.

Germany needs a European Security Strategy that supports the European Union

In light of the current U.S. Administration's withdrawal from leadership, the U.S., as well as the growing economic, security, and political challenges from China, Germany has a choice to make about its European transatlantic partner. Is a weak partner, aligned with its interests or a more forceful, disagreeing European the second pillar of the transatlantic alliance in its best interests? Haddad and Polyakova have argued that "Europe, for its part, has a similar choice to make. It cannot claim the mantle of independent global leadership and continue to rely on the United States for its security, including in its immediate neighborhood."[346] Making Europe relevant again is the responsibility of European policymakers.

To accomplish that goal, Germany needs a two-fold policy of strategic policymaking. One is to overcome the incoherence in security policy between elites and the general public. The other is to create a political process to coordinate and to strategize German foreign and security policy between the Chancellor's office, relevant ministries, agencies, and NGOs. Such a strategic policy process compliments European initiatives in security, including the European Defense Fund and Permanent Structured Cooperation (PESCO). A stronger Europe reinforces the Transatlantic Alliance.

Can Germany lead, but not dominate Europe? Will Germany and Europe fill the leadership gap left by absent American leadership? Otto von Bismarck quoted Friedrich Schiller recognizing the central question and challenge of his epoch: "I know not where to find the land where the scholarly begins, and the political ends." [347] All the world is watching the German debate from the scholarly to the political to see if Germany shows up for leadership. Who but Germans will successfully manage the stress of these turbulent times in the transatlantic relationship? Is Germany the best hope to sustain the Liberal International Order? Can the German culture of remembrance act as a restraint on policy excess? Can Germany, with its European partners, craft a European security and defense strategy?

---

346 Benjamin Haddad und Alina Polyakova, Is Going Alone the Best Way Forward for Europe? Why Strategic Autonomy Should Be the Continent's Goal, in: Foreign Affairs, Online https://www.foreignaffairs.com/articles/europe/2018-10-17/going-it-alone-best-way-forward-europe, (Washington D.C., 2018).
347 "Part of the Poem: Germany? But where does it lie? I don't know where to find the nation. I know not where to find the land where the scholarly begins, and the political ends." Poem written together with Johann Wolfgang von Goethe. Poem: Das Deutsche Reich, Xenien.

Chapter 9: Germany From Peace to Power?

Democracies are traditionally reluctant to engage in strategic thinking unless events force them to defend democracy, freedom, and the rule of law. We are in one of those times of significant change today. The coronavirus poses one of the most significant threats to humankind. Covid-19, the coronavirus pandemic will change economies, healthcare, the media, and international relations just like after the unification of Germany and the end of the Cold War, the terrorist attacks on 9/11, the 2008 global financial crisis, and earlier pandemics. Earlier existential crises in democratic societies reordered them.

Winston Churchill, at the beginning of the Second World War, was asked about Russia's role. He answered: "I cannot forecast to you the action of Russia. It is a riddle wrapped in a mystery inside an enigma. But perhaps there is a key. That key is Russian national interest."[348] Is German leadership in the EU in their interest? Can the European Union expect Germany to lead it in solidarity with the Member States?

Solidarity in Europe

Covid-19's threat highlighted the EU's need to answer with solidarity. Covid-19 is a humanitarian crisis that moved Pope Francis to call for "finding the courage to create spaces where everyone can recognize that they are called, and to allow new forms of hospitality, fraternity, and solidarity."[349] French President Macron, along with Italian Prime Minister Conte, called for EU solidarity. In the pandemic, hospitals are overwhelmed with patients. Government leaders, to make the world safer, have shutdown cities, closed borders, and curtailed travel. Local

---
348 Winston Churchill, in: BBC Broadcast, Online: https://winstonchurchill.org/publications/finest-hour/finest-hour-150/churchill-on-russia/, (London, 1939).
349 Pope Francis, Urbi et Orbis, Moment of Prayer, Onine: https://www.youtube.com/watch?v=JcUqLrbi9Cg&feature=youtu.be, (Rom, 2020).

leaders shuttered schools, restaurants, and stores, leaving only essential groceries and pharmacies open. The global virus is changing economies, health care, the media, international relations, and societies. Living through Covid-19, countries will again change. Leadership after Corona is needed to re-establish a new balance between government and the market, with relationships among individuals and society. Local, regional, national, and international governance can create a constructive, collaborative order.

Technology will offer tools to guide good governance in re-connecting humanity with society in new lifestyles – but nothing that can replace a good, constructive dialogue among leaders and the people. For three generations, we have had the pleasure of lives worth living, including an appreciation for others, for the outdoors, for everyday living. Government, healthcare, the economy, society, and more will change. Before the 2020 Coronavirus pandemic, governments took lessons from the SARS, Ebola, MERS, and H1N1 (Swine Flu) outbreaks. In the Obama Administration, a Global Health Agenda addressed the threat of pandemics and sought to advance international cooperation with the 2005 International Health Regulations.[350] The World Health Organization took initiatives to prepare for the next pandemic. Nevertheless, government leaders were regretfully unprepared for the pandemic. In the U.S., the Center for Strategic and International Studies (CSIS) Risk and Foresight Group in October 2019 presented government officials with a coronavirus pandemic disaster scenario. They concluded that communication is vital – but a decline in trust makes it harder; that international cooperation is critical, and that the private sector will be essential to managing pandemic crises. Their principal conclusion fits many governments – leaders simply do not take health security seriously enough.[351]

The systemic lesson is that the Covid-19 pandemic has accelerated the unraveling of the world order. However, leaders will shape new realities. "The historic challenge for leaders," Henry Kissinger argues, "is to manage the crisis while building the future. Failure could set the world on fire."[352] The coronavirus outbreak, the worst crisis since the Second World War, as Chancellor Merkel

---

350 Larry Kerr, *Global Health Agenda (GHSA)*, Online: https://www.who.int/influenza_vaccines_plan/objectives/SLPIVPP_Session3_Kerr.pdf, (N.N., 2017).
351 Samuel Brannen and Kathleen Hicks, We Predicted a Coronavirus Pandemic. Here's What Policymakers Could Have Seen Coming, in: POLITICO, Online: https://www.politi-co.com/news/magazine/2020/03/07/coronavirus-epidemic-prediction-policy-advice-121172, (Arlington County, 2020).
352 Henry Kissinger, The Coronavirus Pandemic Will Forever Alter the World Order, in: The Wall Street Journal, Online: https://www.wsj.com/articles/the-coronavirus-pandemic-will-forever-alter-the-world-order-11585953005, (New York City, 2020).

described it, needs European solidarity.[353] Italian Prime Minister Conte echoed that statement and turned to Europe to find answers in the spirit of Robert Schuman, Konrad Adenauer, and Alcide de Gasperi. The debate opened an unfinished European Monetary Union question of mutualization of debt but also of the future of the European Union.[354]

Conte and eight other leaders asked the EU to issue 'Corona-Bonds' to deal with the crisis and to improve economic conditions after the pandemic.[355] Although this pandemic disaster requires enormous effort for European solidarity, the proposed answer, while generously funded, is a patchwork of traditional responses. They include the European Stabilization Fund (ESM) loans, the EU Commission's short-time (*Kurzarbeit*, reimbursement) fund, European Investment Bank (EIB) investments, the EU Solidarity Fund, the European Central Bank, and disaster aid proposed by the Dutch. The German, Dutch, and Austrian governments reject Corona-Bonds. Some economists have argued alternately for community bonds, jointly guaranteed by all eurozone governments.[356] French Finance Minister Bruno Le Maire suggested allowing the European 'Solidarity Fund' for Covid-19, funded by all EU members.[357]

Is the crisis one that can be solved by financial fixes, or is the Coronavirus part of the new normal? If the virus has fundamentally changed our societies, a fundamental change in the EU, perhaps with Coronabonds or Eurobonds, is the more strategic answer. Mutualization of European debt would shift more decision making to the EU Commission, which would need a larger deficit and a funding stream, perhaps an EU tax.[358] President Macron has said the EU has no choice but to set up a fund that "could issue common debt with a common

---

353 Deutschland.de, Merkel urges unity in corona crisis. Coronavirus is Germany's worst crisis since WWII, says German Chancellor and appeals to citizens to help one another, Online: https://www.deutschland.de/en/news/merkel-urges-unity-in-corona-crisis, (Berlin, 2020).
354 Cerstin Gammelin, Thomas Kirchner and Markus Zyndra, Corona-Bonds:Und jetzt alle. Die Zustimmung zu gemeinsamen Corona-Bonds wächst in Europa – und damit auch der politische Druck auf die Bundesregierung, in: Süddeutsche Zeitung, Online: https://www.sueddeutsche.de/wirtschaft/corona-bonds-und-jetzt-alle-1.4864530, (Berlin, 2020).
355 Ibid.
356 Peter Bofinger, Sebastian Dullien, Gabriel Felbermayr, Michael Hüther, Moritz Schularick, Jens Südekum, Jens and Christoph Trebesch, To avoid economic disaster, Europe must demonstrate financial solidarity, in: New Statesman, Online: https://www.newstatesman.com/world/europe/2020/03/avoid-economic-disaster-europe-must-demonstrate-financial-solidarity, (London, 2020).
357 Albrecht Meier, Beendet ein Vorschlag aus Frankreich den Streit um Corona-Bonds?, in: Der Tagesspiegel, Online: https://www.tagesspiegel.de/politik/konflikt-um-corona-hilfen-in-der-e u-beendet-ein-vorschlag-aus-frankreich-den-streit-um-corona-bonds/25727554.html, (Berlin, 2020).
358 Gideon Rachman, Eurobonds are not the answer, Why the Germans and Dutch are right to resist this way of sharing coronavirus costs, in: Financial Times, Online: https://www.ft.com/content/b809685c-77de-11ea-af44-daa3def9ae03, (London, 2020).

guarantee" to finance member states according to their needs rather than the size of their economies. The EU is at a moment of truth in a new reality that will define its identity as a distinctly single economic market or a Union in solidarity during this pandemic. Macron warned the lacking solidarity would likely fuel populist anger, especially in southern Europe. Otherwise, Europe will face populists who will win elections in Italy, in Spain, perhaps in France.[359]

Strategic Foresight

Is it time to think strategically of the future of the EU and the unfinished European Monetary Union? An on-going strategic foresight dialogue is needed to address them. While avoiding the 'mutualization' of debt, the EU Commission proposed extending the scope of the EU Solidarity Fund to include significant public health events. Guy Verhofstadt, with Luis Garican, suggested a 'European Reconstruction Fund' with consolidated annuities financed by levies on digital services, pollution, and tax evaders. That debt management debate is about the future of the European Union. Is it time to think strategically of the future of the EU and the unfinished European Monetary Union? That debt management debate is about the future of the European Union.

The rise of populism, Stephen M. Walt writes, COVID-19 will create a "world that is less open, less prosperous, and less free. It did not have to be this way, but the combination of a deadly virus, inadequate planning, and incompetent leadership has placed humanity on a new and worrisome path."[360] Walt argued resurgent nationalists would adopt emergency measures to 'manage the crisis' and will be loath to relinquish these new powers when the crisis is over. In Hungary, Viktor Orban confirmed Walt's assessment and moved quickly to disenfranchise the parliament and give Orban the power to rule by decree indefinitely.[361] Viktor Orban, the Tyll Eulenspiegel-like figure, has turned his back

---

359 Victor Mallet and Roula Khalaf, Macron warns of EU unravelling unless it embraces financial solidarity, in: Fianancial Times, Online: https://www.ft.com/content/d19dc7a6-c33b-4931-9a7e-4a74674da29a?shareType=nongift, (London, 2020).
360 John Allen, et al., "How the World Will Look After the Coronavirus Pandemic". The pandemic will change the world forever. We asked 12 leading global thinkers for their predictions, in: Foreign Policy, Online: https://foreignpolicy.com/2020/03/20/world-order-after-coroanvirus-pandemic/, (Washington D.C., 2020).
361 Joanna Kakissis, New Law Gives Sweeping Powers To Hungary's Orban, Alarming Rights Advocates, in: National Public Radio, Online: https://www.npr.org/sections/coronavirus-live-updates/202-0/03/30/823778208/new-law-gives-sweeping-powers-to-hungarys-orban-alarming-rights-advocates?utm_term=nprnews&utm_campaign=npr&utm_source=facebook.com&utm_medium=social&fbclid=IwAR3B7SPnRXbO6lgDvrAh-GQD87ZOcx7VwnJsypylwGobBmD85v-JHb98G6g&t=1585899826017, (Budapest, 2020).

on the west's fight for parliamentary democracy that finds its origins in the 1848 Revolution and its conclusion in the 1990 German unification.[362] In Hungary, Viktor Orban moved quickly to disenfranchise the parliament and give himself the power to rule by decree indefinitely. Covid-19 will create a world that is less open, less prosperous, and less free, Stephen M. Walt told Foreign Policy magazine.[363]

Resurgent nationalism and a rising China are only two trends that undermine democracy and the liberal world order in the aftermath of the pandemic. In a rising China, Kishore Mahbubani sees a more China-centric globalization that does not fundamentally alter global economic order. He suggests that the Covid-19 pandemic "will only accelerate a change that had already begun: a move away from U.S.-centric globalization to more China-centric globalization."[364] Resurgent nationalism and a rising China are two trends to add to the pandemic's threat to the EU. They undermine democracy and the liberal world order. The leadership needed after the combination of a deadly virus, inadequate planning, and incompetent leadership has placed humanity on a new and worrisome path, Walt argued. A greater danger lies in other resurgent nationalists who also adopt emergency powers; they will resist relinquishing them when the crisis is over. Democracies that fail to deal effectively with the concerns of the people make themselves vulnerable to appeals from fear-based populists.

Although the outcome of this debate is fraught with problems, this much is certain. Just as the Covid-19 disease has shattered lives, disrupted markets, and exposed the competence (or lack thereof) of governments, it will lead to permanent shifts in political and economic power in ways that will become apparent only later. In this systemic change, Germany is called to lead in Europe to help resolve the Covid-19 crisis in this time of new realities. Who will take leadership after Corona? Will Europe emerge stronger to prevent and end conflicts, promote the rule of law, strengthen justice, and improve the delivery of public and private services?

---

362 Eulenspiegel, the individual gets back at society; the stupid yet cunning peasant demonstrates his superiority to the narrow, dishonest, condescending townsman, as well as to the clergy and nobility. More information can be found in: https://www.britannica.com/topic/Till-Eulenspiegel-German-literature.

363 Joanna Kakissis, New Law Gives Sweeping Powers To Hungary's Orban, Alarming Rights Advocates, in: National Public Radio, Online: https://www.npr.org/sections/coronavirus-live-updates/2020/03/30/823778208/new-law-gives-sweeping-powers-to-hungarys-orban-alarming-rights-advocates?utm_term=nprnews&utm_campaign=npr&utm_source=facebook.com&utm_medium=social&fbclid=IwAR3B7SPnRXbO6lgDvrAh-GQD87ZOcx7VwnJsypylwGobBmD85v-JHb98G6g&t=1585899826017, (Budapest, 2020).

364 John Allen, et al., "How the World Will Look After the Coronavirus Pandemic". The pandemic will change the world forever. We asked 12 leading global thinkers for their predictions, in: Foreign Policy, Online: https://foreignpolicy.com/2020/03/20/world-order-after-coroanvirus-pandemic/, (Washington D.C., 2020).

Politically, Germany has the opportunity to accept leadership responsibility in its 2020 EU Presidency, in close coordination with the President of the European Council and the High Representative of the Union for Foreign Affairs and Security Policy. Chancellor Angela Merkel and Commission President Ursula von der Leyen have an opportunity to move European Integration and a more global role for Europe forward. Beyond crisis management, leaders will face many issues in shaping a new normal. One thing becomes clear when looking back over the past thirty years. Even today, three decades after unification, the country still has a problem in balancing national interests with its reluctance to lead with its national interests and its obligations and responsibilities in foreign policy, leaving the German Problem unanswered.

The far-reaching security challenges and rising populism make it apparent how urgently Germany and Europe need to develop a broad strategic debate. The first issue is re-balancing the market economy and the government. Desire is growing for the retreat into nationalist thinking. Notwithstanding that trend, the world today is intensely interdependent. Institutions and structures for multilateral cooperation that were once needed only to a limited extent are now becoming necessary to confront fundamental political challenges. Political leaders can only solve foreign policy and security issues, from climate change to international terrorism to global streams of refugees as well as their underlying causes, through global cooperation. Sustaining global institutions, an overarching framework for international collaboration, and shaping the newly emerging international order to grapple with today's challenges effectively will require tremendous efforts. There is little doubt that democracies need 'Robust liberalism' to sustain, renew, and reshape transatlantic institutions. It is also a question of political survival of our values-based liberal order.[365]

The EU can no longer hide from the fact that the U.S. is retreating from its role as Europe's security guarantor at a time of mounting political challenges, nor can it ignore the fact that Germany is a critical strategic actor for Europe. Europe's security is, in part, dependent on Germany's ability to develop a coherent strategic vision. The EU can no longer act like a child who covers its eyes and declares no one can see it. To accomplish this, Germany will have to enter into a strategic planning process alongside its partners. Establishing a Council for Strategic Foresight may be an option to support this process by promoting a broad, informed strategic debate and ultimately helping the EU develop a coherent, more effective global strategy.

Germany remains a critical strategic actor in Europe. Can Germany lead in Europe and reshape the European pillar of the transatlantic partnership to fill the

---

[365] Kleine-Brockhoff, Thomas, *Die Welt braucht den Westen: Neustart für eine liberale Ordnung*, (Edition Koerber: Hamburg, 2019).

vacuum that is starting to emerge as the United States retreats from the international stage? Yes, under certain circumstances, Germany can find the right balance between its international responsibilities and its culture of remembrance.

Taking into account the changing external conditions, Germany needs to step up to defend and help reshape the world to sustain Western values. Sigmar Gabriel captured a sense of change in the political will to meet challenges for Germany:

> "Do we have the necessary strength? I don't know. But we have to try, and we have to start by defining our own interests. Then begins the jousting for power and position, which will not be pleasant. But what was it Willy Brandt said? It may be true that power corrupts the character, but powerlessness does so too, to no less a degree. With this in mind, this is not the time to take shelter in our alleged powerlessness."[366]

Whether the EU will become a global player depends on its internal coherence, its ability to act collectively, and authoritatively. Steps toward autonomy require more pooling of sovereignty to the EU hierarchy or more majority-decision-making. Expanding EU governance into new fields such as security will only happen if the voters agree, which with Poland, Hungary, and Great Britain examples, voters seem to feel mostly disempowered by the existing transfer of power to the EU and Commission. The EU legitimacy rests fundamentally on its competence as an economic actor. Foreign policy issues remain national issues. The EU has core functions: an area of freedom, the rule of law, democracy, constitutionalism, human rights, customer protection, and social coherence. In policy, the Member States have some shared responsibility for Africa and provide a role model for former socialist countries. As in the German debate, the EU will only be able to act jointly if it can bring along the public, the popular sovereign. EU voters want a functioning community that is an added value to the limits of the nation-state. The strength of the EU is in its trade and commerce management. However, the bottom line is that the times of passive acquiescence are over. The EU is Germany's partner and the pillar of the transatlantic relationship.

Yes, Germany's path from peace to power remains uncertain. Germany needs to overcome its historical obstacles and address its strategic cultural deficits, not letting them become a hindrance to the country's future. Successfully doing so will require the state to follow a dual approach. First, Germany will need to update its strategic culture and include an overarching concept for long-term strategic thinking, a broad and transparent debate about goals, challenges, and

---

[366] Sigmar Gabriel, Europe in a Less Comfortable World – Speech by Foreign Minister Sigmar Gabriel at the Berlin Foreign Policy Forum at the Körber Foundation, [Rede zur Eröffnung des Berlin Foreign Policy Forum 2017 von Sigmar Gabriel], Online: https://www.youtube.com/watch?v=kcljjSBLBg4, (Berlin).

options of German foreign policy, and a clear strategic vision. The country also requires a security strategy for Europe, one that elevates strategic planning as a priority over its plans for crisis management. Second, Germany's international engagement can only be successful if it manages to combine political leadership with its obligations to Europe. To do so, it will have to ensure its *Leaders in Partnership* approach accounts for European partner countries' interests just as much as for its own.

Strategic foresight is needed to consider and test strategic thinking with the skeptical public to shape opinion in the aftermath of the pandemic. United Germany differs from its predecessors in its unique combination of decisions in West Germany. Konrad Adenauer set its constitution in the liberal world order of the West (*Westbindung*). Self-determination of the Peaceful Revolution in East Germany brought down the East German Government and elected a parliamentary democracy mandated to unify Germany. Sovereign Germany uses its sovereign obligation to Europe, where states have sovereign rights but also have obligations to the EU and NATO. Germany, restrained by history, is well-positioned with its partners, to exercise its sovereign responsibilities. Can strategic foresight, supported by a new institutional body such as a council of experts, help bridge the gap between Germany's conflicting restraints and responsibilities? Can it contribute to an informed public debate that enhances sound policy-making, addresses German power, and strengthens strategic consideration of German foreign policy for Europe? The Bundestag is the best home to debate the risks democracies face.

As an advocate of the transatlantic relationship even in challenging times, Germany can step up to these new realities, and reshape the European pillar of that relationship through an updated *Leaders in Partnership* approach, and shoulder international responsibility with the United States. Germany, changed at unification, is well-positioned to reshape the European cornerstone of the transatlantic partnership. Germany's unique historical sense of responsibility and its present position of power embedded in European and transatlantic structures does present its leaders with a window of opportunity for accepting increased international responsibility and help strengthen European security and foreign policy.

Acknowledgments

The book has many fathers/mothers. Professor Dr. Dr. h.c. Karl Kaiser and Prof. Dr. Dr. h.c. Matthias Herdegen were critical in the creation of the Kissinger Chair at Bonn University. Rectors of the University of Bonn Dr. Ulrich Frohmann and Dr. Michael Hoch initiated and chose to make the Kissinger Chair permanent. Guido Goldman supported the initiative to create a Bonn International Security Forum that tested many security policy ideas with numerous experts in transatlantic relations. I am especially grateful to Prof. Andreas Heinemann-Grüder, who collaborated on strategic foresight, lending his decades of expertise in academic excellence from peace and conflict studies. I appreciate the collaboration of my co-authors on this subject, Philip Ackermann, for the article on strategic foresight for the SIRIUS Journal and Simone Becker for her contributions to articles related to the ideas in the book. I sincerely appreciate Amanda Henson's and Clara Dinkelbach's editing and production of the manuscript. Thanks also to Detlef Puhl, Andreas Heinemann-Grüder, Manfred Stinnes, and Stefan Froehlich, who reviewed the text. My team at the Bonn University Center for International Security and Governance, Karsten Jung, Philip Ackermann, Malte Schrage, Simone Becker, Lea Gernemann, Patrick van der Well, and several student interns provided a sounding board for ideas. They contributed to numerous papers and speeches on the subjects that landed in the book. I also appreciate my Bonn University students who engaged in my seminars where we debated these security subjects and the role of Germany and strategic foresight. I accept full responsibility for any errors in this book and ask for the readers' indulgence for any misspelled names and mistaken dates. I hope the book will be judged by its ideas and arguments. I hope that the book will contribute to the University of Bonn's Center for Advanced Security, Strategy and Integration Studies (CASSIS) research, and teaching.

I dedicate this book to my wife, Jean, and to our lifelong friend Dennis Rose, whose commitment to freedom and democracy sustained us throughout the past half-century in German-American relations.

Bibliography

Primary Sources

Coalition Contract for the Federal Government of Germany (2018): Ein neuer Aufbruch für Europa. Eine neue Dynamik für Deutschland. Ein neuer Zusammenhalt für unser Land. Koalitionsvertrag zwischen CDU, CSU und SPD, Online: https://www.bundesregierung.de/resource/blob/656734/847984/5b8bc23590d4cb2892b31c987ad672b7/2018-03-14-koalitionsvertrag-data.pdf?download=1, (Berlin).

Foreign Ministers of Austria, Belgium, Denmark, France, Italy, Germany, Luxembourg, the Netherlands, Poland, Portugal and Spain (2012): *Final Report of the Future of Europe Report*, Online: https://www.cer.eu/sites/default/files/westerwelle_report_sept12.pdf, (2012).

High Representatives of Austria, Belgium, Bulgaria, Canada, Cyprus, Czechoslovakia, Denmark, Finland, France, the German Democratic Republic, the Federal Republic of Germany, Greece, the Holy See, Hungary, Iceland, Ireland, Italy, Liechtenstein, Luxembourg, Malta, Monaco, the Netherlands, Norway, Poland, Portugal, Romania, San Marino, Spain, Sweden, Switzerland, Turkey, the Union of Soviet Socialist Republics, the United Kingdom, the United States of America and Yugoslavia (1975): *Conference On Security And Co-Operation in Europe Final Act*, Online: https://www.osce.org/helsinki-final-act?download=true, (Helsinki).

The Basic Law of the Federal Republic of Germany (1949): Online: https://www.cvce.eu/content/publication/1999/1/1/7fa618bb-604e-4980-b667-76bf0cd0dd9b/publishable_en.pdf. Translated by Prof. Christian Tomuschat, Professor David P. Currie, Professor Donald P. Kommers and Ramyond Kerr, in cooperation with the Language Service of the German Bundestag.

Treaty between the Federal Republic of Germany and the French Republic on Franco-German Cooperation and Integration (2019): Online: https://www.diplomatie.gouv.fr/en/country-files/germany/france-and-germany/franco-german-treaty-of-aachen/, (Aachen).

Treaty on the Final Settlement with Respect to Germany September 12, 1990. Art. 7 Online: https://usa.usembassy.de/etexts/2plusfour8994e.htm.

Secondary Sources

Alexander, Robin (2012): Merkels Tritte gegen den CDU Wirtschaftsrat, 12, in: Die Welt, Online: https://www.welt.de/politik/deutschland/article106533001/Merkels-Tritte-gegen-den-CDU-Wirtsch-aftsrat.html, (Berlin).

Allen, John/Burns, Nicholas/Garrett, Laurie/Haass, Richard N./Ikenberry, G. John/ Mahbubani, Kishore/ Menon, Shivshankar/Niblett, Robin/Nye Jr., Joseph S./O'Neil, Shannon K./ Schake, Kori/Walt, Stephen M. (2012): How the World Will Look After the Coronavirus Pandemic. The pandemic will change the world forever. We asked 12 leading global thinkers for their predictions, in: Foreign Policy, Online: https://foreignpolicy.com/2020/03/20/world-order-after-coroanvirus-pandemic/, (Washington D.C.).

Alyu, Heide (2012): Aktenverzeichnis zum "Selbständigen Referat Bewaffnung und Chemischer Dienst" (SR BCD) in der Bezirksverwaltung Rostock des Ministeriums fuer Staatssicherheit der DDR, Der Bundesbeauftragte fuer die Unterlagen des Staatssicherheitsdienstes der ehemaligen Deutschen Demokratischen Republik, (Rostock).

Archives of European Integration (1969): *Meeting of the Heads of State or Government*, The Hague, 1–2 December 1969, Online: http://aei.pitt.edu/1451/1/hague_1969.pdf, (The Hague).

Ash, Timothy G. (2009): Britain fluffed the German question. Now Britain is Europe's great puzzle, in: The Guardian, Online: https://www.theguardian.com/commentisfree/2009/oct/21/britain-fluffed-german-question, (London).

Ash, Timothy G. (2017): Think Global Act Regional, in Berlin Pulse, Online: https://www.koerber-stiftung.de/en/the-berlin-pulse/2017/garton-ash, (Berlin).

Aust, Helmut P./Vashakmadze, Mindia (2008): Parliamentary Consent to the Use of German Armed Forces Abroad: The 2008 Decision of the Federal Constitutional Court in the AWACS/Turkey Case, German L.J. 2223, 2223 (Karlsruhe).

Bagger, Thomas (2020): The World According to Germany: Reassessing 1989, [Originally publsished: "The Washington Quarterly",(Milton: Taylor and Francis, 2019)], in: Atlantik Brücke, Online: https://www.atlantik-bruecke.org/the-world-according-to-germany-reassessing-1989/ (Berlin).

Baker, Peter (2019a): Viktor Orban, Hungary's Far Right Leader, Gets Warm Welcome From Trump, in: The New York Time, Online. https://www.nytimes.com/2019/05/13/us/politics/trump-viktor-orban-oval-office.html (New York City).

Baker, Peter (2019b): Trump embraces Polish Leader and Promises Him More U.S. Troops, in: The New York Times, Online: https://www.nytimes.com/2019/06/12/us/politics/andrzej-duda-trump-poland.html, (New York City).

Barber, Tony (2019): Germany's Eurozone gambit could meet a swift death, in: Financial Times, Online: https://www.google.com/search?channel=trow2&client=firefox-b-d&q=Barber%2C+Tony%2C+%E2%80%9CGermany%E2%80%99s+Eurozone+gambit+could+meet+a+swift+death%2C%E2%80%9D+Financial+Times%2C+November+8%2C+2019, (London).

Bates, Stephen (2002): Pierre Werner. The man who dreamed the euro, in: The Guardian, Online: https://www.theguardian.com/news/2002/jun/28/guardianobituaries.euro, (London).

Bibliography

Baun, Michael J. (1996): The Maastricht Treaty as High Politics: Germany, France and European Integration, in: Political Science Quarterly, Vol. 110, No.4, Winter (1995–1996), (New York City), pp. 605–624.

Barroso, José Manuel (2012): State of the European Union 2012 Speech, European Parliament in Strasbourg, France, September 12, Online: https://ec.europa.eu/commission/presscorner/detail/en/SPEECH_12_596 (Straßbourg).

Beetsma, Roel/Thygesen, Niels/Cugnasca, Alessandro/Orseau, Eloïse/Eliofotou, Polyvios/Santacroce, Stefano (2018): Reforming the EU fiscal framework: A proposal by the European Fiscal Board, in: Vox CEPR Policy Portal, Online: https://voxeu.org/article/reforming-eu-fiscal-framework-proposal-european-fiscal-board, (Brussels).

Bergsten, C. Fred (2012): The Outlook for the Euro Crisis and Implications for the United States, United States Congress, Senate, Senate Budget Committee, Concurrent Resolution on the Budget Fiscal Year 2013, (Washington D.C.).

Bergsten, C. Fred (2015): The Revenge of Helmut Schmidt, Speech at the American Academy in Berlin GmbH, Online: https://www.americanacademy.de/videoaudio/germany-euro-revenge-helmut-schmidt/, (Berlin).

Beschloss, Michael R./Talbott, Strobe (1993): At the Highest Levels: The Inside Story of the End of the Cold War, (Little, Brown and Company: Boston).

Bet-El, Ilana (2016): Events, dear boy, events, in: European Voice, Politico Europe, https://www.politico.eu/article/events-dear-boy-events/, (Brussels).

Bindenagel, James D. (2010): Afghanistan. The German Factor, in: PRISM 1, No. 4, (Washington D.C.), pp. 95–112.

Bindenagel, James D. (2014): The Miracle of Leipzig, Online: https://www.aicgs.org/2014/11/the-miracle-of-leipzig/, American Institute for Contemporary German Studies, (American Institute for Contemporary German Studies: Bonn).

Bindenagel, James D. (2015): The Role of the United States in German Unification, Online: http://www.bpb.de/geschichte/zeitgeschichte/deutschlandarchiv/213549/the-role-of-the-united-states-in-german-unification, (Bundeszentrale für politische Bildung: Bonn).

Bindenagel, James D. (2017): *Germany's International Responsibility*, No. 5, July 2017 Commentary – Cisg-bonn.com, Online: https://cisg-bonn.com/wp-content/uploads/2017/07/210717-Commentary-Paper.pdf (Bonn).

Bindenagel, James D. (2018): Kampflos aufgeben? Niemals!, in: Süddeutsche Zeitung, Online: https://www.sueddeutsche.de/politik/aussenansicht-kampflos-aufgeben-niemals-1.3997509, (München).

Bindenagel, James D. (2019): Countering disinformation on German reunification and NATO enlargement, in *Europe's World*, Citizens' Europe, Online: https://www.friendsofeurope.org/insights/countering-disinformation-on-german-reunification-and-nato-enlargement/ (Brussels).

Bindenagel, James D. Bindenagel/Ackermann, Philip A. (2018a): Germany's Troubled Strategic Culture Needs to Change, in: Transatlantic Take, Online: http://www.gmfus.org/sites/default/files/Germany%E2%80%99s%20Troubled%20Strategic%20Culture%20Needs%20to%20Change.pdf (Washington D.C.).

Bindenagel, James D. Bindenagel/Ackermann, Philip A. (2018b): Deutschland strategiefähiger Machen. Ein Sachverständigenrat für strategische Vorausschau ist nötig, in: Sirius 2018, Vol. 2, Nr. 3, (Bonn), pp. 253–260.

Bindenagel, James D./Becker, Simone (2019): Strategic Thinking, Planning, and Culture in Germany as an Integral Part of European Security Policy, in: Gunther Hellmann and Daniel Jacobi, Germany, The German White Paper 2016 and the Challenge of Crafting Security Strategies, Online: https://www.fb03.uni-frankfurt.de/76345851/Band_Crafting_Security_Strategies_Aspen_englisch.pdf, (Berlin/Frankfurt am Main), pp. 115–122.

Bobbitt, Philip (2002): *The Shield of Achilles: War, Peace and the Course of History*, (Penguin Group: London).

Bolton, Sally (2001): A History of Currency Unions, in: The Guardian, Online: https://www.theguardian.com/world/2001/dec/10/euro.eu, (London).

Bofinger, Peter/Dullien, Sebastian/Feldmayr, Gabriel/Hüther, Michael/Schularick, Moritz/Südekrum, Jens/Trebesch, Christoph (2020): To avoid economic disaster, Europe must demonstrate financial solidarity, in: New Statesman, Online: https://www.newstatesman.com/world/europe/2020/03/avoid-economic-disaster-europe-must-demonstrate-financial-solidarity, (London).

Brannen, Samuel/Hicks, Kathleen (2020): We Predicted a Coronavirus Pandemic. Here's What Policymakers Could Have Seen Coming, in: POLITICO, Online: https://www.politico.com/news/magazine/2020/03/07/coronavirus-epidemic-prediction-policy-advice-121172, (Arlington County).

British Broadcast Channel (2016): Trump says Putin 'a leader far more than our president', Online: https://www.bbc.com/news/election-us-2016-37303057, (London).

Brockmeier, Sarah (2019): A German National Security Council: If Kramp-Karrenbauer is Serious, Her Work Starts Now, in: Global Public Policy Institute, Online: https://www.gppi.net/2019/12/05/a-german-national-security-council-if-kramp-karrenbauer-is-serious-her-work-starts-now, (2019).

Brzezinski, Zbigniew (2015): On Global Crisis, Center for Strategic and International Studies, Online: https://ontheworld.csis.org/2015/09/22/on-global-crisis/, (Washington D.C.).

Bundesverfassungsgericht [BVerfG] (1994): July 12, 1994, 90 Entscheidungen des Bundesverfassungsgerichts [BVerfGE] 286 (F.R.G)], Online: https://www.servat.unibe.ch/dfr/bv090286.html, (Karlsruhe).

Bush, Georg H. W. (1989a): Remarks to the Citizens of Mainz, Federal Republic of Germany, Mainz, 31. May 1989. in: Public Papers of the President of the United States, (Washington D.C.), p. 652.

Bush, George H. W. (1989b): Georg Herbert Walker Bush's Conditions for Unification (December 4, 1989), Online: http://ghdi.ghi-dc.org/sub_document.cfm?document_id=2874, (Brussels).

Buti, Marco/Deroose, Servaas/Laendro, José/Giudice, Gabriele (2017): Completing EMU, in: Vox. CEPR Policy Portal, Online: https://voxeu.org/article/completing-emu, (London).

Byrant, Chris (2012): Schäuble backs wage rises for German, in: Financial Times, Online: https://www.ft.com/content/54aa8246-9772-11e1-83f3-00144feabdc0, (London).

Cafruny, Alan W. (2015): European integration studies, European Monetary Union, and resilience of austerity in Europe: Post-mortem on a crisis foretold, in: Competition and Change. Vol. 19, No. 2, (Washington D.C.), p.p. 161–177.

Calamur, Krishnadev (2017):, Merkel Urges 'Europe to Take Our Fate Into Our Own Hands. The German chancellor's remarks come as President Trump doubled down on his

Bibliography

criticism of Germany, in: The Atlantic, Online: https://www.theatlantic.com/news/archive/2017/05/merkel-europe-trump/528468/, (Washington D.C.: 2017).

Center for International Security and Governance (2019): *International Security Forum 2018 Report*, (Rheinische Friedrich Wilhelms Universität: Bonn).

Chronik der Mauer (2015), Chronicle 1989, Online: http://www.chronik-der-mauer.de/en/chronicle/_year1989/_month9/?moc=1, (Bonn).

Churchill, Winston (1939): Churchill on Russia, in: BBC Broadcast, Online: https://winstonchurchill.org/publications/finest-hour/finest-hour-150/churchill-on-russia/, (London).

Clauson, Ken (1990): Berlin's Checkpoint Charlie closes, in: Stars and Stripes, Online: https://www.stripes.com/news/berlin-s-checkpoint-charlie-closes-1.12086, (Washington D.C.).

Clifton, Jon (2013): Germany Ties U.S. Again in Leadership Approval Ratings. Approval declines among most global powers, in: Gallup, Online: https://news.gallup.com/poll/161369/germany-ties-again-leadership-approval-ratings.aspx, (Washington, D.C.).

Clinton, William J. (1994): *Public Papers of the Presidents of the United States 1994, Book I*, U.S. Government Publishing Office, Online: https://www.govinfo.gov/content/pkg/PPP-1994-book1/pdf/PPP-1994-book1.pdf, (Washington D.C.).

Cohen, Roger (2011): France Flies, Germany Flops, in: The New York Times, Online: https://www.nytimes.com/2011/04/17/opinion/17cohen.html, (New York City), p. 10.

Cohen, Roger (2017): Donald Trump and the Erosion of American Greatness, in: Spiegel International, Online: http://www.spiegel.de/international/world/roger-cohen-on-trump-and-the-erosion-of-american-greatness-a-1176642.html, (Hamburg).

Council of Europe (1990): Speech by Mikhail Gorbachev, Council of Europe – Parliamentary Assembly. Official Report. Fourty-first ordinary session. 8–12 May and 3–7 July. Volume I. Sittings 1 to 9. 1990. Strasbourg: Council of Europe. (Straßbourg), pp. 197–205.

De Maiziere, Lothar (2010): *Ich will, dass meine Kinder nicht mehr lügen müssen*, (Verlag Herder GmbH: Freiburg im Breisgau).

Dempsey, Judy (2012): Is European Integration Still a Question of War and Peace?, in: Carnegie Europe, Online: https://carnegieeurope.eu/strategiceurope/49651, (Brussels).

Dettke, Dieter (2009): *Germany Says "No": The Iraq War and the Future of German Foreign and Security Policy*, (Johns Hopins University Press: Baltimore).

Deutsche Bundesregierung (2016): *Weissbuch zur Sicherheitspolitik und zur Zukunft der Bundeswehr, 2016.*, Online: https://www.bmvg.de/de/themen/weissbuch, (Berlin).

Deutscher Bundestag (1989): Stenographischer Bericht, 177. Sitzung, Plenarprotokoll 11/177, (Bonn).

Deutscher Bundestag (1990): Stenographischer Bericht, 11. Wahlperiode, 210. Sitzung. Bonn, Donnerstag, den 10. Mai 1990, (Bonn).

Deutscher Bundestag (1994), Beschlußempfehlung und Bericht des 1. Untersuchungsausschusses nach Art. 44 des Grundgesetzes, 12.Wahlperiode, Drucksache 12/7600, (Bonn).

Deutscher Bundestag (1997): Rede von Dr. Helmut Kohl, Bundeskanzler a.D., Online: https://www.bundestag.de/parlament/geschichte/gastredner/gorbatschow/kohl-247410 (Berlin).

Deutsche Bundeswehr (2020): Aktuelle Einsätze der Bundeswehr, Online: https://www.bundeswehr.de/de/einsaetze-bundeswehr, (Berlin, 2020).

Deutsche Welle (2011): Recognizing Slovenia, Croatia brought peace, Genscher says, in: Deutsche Welle, Online: https://www.dw.com/en/recognizing-slovenia-croatia-brought-peace-genscher-says/a-15182463, (Bonn).

Deutsche Welle (2017): More leading German politicians land into Trump, Online: https://www.dw.com/en/more-leading-german-politicians-land-into-trump/a-39038441, (Bonn).

Deutsche Welle (2019a) Krampkarrenbauer im Interview mit der Deutschen Welle: Eine internationale Sicherheitszone in Syrien, Annegret Kramp-Karrenbauer im Interview, Online: https://www.youtube.com/watch?v=VK8t0Ti9WfQ, (Bonn).

Deutsche Welle (2019b): Germany calls for international safe zone Syria, in: Deutsche Welle, Online: https://www.dw.com/en/german-defense-chief-recommends-international-security-zone-in-syria/a-50924304, (Bonn).

Deutschland.de (2020): Merkel urges unity in corona crisis. Coronavirus is Germany's worst crisis since WWII, says German Chancellor and appeals to citizens to help one another, Online: https://www.deutschland.de/en/news/merkel-urges-unity-in-corona-crisis, (Berlin).

Diez, Georg (2011): Habermas, the Last European: A Philosopher's Mission to Save the EU, in: Spiegel Online: https://www.spiegel.de/international/europe/habermas-the-last-european-a-philosopher-s-mission-to-save-the-eu-a-799237.html, (Hamburg).

Doran, Michael Scott (2011): The Heirs of Nasser. Who Will Benefir From thhe Second Arab Spring, in: Foreign Affairs, Online: https://www.foreignaffairs.com/authors/michael-scott-doran, (May/June 2011), (Congers).

European Commission (2017): *Reflection Paper on the Deepening of the Economic and Monetary Union*, European Commission COM(2017) 291, (Brussels).

European Union (2020): The history of the European Union, Online: https://europa.eu/european-union/about-eu/history_en, (Brussels).

Feldstein, Martin Feldstein (2012): The Failure of the Euro. The Little Currency That Couldn't, in: Foreign Affairs, Vol. 91, No.1, (January-February 2012), (Washington D.C.). pp. 105–116.

Fels, Enrico (2017): *Shifting Powers in Asia-Pacific*? The Rise of China, Sino-US Competition and Regional Middle Power Allegiance, (Springer Verlag VS: Wiesbaden).

Ferguson, Niall (2015): *Kissinger: 1923–1968: The Idealist*, (Penguin Press: London).

Frankfurter Allgemeine Zeitung (2019): Maas kritisiert Kramp-Karrenbauers "SMS-Diplomatie", in: Frankfurter Allgemeinen Zeitung, Online: https://www.faz.net/aktuell/politik/ausland/syrien-maas-beschwert-sich-ueber-kramp-karrenbauers-sms-diplomatie-16445725.html, (Frankfurt am Main).

Fried, Nico (2010): "Ich habe gelernt: Nie wieder Auschwitz", in: Süddeutsche Zeitung, Online: https://www.sueddeutsche.de/politik/fischer-ich-habe-gelernt-nie-wieder-auschwitz-1.915701, (München).

Friedman, George (2012): The Elections, Gridlock and Foreign Policy, in: Stratfor, Online: https://worldview.stratfor.com/article/elections-gridlock-and-foreign-policy, (Austin).

Friedman, Thomas L. (1989): Baker, in Berlin, Outlines a Plan To Make NATO a Political Group., in: The New York Times, Online: http://www.nytimes.com/1989/12/13/world/upheaval-east-baker-berlin-outlines-plan-make-nato-political-group.html?pagewanted=all, (The New York Times: New York).

Friedman, Thomas L. (2018): "The End of Europe?", in: The New York Times, Online: https://www.nytimes.com/2018/12/18/opinion/europe-france-economy.html, (New York City).

Fröhlich, Stephan (2019): *Das Ende der Selbstentfesselung*, (Springer Verlag S.V.: Frankfurt am Main).

Bibliography

Frum, David (2016): America's Friendship With Europe Has Been Horribly Damaged It's not all Donald Trump's fault. But he has in every way already made the situation gravely worse, in: The Atlantic, Online: https://www.theatlantic.com/international/archive/2016/11/trump-merkel-germany-europe/507773/, (Washington, D.C.).

Fulbrook, Mary (1991): Wir sind ein Volk? Reflections on German Unification in: *Parliamentary Affairs*, Volume 44, Issue 3, (Oxford University Press: Oxford), pp. 389–404.

Gabriel, Sigmar (2017): Europe in a Less Comfortable World – Speech by Foreign Minister Sigmar Gabriel at the Berlin Foreign Policy Forum at the Körber Foundation, [Rede zur Eröffnung des Berlin Foreign Policy Forum 2017 von Sigmar Gabriel], Online: https://www.youtube.com/watch?v=kcljjSBLBg4, (Berlin).

Gammelin, Cerstin/Kirchner, Thomas/Zyndra, Markus (2020): Corona-Bonds:Und jetzt alle. Die Zustimmung zu gemeinsamen Corona-Bonds wächst in Europa – und damit auch der politische Druck auf die Bundesregierung, in: Süddeutsche Zeitung, Online: https://www.sueddeutsche.de/wirtschaft/corona-bonds-und-jetzt-alle-1.4864530, (Berlin).

Gauck, Joachim (2014): Gauck, Eröffnung der 50. Münchner Sicherheitskonferenz, Online: https://www.bundespraesident.de/SharedDocs/Reden/DE/Joachim-Gauck/Reden/2014/01/140131-Muenchner-Sicherheitskonferenz.html, (München).

Gewen, Barry (2017): Kissinger's Moral Example, Kissinger examined whether intellectuals should get their hands dirty making policy, or preserve their integrity at the price of influence, in: The National Interest, 2017, Online: https://nationalinterest.org/feature/kissingers-moral-example-20225?nopaging=1, (Washington D.C.).

GHDT (1986): Federal President Richard von Weizsäcker on the Meaning of Being German (1986), Online: http://germanhistorydocs.ghi-dc.org/docpage.cfm?docpage_id=2111, (Bonn).

GHDT (1989): Mass Rally on Alexanderplatz in East Berlin (Novemver 4, 1989), Online: http://ghdi.ghi-dc.org/sub_image.cfm?image_id=124, (East-Berlin).

Grachev, Andrey (2019): Europe and Russia 30 years after the fall of the Berlin Wall: Hopes, chances, failures with Andrey Grachev, Online: https://doc-research.org/2019/10/europe-russia-30-years-fall-berlin-wall/, (DOC Research Institute: Berlin).

Greenwald, G. Jonathan (1993): *Berlin Witness: An American Diplomat's Chronicles of East German's Revolution*, (Pennsylvania State University Press: Pennsylvania).

Grof, Wolfgang (2020): In der frischen Tradition des Herbstes 1989, in: Sozialdemokratische Partei, 7. Oktober 1989. Morgenröte in Schwante, Online: https://www.spd.de/aktuelles/30-jahre-sdp/morgenroete-in-schwante/ (Archiv der sozialen Demokratie (AdsD) der Friedrich-Ebert-Stiftung: Bonn).

Gu, Xuewu (2016): Die weltpolitische Dreiecksbeziehung Beijng, Moskau, Washington, in: Aus Politik und Zeitgeschehen, Vol. 66, 23/2016 (Bonn), pp. 27–32.

Haass, Richard N. (2017): World Order 2.0, The Case for Sovereign Obligation, in: Foreign Affairs, January/February 2017, Online: https://www.foreignaffairs.com/articles/2016-12-12/world-order-20, (Congers).

Haass, Richard N. Haass (2018): Liberal World Order, R.I.P., in: Project Syndicate, Online: https://www.project-syndicate.org/commentary/end-of-liberal-world-order-by-richard-n-haass-2018-03/german?barrier=accesspaylog, (New York City).

Haddad, Benjamin/Polyakova, Alina (2018): Is Going Alone the Best Way Forward for Europe? Why Strategic Autonomy Should Be the Continent's Goal, in: Foreign Affairs,

Online https://www.foreignaffairs.com/articles/europe/2018-10-17/going-it-alone-best-way-forward-europe, (Washington D.C.).

Hayton, Bill (2018): Two Years On, South China Sea Ruling Remains a Battleground for the Rules-Based Order, in: Chatam House, Online: https://www.chathamhouse.org/expert/comment/two-years-south-china-sea-ruling-remains-battleground-rules-based-order, (London).

Heipertz, Martin/Verdun, Amy (2004): The dog that would never bite? What we can learn from the origins of the Stability and Growth Pact, in: Journal of European Public Policy, Vol. 11, No. 5, (Taylor & Francis: Milton), pp. 765–780.

Hemingway, Ernest (1966): *The Sun Also Rises*, Scribner Classics, first published 1926, (New York City).

Herdegen, Matthias (2018): *Der Kampf um die Weltordnung*, (C.H. Beck: München).

Hertle, Hans Hermann (2015): *Die Berliner Mauer. Biografie eines Bauwerks*, 2. durchgesehene und aktualisierte Aufl., (Ch. Links Verlag: Berlin).

Heumann, Hans-Dieter (2011), *Hans-Dieter Genscher, Die Biographie*, (Ferdindand Schönigh: Meppen/Emsland).

Hilz, Wolfram (2017): *Deutsche Außenpolitik*, (W. Kohlhammer GmbH: Stuttgart).

Holbrooke, Richard (1998): *To End a War: The Conflict in Yugoslavia–America's Inside Story*, (Modern Library: New York City).

Howarth, David J. (2005): Making and Breaking the Rules: French policy on EU 'gouvernement économique' and the Stability and Growth Pact, in: European Integration Online Papers, Vol. 9, No. 15, (Vienna).

Issing, Otmar (2018): Wie die Deutsch-französische Achse neue Impulse für Europa setzen könnte, in: Wohlstand für Alle, 70 Jahre Währungsreform, Ludwig-Erhard Stiftung, (Bonn), pp. 32–33.

Jacobs, Ben (2017): Donald Trump: Marine Le Pen is 'strongest candidate' in French elections, in: The Guardian, Online: https://www.theguardian.com/us-news/2017/apr/21/donald-trump-marine-le-pen-french-presidential-election, (Washington D.C.).

Janus, Charlotte (2019): Der Staat war dem Untergang geweiht, Online: https://www.t-online.de/nachrichten/wissen/geschichte/id_86775462/jens-reich-im-interview-wie-das-neue-forum-die-ddr-veraendern-wollte.html (Frankfurt am Main).

Jarausch, Konrad H. Jarausch (1994): The Rush to German Unity, (Oxford University Press: Oxford).

Mitteldeutscher Rundfunk (1990): Die Volkskammer beschließt den Beitritt zur Bundesrepublik, Online: https://www.mdr.de/zeitreise/beschluss-beitritt-brd100.html, (MDR, zuletzt aktualisiert 2018).

Jennerjahn, Yvonne (2019): Wendejahr 1989. Es begann in Brandenburg: Vor 30 Jahren wurde die SPD gegründet, in: Märkische Zeitung, Online: https://www.maz-online.de/Brandenburg/Es-begann-in-Brandenburg-Vor-30-Jahren-wurde-die-SDP-gegruendet, (Brandenburg, 2019).

Kaelberer, Matthias (2004): The Euro and European identity: symbols, power and the politics of European monetary union, in: Review of International Studies, Vol. 30, No. 2, (Cambridge), pp. 161–178.

Kakissis, Joanna (2020): New Law Gives Sweeping Powers To Hungary's Orban, Alarming Rights Advocates, in: National Public Radio, Online: https://www.npr.org/sections/coronavirus-live-updates/2020/03/30/823778208/new-law-gives-sweeping-powers-to-hun garys-orban-alarming-rights-advocates?utm_term=nprnews&utm_campaign=npr&utm_source=facebook.com&utm_medium=social&fbclid=IwAR3B7SPnRXbO6lgDvrAh-GQD87ZOcx7VwnJsypylwGobBmD85v-JHb98G6g&t=1585899826017, (Budapest).

Kempster, Norman (1989): Baker Vows Support for E. Germany: Diplomacy: Regime calls dramatic visit the start of a 'dialogue.' Reforms praised by secretary of state, in: Los Angeles Times, Online: https://www.latimes.com/archives/la-xpm-1989-12-13-mn-106-story.html, (Los Angeles).

Kerr, Larry (2017): *Global Health Agenda (GHSA)*, Online: https://www.who.int/influenza_vaccines_plan/objectives/SLPIVPP_Session3_Kerr.pdf, (N.N.).

Kissinger, Henry (2014): *World Order*, (Penguin Books: London).

Kissinger, Henry (2020): The Coronavirus Pandemic Will Forever Alter the World Order, in: The Wall Street Journal, Online: https://www.wsj.com/articles/the-coronavirus-pandemic-will-forever-alter-the-world-order-11585953005, (New York City).

Kirste, Knut/Maull, Hanns (1996): Zivilmacht und Rollentheorie, in: Zeitschrift für Internationale Beziehungen, 3. Jhrg. (Nomos Verlagsgesellschaft: Wuppertal), pp. 283–312.

Kleine-Brockhoff, Thomas (2019): *Die Welt braucht den Westen: Neustart für eine liberale Ordnung*, (Edition Koerber: Hamburg, 2019).

Kohl, Helmut (1997): Statement by Helmut Kohl, Chancellor of Germany at the Signing Ceremony of the NATO-Russia Founding Act, in: NATO, Online: https://www.nato.int/cps/en/SID-27AF5864-EE4A5D0C/natolive/opinions_25643.htm, (Brussels).

Kohl, Helmut Kohl (2012): Wie soll das Europa der Zukunft aussehen?, in: Bild Zeitung, Online: https://www.bild.de/politik/inland/helmut-kohl/wie-soll-europa-in-zukunft-aussehen-22864952.bild.html, (Hamburg).

Koremenos, Barbara (2016): Escape clauses and withdrawal clauses. In: *The Continent of International Law: Explaining Agreement Design* (Cambridge University Press: Cambridge), pp. 124–157.

Körber Stiftung (2019): *The Berlin Pulse 2019/20. German Foreign Policy in Perspective*, (Berlin: Körber Stiftung).

Krasner, Stephen D. (2009): Think Again: Sovereignty, in: Foreign Policy, Online: https://foreignpolicy.com/2009/11/20/think-again-sovereignty/, (Washington D.C., 2009).

Kraus, Karl (2019): Kraus Online, Ludwig Boltzmann Institut für Geschichte und Theorie der Biographie, Online: https://www.kraus.wienbibliothek.at/content/wenn-die-welt-untergeht-dann-gehe-ich-nach-wien-dort-passiert-alles-zehn-jahre-spaeter, (Wien, 2019).

Kühnhardt, Ludger (2010): European Union – The Second Founding: The Changing Rationale of European Integration, in: Schriften des Zentrums für Europäische Integrationsforschung (ZEI), 2. Edition, (Bonn), pp. 481–574.

Lau, Jörg (2019): Der kalte Krieg taut auf, Deutschland muss sich in einer Welt neuer Großmachtkonflikte behaupten. Berlins Außenpolitiker versuchen, sich dafür zu rüsten, in: Die Zeit, Nr. 7/2019, Online: https://www.zeit.de/2019/07/grossmachtkonflikte-deutschland-aussenpolitik-brexit-inf-vertrag, (Hamburg).

Lenzner, Robert (2011): Europe In 2011 A Worse Crisis Than The U.S. In 2008, in: Forbes, Online: https://www.forbes.com/sites/robertlenzner/2011/09/30/europe-in-2011-a-worse-crisis-than-the-u-s-in-2008/#3963414a6958, (New York City).

Link, Arthur S. (1984): *The Papers of Woodrow Wilson*, Vol. 45 (Princeton University Press: Princeton).

Liptak, Kevin (2019): Trump declare himself a 'big fan' of Turkey's strongman leader Erdoğan, in: CNN, Online: https://edition.cnn.com/2019/11/13/politics/donald-trump-recep-tayyip-erdogan-turkey-impeachment/index.html, (New York City).

Los Angeles Times (1989): *Berlin Wall Will Stand 100 Years, Honecker Vows*, East Germany's official news agency, Online: https://www.latimes.com/archives/la-xpm-1989-01-20-me-1130-story.html, (Los Angeles).

Maas, Heiko (2018): Rede von Außenminister Heiko Maas am National Graduate Institute for Policy Studies in Tokyo, Japan, 25.07. 2018, Online: https://www.auswaertiges-amt.de/de/newsroom/maas-japan/2121670, (Tokyo).

Macron, Emmanuel (2017): Initiative for Europe, Online: http://international.blogs.ouest-france.fr/archive/2017/09/29/macron-sorbonne-verbatim-europe-18583.html, (Paris, 2017).

Main Post (2011): Merkel hat politisch richtig agiert, in: Main Post, Online: https://www.mainpost.de/ueberregional/meinung/leitartikel/Merkel-hat-politisch-richtig-agiert;art9517,6494325, (Würzburg).

Mallet, Victor/Khalaf, Roula (2020): Macron warns of EU unravelling unless it embraces financial solidarity, in: Fianancial Times, Online: https://www.ft.com/content/d19dc7a6-c33b-4931-9a7e-4a74674da29a?shareType=nongift, (London).

Malycha, Andreas (2011): *Auf dem Weg in den Zusammenbruch*, Online: https://www.bpb.de/izpb/48560/auf-dem-weg-in-den-zusammenbruch-1982-bis-1990?p=all, (Bundeszentrale für politische Bildung: Bonn).

Marsh, David (2011): *The Euro – The Battle for the New Global Currency*, (Yale University Press: Providence).

Martin, Michelle/Chambers, Madeline (2016): Merkel offers to work with Trump on basis of democratic values, in: Reuters, Online: https://in.reuters.com/article/usa-election-reaction-merkel-idINKBN1341ZQ?feedType=RSS&feedName=worldNews, (Berlin).

Maull, Hanns W. (2012): Außenpolitische Entscheidungsprozesse in Krisenzeiten, in: Bundeszentrale für politische Bildung, Online: http://www.bpb.de/apuz/75797/aussenpolitische-entscheidungsprozesse-in-krisenzeiten?p=all, (Bonn).

McMaster, H.R./Cohn, Gary D. (2017): America First Doesn't Mean America Alone, in: Wall Street Journal, Online: https://www.wsj.com/articles/america-first-doesnt-mean-america-alone-14961874262017, (New York City).

Mead, Walter Russel (2019): Trump's Case Against Europe, in: Wall Street Journal, Online: https://www.wsj.com/articles/trumps-case-against-europe-11559602940, (New York City).

Meier, Albrecht (2020): Meier, Beendet ein Vorschlag aus Frankreich den Streit um Corona-Bonds?, in: Der Tagesspiegel, Online: https://www.tagesspiegel.de/politik/konflikt-um-corona-hilfen-in-der-eu-beendet-ein-vorschlag-aus-frankreich-den-streit-um-corona-bonds/25727554.html, (Berlin).

Mearsheimer, John J. (2017): Liberal Ideals and International Realities, Stimson Lectures, Yale University, Online: https://macmillan.yale.edu/news/john-j-mearsheimer-liberal-ideals-and-international-realities, (Providence).

Mearsheimer, John J. (2019): Bound to Fail, The Rise and Fall of the Liberal International Order, in: International Security, Vol. 43, No. 4 (Cambridge, U.S.A), pp. 7–50.

Menzel, Claus (2009): "Wer zu spat kommt, den bestraft das Leben" Vor 20 Jahren sagte Gorbatschow das Ende der DDR voraus, Online: https://www.deutschlandfunk.de/wer-zu-spaet-kommt-den-bestraft-das-leben.871.de.html?dram:article_id=126749, (Köln).

Merkel, Angela (2012): Chancellor Merkel European Parliament Address, Online: https://www.c-span.org/video/?309369-1/chancellor-merkel-european-parliament-address, (Brussels).

Merkel, Angela (2019): Speech by Federal Chancellor Dr Angela Merkel on 16 February 2019 at the 55th Munich Security Conference, Online: https://www.bundeskanzlerin.de/bkin-en/news/speech-by-federal-chancellor-dr-angela-merkel-on-16-february-2019-at-the-55th-munich-security-conference-1582318, (Munich).

Mitchell, William (2015): *Eurozone Dystopia. Groupthink and Denial on a Grand Scale*, (Edward Elgar Publishing: Cehltenham).

Mody, Ashoka (2018): *EuroTragedy: A Drama in Nine Acts*, (Oxford University Press: New York City).

Mohseni, Payam/Kalout Hussein (2017): Iran's Axis of Resistance Rises. How It's Forging a New Middle East, in: Foreign Affairs, Online: https://www.foreignaffairs.com/articles/iran/2017-01-24/irans-axis-resistance-rises, (Washington D.C.).

Momper, Walter (2014): *Berlin, Nun Freue Dich! Mein Herbst 1989*, (Das Neue Berlin: Berlin), p. 221.

Monti, Mario (2012): Mario Monti on Challenges for the Euro and the Future of European Integration, in: Council on Foreign Relations, Online: https://www.cfr.org/event/mario-monti-challenges-euro-and-future-european-integration, (Washington D.C.).

Mourlon-Druol, Emmanuel (2014): Don't Blame the Euro : Historical Reflections on the Roots of the Eurozone Crisis, in: West European Politics, Vol. 37, No. 6., (Abingdon-on-Thames), pp. 1287–1288.

Moravcsik, Andrew (2012): Europe After the Crisis, How to Sustain a Common Currency, in: Foreign Affairs, Online: https://www.foreignaffairs.com/articles/europe/2012-05-01/europe-after-crisis, (Congers).

Müller, Harald (2016): *Diplomatie als Instrument deutscher Außenpolitik*, Online: http://m.bpb.de/apuz/230577/diplomatie-als-instrument-deutscher-aussenpolitik?p=all, (Bundeszentrale für politische Bildung: Bonn).

Münchau, Wolfgang (2012a): A real banking union can save the Eurozone, in: Financial Times, Online: https://www.ft.com/content/45b36a66-abd4-11e1-a8a0-00144feabdc0, (London).

Münchau, Wolfgang (2012b): Draghi is the devil in Weidmann's Eurozone drama, in: Financial Times, Online: https://www.ft.com/content/9095a970-03dd-11e2-9322-00144feabdc0, (London).

Münkler, Herfried (2015): *Macht der Mitte. Die neuen Aufgaben Deutschlands in Europa*, (Koerber Stiftung: Hamburg).

Naß, Matthias (2016): Amerikas Rückzug auf Raten. Eine Kolumne von Matthias Naß, in: Zeit Online, Online: https://www.zeit.de/politik/ausland/2016-03/barack-obama-rueckzug-usa-mittlerer-osten-verantwortung-europa, (Hamburg).

Nelsson, Richard (2019): How Milosevic stripped Kosovo's autonomy – archive, 1989, in: The Guardian, https://www.theguardian.com/world/from-the-archive-blog/2019/mar/20/how-milosevic-stripped-kosovos-autonomy-archive-1989, (London).

Neues Deutschland (1989a): Freundschaftliche Begegnung mit dem Außenminister der VR China, in: Neues Deutschland, Organ des Zentralkommitees der Sozialistischen Einheitspartei Deutschlands, Online: https://www.nd-archiv.de/ausgabe/1989-06-13, (East-Berlin), p. 1.

Neues Deutschland (1989b): Baker informierte über die Lage in der DDR: Tempo der Entwicklung atemberaubend", 9–10.12.1989, (East-Berlin), p. 5.

North-American Treaty Organisation (2020): Ismay in NATO, Online: https://www.nato.int/cps/en/natohq/declassified_137930.htm, (Brussels).

Paravicini, Guilia (2017): Angela Merkel: Europe must take 'our fate' into own hands, in: Politico Magazine, Online: https://www.politico.eu/article/angela-merkel-europe-cdu-must-take-its-fate-into-its-own-hands-elections-2017/, (Arlington County).

Peel, Quentin (2012): Germany and Europe: A very Federal Formula, in: Financial Times, Online: https://www.ft.com/content/31519b4a-5307-11e1-950d-00144feabdc0, (London).

Persio, Sofia Lotto (2019): This Sparkling Wine Survived Nationalization And Privatization To Become Germany's Favorite, in: Forbes, Online: https://www.forbes.com/sites/sofialottopersio/2019/11/11/this-sparkling-wine-survived-nationalization-and-privatization-to-become-germanys-favorite/, (New York City).

Pew Research Center (2017): Divisions within NATO on defending an allaice ally, Online: https://www.pewresearch.org/global/2017/05/23/natos-image-improves-on-both-sides-of-atlantic/pg_2017-05-23-nato-00-06/, (Washington D.C.).

Pinzel, Petra/Schieritz, Mark (2018): Euro-Einführung. Wir waren doch keine Idioten, in: Zeit Online, Online: https://www.zeit.de/2018/27/euro-einfuehrung-waehrungsunion-eu-reformInterview, (Hamburg).

Piper, Ernst (2018): *Deutsche Revolution*, Online: https://www.bpb.de/izpb/274840/deutsche-revolution (Bundeszentrale für politische Bildung: Bonn).

Polyakova, Alina/Haddad, Benjamin Haddad (2019): Europe Alone, What comes After the Transatlantic Alliacne, in: Foreign Affairs, Online: https://www.foreignaffairs.com/articles/europe/2019-06-11/europe-alone (New York City).

Pomeranz, Henrik (2019), Interview with Egon Krenz, "Also, dann hoch mit den Schlagbäumen!" in: Frankfurter Allgemeine Sonntagszeitung, Nr. 21, (Frankfurt am Main).

Pope Francis (2020): *Urbi et Orbis, Moment of Prayer,* Online: https://www.youtube.com/watch?v=JcUqLrbi9Cg&feature=youtu.be, (Rom).

Putin, Vladimir (2017): Speech and the Following Discussion at the Munich Conference on Security Policy, Online: http://en.kremlin.ru/events/president/transcripts/24034, (Munich, 2017).

Rachman, Gideon (2020): Eurobonds are not the answer, Why the Germans and Dutch are right to resist this way of sharing coronavirus costs, in: Financial Times, Online: https://www.ft.com/content/b809685c-77de-11ea-af44-daa3def9ae03, (London).

Rooney, Ben (2012): Draghi to the rescue, in: CNN Money Invest, Online: https://money.cnn.com/2012/07/26/investing/draghi-ecb/index.htm, (Atlanta).

Rödder, Andreas (2018): *Wer hat Angst vor Deutschland? Geschichte eines europäischen Problems*, (S. Fischer Verlag: Frankfurt am Main).

Rubin, James P. (2017): The Leader of the Free World Meets Donald Trump, in: Politico, Online: https://www.politico.com/magazine/story/2017/03/the-leader-of-the-free-world-meets-donald-trump-2-14924, (Arlington County).

Rudd, Kevin (2010): How to Avoid an Avoidable War, in: Foreign Affairs, Online: https://www.foreignaffairs.c-om/articles/china/2018-10-22/how-avoid-avoidable-war, (Washington D.C., 2018).

Rühe, Volker (1992): Opening NATO's Door, in: Daniel S. Hamilton and Kristina Spohr, Open Door: Nato and euro-atlantic security after the Cold War, (Brookings Institution Press: Washington D.C.).

Rühl, Lothar (2011): Debatte über Militärintervention. Soll der Westen in Libyen eingreifen?, in: Frankfurter Allgemeiner Zeitung, Online: https://www.faz.net/aktuell/politik/ausland/naher-osten/debatte-ueber-militaerintervention-soll-der-westen-in-libyen-eingreife-n-1610254.html, (Frankfurt am Main).

Samuels, Brett (2019): Global image of US leadership trails China: Gallup, in: The Hill, Online: https://thehill.com/blogs/blog-briefing-room/news/431973-global-image-of-us-lea-dership-now-trails-china-gallup, (Washington D.C.).

Sauga, Michael/Simons, Stefan/Wiegrefe, Klaus (2010): The Price of Unity. Was the Deutsche Mark Sacrificed for Reunifcation, in: Spiegel International, Online: https://www.spiegel.de/international/germany/the-price-of-unity-was-the-deutsche-mark-sacrificed-for-reunification-a-719940.html, (Hamburg).

Savranskaya, Svetlana/Blaton, Thomas/Zubok, Vladislav (Eds.) (2010), *Masterpieces of History,* Online: https://books.openedition.org/ceup/2895?lang=de, (Central European University Press: Budapest).

Schmidt, Helmut (2011): Germany in and with and for Europe. Speech at the SPD party conference, 4 December 2011, Berlin, Online: https://library.fes.de/pdf-files/id/ipa/08888.pdf, (Berlin).

Scholz, Olaf (2019): Germany will consider EU-wide bank deposit reinsurance, in: Financial Times, Online: https://www.ft.com/content/82624c98-ff14-11e9-a530-16c6c29e70ca, (London).

Schuler, Ralf (2015): Nachruf auf Alexander Schalck-Golodkowski (+ 82). Er war die graue Eminenz der DDR!, in: BILD Zeitung, Online: https://www.bild.de/politik/inland/devisenhandel/schalck-golodkowski-die-graue-eminenz-der-ddr-41457982.bild.html (Axel Springer Verlag: Berlin).

Schuman, Robert (1950): Schuman Declaration and the Birth of Europe, Speech of May 9, Online: http://www.schuman.info/9May1950.htm, (Brussels).

Schwarz, Hans-Peter/Schneider, Deborah Lucas (1994): Germany's National and European Interests. In: Daedalus, Vol. 123, No. 2 (Cambridge), pp. 81–105.

Shakdam, Catherine (2017): The New Thaw: Donald Trump and the Iranian Resistance Block, in: NEO. New Eastern Outlook, Online: https://journal-neo.org/2017/02/12/the-new-thaw-donald-trump-and-the-iranian-resistance-block/, (Moscow).

Shapiro, Jeremy/Browne, Matthew/Closa, Carlos/Dosenrode, Søren/ Draus, Franciszek/de Schoutheete, Philippe (2006): A View from Outside the Franco-German Couple as seen by their Partners. Our Europe, President: Jacques Delors Institute, Group E'tude et de Recherches, (Brussels).

Radio Free Europe (2006): *Timeline: The Political Career of Slobodan Milosevic,* Online: https://www.rferl.org/a/1066641.html, (Prague).

Sikorski, Radoslaw (2011a): I fear Germany's power less than her inactivity. Eurozone break-up would be apocalyptic, writes Radoslaw Sikorski, in: Financial Times, https://www.ft.com/content/b753cb42-19b3-11e1-ba5d-00144feabdc0, (London).

Sikorski, Radoslaw (2011b): Deutsche Macht fürchte ich weniger als Deutsche Untätigkeit, Speech at the Deutsche Gesellschaft für Auswärtige Politik, Online: https://dgap.org/de/veranstaltungen/deutsche-macht-fuerchte-ich-heute-weniger-als-deutsche-untaetigkeit, (Berlin).

Sikorski, Radek/Westerwelle, Guido (2012): A New Vision of Europe, in: The New York Times, Online: https://www.nytimes.com/2012/09/18/opinion/a-new-vision-of-europe.html (New York City).

Simms, Brendan (2013): Cracked heart of the old World, in: The New Statesman, Online: https://www.newstatesman.com/world-affairs/europe/2013/03/cracked-heart-old-world, (London).

Simms, Brendan (2014): Europe The Struggle for Supremacy from 1453 to the Present, (Basic Book: New York City).

Smyser, William. R. (1999): *From Yalta to Berlin: The Cold War Struggle over Germany*, (St. Martin's Press: New York City).

Solana, Javier (2003): *European Security Strategy A Secure Europe in a Better World*, (EU Institute for Security Studies: Paris).

Soros, George (2012): The Tragedy of the European Union and how to Resolve it, in: New York Review, Online: https://www.nybooks.com/articles/2012/09/27/tragedy-european-union-and-how-resolve-it/, (New York City).

Spiegel Online (1994): Ganz verbindlich, in: Der Spiegel, Online: https://www.spiegel.de/spiegel/print/d-13686555.html, (Hamburg).

Spiegel Online (2009a): Oct. 7, 1989. "How 'Gorbi' Spoiled East Germany's 40th Birthday Party", in: Spiegel Online, Online: https://www.spiegel.de/international/germany/oct-7-1989-how-gorbi-spoiled-east-germany-s-40th-birthday-party-a-653724.html, (Hamburg).

Spiegel Online (2009b): The Guard Who Opend the Berlin Wall. I Gave my People the Order – Raise the Barrier, Online: https://www.spiegel.de/international/germany/the-guard-who-opened-the-berlin-wall-i-gave-my-people-the-order-raise-the-barrier-a-660128.html, (Hamburg).

Spiegel Online (2010): Interview With Conductor Kurt Masur – The Spirit of 1989 Has Been Exhausted, Online: https://www.spiegel.de/international/germany/interview-with-conductor-kurt-masur-the-spirit-of-1989-has-been-exhausted-a-721851.html (Hamburg).

Spiegel Online (2011): 'If the Euro Fails, Europe Fails' Merkel Says EU Must Be Bound Closer Together, in: Spiegel online, Online: https://www.spiegel.de/international/germany/if-the-euro-fails-europe-fails-merkel-says-eu-must-be-bound-closer-together-a-784953.html, (Hamburg).

Spiegel Online (2012): Europe Remains a Question of War and Peace. Kohl Urges Germans to Stay Committed to Europe , in: Spiegel Online, Online: https://www.spiegel.de/international/europe/europe-remains-a-question-of-war-and-peace-kohl-urges-germans-to-stay-committed-to-europe-a-818095.html, (Hamburg).

Spiegel Online (2019), Maas greift Kramp-Karrenbauer erneut an – scharfe Kritik aus der Union, in: Der Spiegel, Online: https://www.spiegel.de/politik/deutschland/nordsyrien-vorstoss-heiko-maas-greift-annegret-kramp-karrenbauer-erneut-an-a-1294934.html, (Hamburg).

Steinmeier, Frank-Walter (2014): Rede von Außenminister Frank-Walter Steinmeier anlässlich der 50. Münchner Sicherheitskonferenz, Online: https://www.auswaertiges-amt.de/de/newsroom/140201-bm-muesiko/259554, (München).

Steinmeier, Frank-Walter (2015): Review 2014 – A Fresh Look at German Foreign Policy – Closing Remarks by Foreign Minister Frank-Walter Steinmeier. 20.05.2015, Online: https://www.auswaertiges-amt.de/en/newsroom/news/140520-bm-review2014-abschlussrede/262346, (Berlin).

Steinmeier, Frank-Walter (2016): Germany's New Global Role, Berlin Steps Up, In: Foreign Affairs, July/August 2016, Online: https://www.auswaertiges-amt.de/de/newsroom/160615-bm-foreignaffairs/281216, (New York).

Steinmeier, Frank-Walter (2017): Interview mit dem Magazin Stern, Online: http://www.bundespraesident.de/SharedDocs/Reden/DE/Frank-Walter-Steinmeier/Interviews/2017/170720-stern-Interview.html, (Berlin).

Steinmeier, Frank-Walter (2018): Frank-Walter Steinmeier beim Abendessen zu Ehren von Henry A. Kissinger aus Anlass seines 95. Geburtstages am 12. Juni 2018 in Schloss Bellevue, Online: https://www.bundespraesident.de/SharedDocs/Downloads/DE/Reden/2018/06/180612-AE-Kissinger.pdf;jsessionid=0438C561DB22F2BEE649C43CE07BB888.1_cid387?__blob=publicationFile, (Berlin).

Steinmeier, Frank-Walter (2020): Eröffnung der Münchner Sicherheitskonferenz, Online: https://www.bundespraesident.de/SharedDocs/Reden/DE/Frank-Walter-Steinmeier/Reden/2020/02/200214-MueSiKo.html, (München).

Stelzenmüller, Constanze (2011): Libyen, eine Deutschstunde; Vielen Gegnern des Militäreinsatzes fehlt auffälliger weise das Mitgefühl mit den Unterdrückten in Gaddafis Reich. Außenansicht, in: Süddeutsche Zeitung, (München), p. 2.

Sternberg, Claudia/Gartzou-Katsouyanni, Kira/Nicolaidis, Kalypso (2018): *The Greco-German Affair in the Euro Crisis: Mutual Recognition Lost?* (Palgrave Macmillan: London).

Stiglitz, Joseph E. (2016): *The Euro: How a Common Currency Threatens the Future of Europe* (W.W. Norton: New York City).

Stokes, Bruce/Kehaulani Goo, Sara (2015): 5 facts about Greece and the EU, in: Pew Research Center, Online: http://www.pewresearch.org/fact-tank/2015/07/07/5-facts-about-greece-and-the-eu/, (Washington D.C.).

Talbott, Strobe/Solana, Javier (2016): The Decline of the West, and How to Stop It, in: The New York Times, Online: https://www.nytimes.com/2016/10/20/opinion/the-decline-of-the-west-and-how-to-stop-it.html, (New York City).

Techau, Jan (2017): Greater Ambition, Please!, in: Berlin Policy Journal, Online: https://berlinpolicyjournal.com/greater-ambition-please/, (Berlin, 2017).

The Guardian (2011): European debt crisis is worst time since second world war, says Angela Merkel, in: The Guardian, Online: https://www.theguardian.com/business/2011/nov/14/eurozone-debt-crisis-angela-merkel, (London).

The New York Times (1988): *The Gorbachev Visit; Excerpts From Speech to U.N. on Major Soviet Military Cuts,* (NY Times: New York City).

The New York Times (1989): Upheaval in the East; Excerpts From Baker's Speech on Berlin and U.S. Role in Europe's Future, Online: http://www.nytimes.com/1989/12/13/world/upheaval-east-excerpts-baker-s-speech-berlin-us-role-europe-s-future.html?pagewanted=3, (West Berlin).

The Times (2010): Diplomacy without Arms, Online: https://www.thetimes.co.uk/article/diplomacy-without-arms-39flhbg09jz, (London).

Tsoukalis, Loukas (1998), The European Agenda: Issues of Globalization, Equity and Legitimacy, in: The Robert Schuman Centre, Jean Monnet Chair, Vol. 49, Online: https://core.ac.uk/download/pdf/45681007.pdf, (San Domenico).

Trenin, Dimitri/Techau, Jan (2013): Germany's Changing Role in a Changing Europe, in: Carnegie Europe, Online: https://carnegieeurope.eu/2013/03/27/germany-s-changing-role-in-changing-europe-event-4034, (Brussels).

Trippe, Christian/Knight, Ben (2019): Munich Security Report: The world is in crisis, in: Deutsche Welle, German News Service, Online: https://www.deutschland.de/en/topic/politics/munich-security-report-the-world-is-in-crisis, (Frankfurt am Main).

Urmersbach, Viktoria (2009): Glasnost in Kavelstorf, in: Nord Deutscher Rundfunk, (Hamburg).

USBerlin NIACT Immediate cable 3430, 051213Z December, "Momper's Grim Analysis of GDR Situation".

U.S. Department of State (2001a): *Gorbachev and New Thinking in Soviet Foreign Policy, 1987–88*, Online: https://2001-2009.state.gov/r/pa/ho/time/rd/108225.htm (U.S. Department of State Archive: Washington D.C.).

U.S. Department of State (2001b): *Interim Agreement for Peace and Self-Government in Kosovo*, Online: https://1997-2001.state.gov/regions/eur/ksvo_rambouillet_text.html, (Was U.S. Department of State Archive: Washington D.C hington D.C.).

United States Government Printing Office (1958): *Containing the Public Messages, Speeches, and Statements of the President, Jan. 01 to Dec. 31, 1957, Public Papers of the Presidents of the United States, Dwight D. Eisenhower*, (Washington D.C.).

van Laak, Claudai (2009): Es geschah in Schwante: Die Gründung der SDP der DDR vor 20 Jahren, in: Deutschlandfunk Kultur, Online: https://www.deutschlandfunkkultur.de/es-geschah-in-schwante.1001.de.html?dram:article_id=156898 (Berlin).

Volkrey, Carsten (2009): Maggie Thatcher und die Wiedervereinigung. Die Deutschen sind wieder da, in: Spiegel Online: https://www.spiegel.de/geschichte/maggie-thatcher-und-die-wiedervereinigung-a-948498.html, (Hamburg).

von der Leyen, Ursula (2018): Rede der Bundesministerin der Verteidigung Dr. Ursula von der Leyen auf der 54. Münchner Sicherheitskonferenz, Online: https://www.bmvg.de/resource/blob/22178/909a56e9af7501819eba0563f9724109/20180216-download-eroeffnungsrede-deutsch-data.pdf, (München).

von Weizsäcker, Richard (1986) Was ist das eigentlich: deutsch? ["What is that actually: German?"], in Reden und Interviews [Speeches and Interviews], vol. 2, pp. 395–412 (Bonn). Translation: GHDT, Federal President Richard von Weizsäcker on the Meaning of Being German (1986), Online: http://germanhistorydocs.ghi-dc.org/docpage.cfm?docpage_id=2111.

Martina Waiblinger (2009): Dass die DDR ausgerechnet an der Kirche scheitern sollte. Christian Führer und die Nikolaikirche. Bericht aus einer Tagung in Bad Boll von 6.-9. Januar 2009, Online: http://www.kirche-fuer-alle-web.de/christianfuehrer-nikolaikirche.pdf, (Bad Boll).

Wall Street Journal (2008), Online: Rahm Emanuel on the Opportunities of Crisis, https://www.youtube.com/watch?v=_mzcbXi1Tkk, (Washington D.C.: 2008).

Wilkinson, Angela (2017): *Strategic Foresight Primer*, European Political Strategy Centre, (Brussels).

Winkler, Heinrich August (2015): Denk ich an Deutschland. Was den Westen zusammenhält, in: Frankfurter Allgemeine Zeitung, Online: https://www.faz.net/aktuell/politik/inland/heinrich-august-winkler-was-den-westen-zusammenhaelt-13815991.html, (Frankfurt am Main).

Wolf, Martin (2012): The riddle of German self-interest, in: Financial Times, Online: https://www.ft.com/content/4fe89d8c-a8df-11e1-b085-00144feabdc0, (London).

Wong, Catherine (2016): Nothing more than a piece of paper': former Chinese envoy dismisses upcoming ruling on South China Sea claims. China will not be intimated even if US sends 10 aircraft carriers to region, says Dai Bingguo amid rising tensions over rival territorial claims to disputed waters, in: South China Morning Post, Online: https://www.scmp.com/news/china/diplomacy-defence/article/1986029/nothing-more-piece-paper-former-chinese-envoy-dismisses, (Hong Kong).

Wolfrum, Edgar (2020): *Der Aufsteiger Eine Geschichte Deutschlands von 1990 bis heute*, (Klett-Cotta Verlag: Stuttgart).

ZDF (2019): US-Reporter beim Mauerfall. Mein Gott, der hat gerade gesagt, dass die Mauer fällt, Online: https://www.zdf.de/nachrichten/heute/interview-us-reporter-tom-brokaw-nbc-news-berichtete-1989-aus-berlin-live-vom-mauerfall-100.html (Berlin).